THE VITAL ESSENCE OF DZOGCHEN

The Vital Essence of Dzogchen

A Commentary on Düdjom Rinpoché's
Advice for a Mountain Retreat

B. Alan Wallace

SHAMBHALA

Shambhala Publications, Inc.
2129 13th Street
Boulder, Colorado 80302
www.shambhala.com

Cover art: *King of Shambhala* from Shechen Archives, photographed by Matthieu Ricard
Cover design: Daniel Urban-Brown
Interior design: Kat Ran Press

9 8 7 6 5 4 3 2 1

First Edition
Printed in the United States of America

Shambhala Publications makes every effort to print on acid-free, recycled paper. Shambhala Publications is distributed worldwide by Penguin Random House, Inc., and its subsidiaries.

LIBRARY OF CONGRESS CATALOGING-IN-PUBLICATION DATA
Names: Wallace, B. Alan, author.
Title: The vital essence of Dzogchen: a commentary on Düdjom Rinpoché's advice for a mountain retreat / B. Alan Wallace.
Description: First edition. | Boulder: Shambhala, 2025 | Includes bibliographical references and index.
Identifiers: LCCN 2024041688 | ISBN 9781645473732 (trade paperback)
Subjects: LCSH: Spiritual life—Rnying-ma-pa (Sect) | Rnying-ma-pa (Sect)—Doctrines. | Rdzogs-chen. | Bdud-'joms 'Jigs-bral-ye-shes-rdo-rje, 1904–1987. Bdud 'dul dbang drag rdo rje gro lod kyi rdzogs rim ka dag gi khrid yig ye shes snang ba.
Classification: LCC BQ7662.6 .W36 2025 | DDC 294.3/444—dc23/eng/20241209
LC record available at https://lccn.loc.gov/2024041688

The authorized representative in the EU for product safety and compliance is eucomply OÜ, Pärnu mnt 139b-14, 11317 Tallinn, Estonia, hello@eucompliancepartner.com.

This precious lineage of ours is not just ancient history, for even these days there are individuals who come to the highest state of realization by following the paths of cutting through and the direct crossing over, and their material bodies dissolve into a mass of rainbow light.

Düdjom Rinpoché

CONTENTS

PREFACE

This is not your first book on the practice of Buddhadharma. You come to this book because you have been seeking, studying, and practicing for years, always yearning for ways to go deeper in your understanding and personal experience of the Buddha's teachings. You come to this book because you have some intuitive reverence for the path of the Great Perfection, the pinnacle of the teachings transmitted by Guru Rinpoché—Padmasambhava—when he came to Tibet in the eighth century and transformed the hearts and minds of Tibetans, establishing a pure lineage of Vajrayāna Buddhism that would be passed from generation to generation until the current day. And you come to this book because, whether you know much or little about Düdjom Rinpoché, you understand enough to trust that he carried the full majesty, purity, and transcendent realization of Guru Padmasambhava directly into the present era, establishing the Nyingma teachings of Tibetan Buddhism throughout the modern world in the late twentieth century.

Düdjom Rinpoché, Jigdral Yeshé Dorjé (1904–1987) was a monumental figure in the history of Tibetan Buddhism, who, like many of the greatest lamas, can be viewed from different perspectives in accord with different dimensions of reality. From the perspective of the way in which he is understood by his own tradition, he is seen as a pivotal figure within a long trajectory of extraordinary lifetimes—from that of Śāriputra, one of the leading disciples of Buddha Śākyamuni, to that of Drokben Khyeuchung Lotsāwa, one of the twenty-five Tibetan disciples of Guru Padmasambhava, to that of Düdjom Lingpa, the astounding nineteenth-century treasure revealer. This transcendent being appeared throughout Indian and Tibetan history as mahāsiddhas, such as Saraha and Hūṃkāra, and as pivotally important figures across the great traditions of Tibet, such as the Sakya leader Drogön Pakpa Lodrö Gyaltsen, the Drukpa Kagyü yogin Lingjé Repa Pema Dorjé, and the Nyingma treasure revealer Düdul Dorjé.

Moreover, in a previous great eon, long before this current fortunate eon, in which it is prophesied that one thousand buddhas will appear, it is said that this same transcendent being manifested from the primordial buddha Samantabhadra as the Vajrayāna yogin, Vidyādhara Nüden Dorjé, who became the lord of the Dharma family of all the bodhisattvas who would become the one thousand buddhas of this current eon by granting them empowerment and prophecies regarding the time of their enlightenment. According to this account, all one thousand bodhisattvas were born as sons of a single king—who himself would be the Buddha Dīpaṃkāra—who sought the help of Vidyādhara Nüden Dorjé in predicting the time of each of his sons' enlightenment.

Düdjom Rinpoché's mental continuum is also said to have been embodied in the youngest of those sons, named Lodrö Tayé, "Limitless Intelligence," who was then prophesied to manifest perfect and complete enlightenment as the last of the thousand buddhas, with the name Möpa Tayé, "Infinite Resolve" (Buddha Adhimukta). According to a narrative drawn from the *Ratnakūṭa Sūtra*, this will be the buddha who, when he was Lodrö Tayé, made the aspiration before all his brothers that his deeds, lifespan, and the number of his followers would be equal to the collection of the deeds, life-spans, and number of followers of all them as the buddhas that each of them would become before him. Thus, he had the courage to form the resolve that because the Buddhadharma is like space, and because sentient beings are without end, there would still be the need for him to perform deeds equal to all the deeds of the buddhas who would precede him in this fortunate eon. Such is the massive wave of realization, virtuous activity, determination, and prayers upon which Düdjom Rinpoché's mindstream rides.[1]

At the level of personal history, Düdjom Rinpoché was born into a family steeped in Dharma and nobility—his father was of ancient Tibetan royal lineage and also a major tulku of Katok Monastery, while his mother was of Bhutanese origin, descended from the great treasure revealer Ratna Lingpa. That the boy was an emanation of Düdjom Lingpa was unmistakable: Soon before dying, Düdjom Lingpa told his disciples to go to the hidden land of Pemakö, promising that before they would arrive, he would be there. Indeed, it appears that Düdjom Rinpoché was conceived in the region of Pemakö before Düdjom Lingpa had even passed away in eastern Tibet. When two of Düdjom Lingpa's disciples met the three-year-old boy whom they would recognize as Düdjom Rinpoché, the boy already knew their names and spoke in an accent that was odd for the region of Pemakö—but it turned out this was a remnant of his Golok accent from his previous lifetime as Düdjom Lingpa.

As a child, Düdjom Rinpoché received an extraordinary number of teachings, empowerments, transmissions, and pith instructions, especially from the two lamas who had been disciples of Düdjom Lingpa and who first recognized him, Ling Lama Chönjor Gyatso and Puktrul Gyurmé Ngedön Wangpo. The boy was trained in the full array of Nyingma practices that were upheld in living lineages at that time, and by the age of five, Düdjom Rinpoché was discovering authentic treasure objects. When he was thirteen, he discovered the treasure cycle of Dorjé Drolö, a wrathful form of Guru Rinpoché, the first of four major treasure cycles that he would reveal while still a young man. Nevertheless, with respect to each treasure cycle, Düdjom Rinpoché quietly practiced these treasures for many years before venturing to share them widely with others. Throughout much of his life, he focused more on preserving and clarifying the treasures revealed by the other great treasure revealers of Tibetan history than he did on spreading his own treasure cycles.

In 1925, amid his abundant studies as a youth, Düdjom Rinpoché met the treasure revealer Zilnön Namkhai Dorjé at Mindröling Monastery in central Tibet. Düdjom Rinpoché received from Zilnön Namkhai Dorjé an empowerment of Dorjé Drolö that would uncover the depths of his own realization from past lifetimes. According to Düdjom Rinpoché's own account,[2]

[Tertön Zilnön Namkhai Dorjé] bestowed Jamgön Kongtrul's secret empowerment of Dorje Drolö. He looked at me with eyes wide open and shouted, "Phet!" In that instant my body, perception, and mind became unimpeded, all notions of solidity disappeared. "That is the absolute wisdom empowerment. *Supra tishta ye soha!*"[3] Saying this, he tossed barley grains skyward. From that time on, my mind remained relaxed and open. I felt no need to boast about spending months and years in retreat; nor did I feel the need to focus forcefully in my meditation, nor cling to practice schedules. I knew the power of the lineage realization of absolute truth had been transferred to me. This karmically connected great teacher was none other than Guru Padmasambhava.

Thus, by the kindness of his guru—whom he recognized as being an embodiment of Guru Rinpoché himself—Düdjom Rinpoché reawakened his ancient realization of pristine awareness and had no need to spend extensive periods in retreat in that lifetime. Therefore, he was able to pour the full force of his energy into teaching, granting empowerments and transmissions, composing and compiling the twenty-five volumes of his own collected works, compiling and editing fifty-eight volumes of the Nyingma Kama (canonical scriptures), and establishing centers for the practice of Dharma, both in Tibet and eventually in India and around the world.

While still a teenager, Düdjom Rinpoché founded a monastery and an associated community for lay Vajrayāna practitioners (or *ngakpa*) in Pemakö. As these communities flourished, Düdjom Rinpoché met with sectarian opposition claiming that his Dharma activities in Pemakö had no sanction from the central Tibetan government. Düdjom Rinpoché traveled to central Tibet to seek such permission, but as it was never granted, he instead spent his twenties touring the sacred sites and monasteries of central Tibet, both receiving and granting teachings and transmissions. In 1937, he traveled to Bhutan, and at the sacred site of Paro Taktsang, he revealed the Vajrakīlaya treasure cycle known as Putri Rekpung and also rediscovered his earlier treasures focused on Yeshé Tsogyal, known as the Khandro Tuktik, and on Guru Rinpoché in the form of the Lake-Born Vajra, known as the Tsokyé Tuktik.

Upon returning to Tibet in the late 1930s, Düdjom Rinpoché founded a constellation of Dharma centers including Zangdok Palri Monastery, which was located on a hill in a sacred region of southern Tibet—known as Kongpo Buchu—where temples had existed since the seventh century. Kongpo Buchu was understood as a key place of power, something like an acupuncture point within the geography of the whole of Tibet. The centers founded there by Düdjom Rinpoché included Sangchen Ösel Namdröl Ling, a monastery for ordained sangha, as well as Lama Ling, which was a *drubdra*, or contemplative community, for ngakpa retreatants and committed lay practitioners. It was there, likely around 1956, that Düdjom Rinpoché taught his now-famous pith instructions for how to practice in an isolated retreat, translated here as *Extracting the Vital Essence of Accomplishment: Concise and Clear Advice for Practice in a Mountain Retreat*. This text is also sometimes known simply as *Ri chö*, or "Mountain Dharma."

It was in the 1990s that I first encountered this text by Düdjom Rinpoché, *Extracting the Vital Essence of Accomplishment*, and I was immediately struck by the depth, precision, brevity, and clarity with which this great *paṇḍita*, Kyabjé Düdjom Rinpoché, expressed these teachings. I then took it upon myself to translate the text, after which my root Dzogchen lama, Venerable Gyatrul Rinpoché, authorized me to teach it. Since then, I have revised and polished my translation several times and enhanced my understanding through the clarifying oral commentaries of two marvelous holders of this Düdjom lineage: Lama Tharchin Rinpoché and Tulku Thadral Rinpoché.

Lama Tharchin Rinpoché (1936–2013) was born in the Kongpo region of southern Tibet in the vicinity of Lama Ling Rigdzin Gatsal Drubdra, that thriving center for Vajrayāna practice founded by Düdjom Rinpoché. As a youth, Lama Tharchin Rinpoché came to study and practice under Düdjom Rinpoché's personal guidance at Lama Ling, completing five years of solitary retreat followed by a three-year retreat performed with three other practitioners. Lama Tharchin Rinpoché recounted that he received this specific instruction on *Extracting the Vital Essence of Accomplishment* while he was in his early twenties, during his three-year retreat. Düdjom Rinpoché himself departed from Tibet due to mounting dangers from Communist China in 1957, so given Lama Tharchin's year of birth, this teaching must have taken place sometime around 1956, when Düdjom Rinpoché was in central Tibet. By this time, major parts of the Zangdok Palri temple complex had already been destroyed by the great earthquake of 1950, and Düdjom Rinpoché was asked to perform protective rituals in key areas of central Tibet to try to rebalance the points of geomantic power that had been so deeply disrupted. It is significant to recognize that the teachings on unshakable courage in the face of obstacles that Düdjom Rinpoché offers in this very text were granted to his own select group of disciples at a time when the very future of Tibet was in peril. Precisely in the face of such danger, the priority for the deepest practice remained, and it was in that context that Düdjom Rinpoché taught this text to a particular group of disciples, including Lama Tharchin Rinpoché, who were engaged in an advanced Vajrayāna three-year meditation retreat at Ogmin Pema Öling, the retreat section of Lama Ling. This retreat would have included the Dzogchen practices of cutting through to the original purity of pristine awareness (*trekchö*) and the direct crossing over to spontaneous actualization (*tögal*). It was certainly not for beginners. While it is possible that Düdjom Rinpoché had actually composed this text earlier, during the 1940s, when the entire Zangdok Palri complex was still flourishing under less ominous circumstances, it is poignant that he was teaching it as late as 1956, when Lama Tharchin Rinpoché was at least twenty and catastrophe had already begun to strike Tibet.

The other oral commentary I received on this text was offered by the contemporary teacher, Tulku Thadral Rinpoché (b. 1970), who was identified by Düdjom Rinpoché as an incarnation of Lama Thadral Dorjé, one of the thirteen disciples of Düdjom Lingpa who achieved rainbow body. Tulku Thadral Rinpoché primarily lives in Nepal, where he is the principal and director of education at a monastic college founded by Düdjom Rinpoché himself, and he also teaches in association with the Vajrayana Foundation founded by Lama Tharchin Rinpoché. Whatever understanding I, personally, may have of Düdjom Rinpoché's text is above all from my own teacher Gyatrul Rinpoché, but I have also returned to the text with deep reverence and gratitude for the wisdom shared by both Lama Tharchin Rinpoché and Tulku Thadral Rinpoché.

In his commentary to *The Sharp Vajra of Conscious Awareness Tantra*, Düdjom Lingpa states that if we are to set out on this path of the Great Perfection, we optimally need a *vidyādhara* to guide us effectively and unerringly. He adds that for those of us who have not had direct, personal access to a vidyādhara—that is, one who has directly realized and made manifest pristine awareness—then we should rely on the teachings of an actual vidyādhara. In that case, the unsurpassed skill and realization of Düdjom Lingpa and his mind emanation, Düdjom Rinpoché, make them exemplary guides on this path of the Great Perfection through their writings. The extraordinary deeds of Düdjom Rinpoché after he departed from Tibet and began to preserve and spread the transmissions of the entire Nyingma tradition in exile have been thoroughly recounted elsewhere.[4]

My recent book *Dzokchen: A Commentary on Düdjom Rinpoché's Illumination of Primordial Wisdom* (Wisdom, 2024) may be regarded as a prequel to this present volume because that is where the practices of śamatha[5] and vipaśyanā[6] are explained in more detail—both in the root text and my commentary—whereas some understanding of śamatha and vipaśyanā is assumed here. The advanced text here, explicitly composed for the seasoned yogis of Ogmin Pema Öling in Kongpo, Tibet, was intended for contemplatives who had already received extensive training in Mahāyāna Buddhism and in the theory and practice of the Nyingma teachings of Vajrayāna as well. Moreover, in Düdjom Rinpoché's *Extracting the Vital Essence of Accomplishment*, there is no expanded explanation of the Dzogchen view because it is a commentary that assumes its recipients are already familiar with these teachings. Ideally, these are pith instructions for retreat, where what is included is exactly what you need to remember for actual practice.

The commentary in this volume is based on a series of private online talks that I presented throughout 2022 to an international group of senior students, all of whom were already dedicated to intensive meditation practice and retreats. Therefore, my own commentary here is in the spirit of personal instructions to those already dedicated to engaging in extensive practice in this lifetime, whether they are in formal retreat or not. I see my own role as being primarily that of a facilitator. Not only have I spent the last fifty years as a translator of Tibetan Buddhism—both as an oral interpreter and translator of written texts—but for those who have not yet had the opportunity to receive meditation instruction from one of the great Tibetan masters of the past or present, I seek to share what I myself have received directly from such great masters in a way that is readily understandable, even if one does not know the Tibetan language. Moreover, I try to bridge the significant gaps in understanding that can occur when Buddhist ideas are shared in the context of a twenty-first-century global culture, where most people hearing those ideas did not grow up with a Buddhist worldview or religious practice. Thus, I explain these ideas in contemporary language for modern people, especially in relationship to science, but also with reference to the broad idioms and zeitgeist of the twenty-first century. At times, I follow the traditional sequence of Buddhist debate, wherein one first refutes ideas contrary to the teaching one is about to present, one then presents the authentic teaching, and finally one refutes potential rebuttals to that presentation. While I do not explicitly point out these steps within this commentary, it is important to keep in mind that when I do enter into a mode of debate, I am not refuting "straw men" but rather actual mistaken ideas and approaches to practice that I have encountered over the course of the last five decades.

Furthermore, I occasionally offer guided meditations or practices that enable the reader to bring the teaching into his or her experience immediately upon receiving the teaching. This is meant to echo what occurs in formal oral teachings, when I regularly balance instruction in the theoretical ideas with direct experiential instructions for practice in meditation.

While the medium of oral teachings is quite different from that of the written word, it was with the encouragement of my student and editor Virginia Craft that I decided to turn the original lectures that I offered to aspiring yogis in 2022 into a written commentary. I am indebted to Martha J. Hanna for her meticulous work in the initial step of transcribing those lectures. Then Virginia took on the formidable task of transforming those transcripts into a publishable manuscript. I am also deeply grateful to Dr. Eva Natanya for polishing my translation of Düdjom Rinpoché's root text and for her expert editing of my commentary as a whole. We are all also very grateful to Anna Wolcott Johnson of Shambhala Publications for her excellent copyediting of the entire manuscript. Finally, I would like to acknowledge the wonderful service offered by the Buddhist Digital Resource Center in making this root text and countless other Tibetan manuscripts available in digital form, as well as the Treasury of Lives for making available scholarly biographies of hundreds of Tibetan figures. These are inexpressibly valuable services to all scholars of Tibetan Buddhism.

B. Alan Wallace
Miyo Samten Ling Hermitage
The Center for Contemplative Research in Crestone, Colorado

The Vital Essence of Dzogchen

Düdjom Rinpoché, Jigdral Yeshé Dorjé (1904–1987)

PART ONE

The Root Text

Extracting the Vital Essence of Accomplishment

Concise and Clear Advice for Practice in a Mountain Retreat

Düdjom Rinpoché, Jigdral Yeshé Dorjé

*Translated by B. Alan Wallace and
edited by Eva Natanya*

[444] I reverently bow and take refuge at the feet of the sublime and glorious guru, whose kindness is beyond compare. Bless me and my disciples so that unmistaken realizations of the profound path may swiftly arise in our mindstreams and that we may take hold of the primordial citadel in this very lifetime.

There are three general topics in this concise and clear presentation of advice for the practice of the very secret Great Perfection, [445] consisting of training in the crucial points for a mountain retreat. This provides an entrance for those fortunate individuals in whom previous prayers and pure, residual karma are united; for those who have heartfelt trust in the profound, secret Dharma of the Great Perfection and in the guru who reveals it; and for those who are intent on pursuing this practice to its culmination. These are the three general topics to be understood: (1) the preparation: how to cut the ties of attachment and clinging, direct your mind to Dharma, and purify your mindstream; (2) the main practice: how to cut through false superimpositions regarding the view, meditation, and conduct and then set out on the road of practice; and (3) the post-meditative practice: how to keep your samayas and vows and how to incorporate all your activities of this life into the Dharma.

I. The Preparation

Now I will say a little about the first topic. Alas! From the very first, the vivid, clear, swift knowing of this so-called mind of ours has emerged simultaneously with Samantabhadra. But Samantabhadra is free because he knows his own nature, while we sentient beings endlessly wander in samsara because we do not. [446] We have become embodied countless times among the six types of existence, and everything we have done has turned out to be meaningless. Now, for once out of a hundred times, on this occasion when we have taken human form, if we fail to achieve the means to avoid taking rebirth in samsara and the miserable realms, after we die, there is no certainty as to where we will be reborn. Wherever we take birth among the six types of beings, there is nothing but suffering. It is not enough to have acquired this human form, and since the time of death is unknown, we must practice authentic Dharma right now. So that we do not feel remorse in the face of death and are not ashamed of ourselves, we must be like the venerable Milarepa, who declared,

> In my Milarepa Dharma tradition,
> we are not ashamed of ourselves.

So that our Dharma practice leads to the path, it is not enough to maintain an outer facade of Dharma. Rather, we must set aside all activities that are concerned with this life and cut all ties to the allures of the desire realm. Without cutting them, even though we enter the gateway of Dharma, if we enter with a merely wishy-washy attitude while being attached to our homeland, possessions, relatives, friends, loved ones, and so on, then with the conjunction of that mind of attachment acting as the primary cause and those objects of attachment acting as the cooperative conditions, māras will create obstacles, we will mix again with worldly people, and the outcome of our deeds will go awry.

Therefore, sacrificing our concern for food, clothing, and conversation, and relinquishing attachment to the eight mundane concerns, [447] we should apply our minds single-pointedly to Dharma, like Gyalwa Yang Gönpa, who declared,

> In solitude, where awareness of death penetrates one's heart,
> the adept, who utterly renounces clinging,
> draws the boundaries of retreat by renouncing concerns of this
>   life.
> Thus one does not encounter people
> whose minds are filled with the eight mundane concerns.

Otherwise, Dharma that is mixed with those eight concerns is like consuming food mixed with poison, and this is extremely dangerous.

Those eight concerns can be understood succinctly in terms of hope and fear, which basically refer to attachment and aversion. Inner attachment and aversion take on the guise of outer male and female demons. As long as your mind is not freed from attachment and aversion, you will never be free of those demons, and there will be no end to obstacles. So you must repeatedly examine your own minds to see if, in your innermost thoughts, there is any conceited clinging to the eight concerns of this life, and if it arises, you must take care to get rid of it. If these eight concerns hold you in their grip while you fabricate a facsimile of Dharma, even your acquisition of goods will constitute wrong livelihood because they were obtained through deceit. In accordance with the aphorism, "By leaving your homeland behind, half the Dharma is accomplished," turn your back on your homeland and wander among unfamiliar lands.

Amicably part ways from your friends and relatives, and do not listen to those who seek to dissuade you from practicing Dharma. Give away your wealth and possessions, [448] and rely on whatever alms come your way. Recognize all desirable things to be obstacles linked with bad habits, and arouse disinclination for them. If you are not satisfied with just a little of such things as material possessions, then if you get one thing, you will want two; and for as long as that goes on, you will easily be possessed by the devious māras of the allures of the desire realm. Whatever good or bad things people say, do not take them to be true or respond to them with hope or fear, affirmation or denial. Rather, let them say what they will, as if they were speaking about someone who is dead and gone.

No one but a qualified guru—not even your parents—can give you sound advice, so hold your own ground, and do not let anyone else take hold of your nose rope. Remaining outwardly good-natured, know how to engage harmoniously with others without "burning anyone's noses." If anyone—strong or weak—actually becomes an obstacle to your practice, you must not be moved by that individual, as if you were an iron boulder pulled by a silk scarf. It won't do to be of a weak character, bending your head in whatever direction the wind blows, like grass on a mountain pass.

For any practice, from the time you begin until you come to its culmination—whether thunderbolts fall from above, a lake springs up from below, or boulders cave in from all sides—carry through to the end, keeping your promise to act in accordance with your samayas, even at the cost of your life. [449] From the very beginning, gradually establish your schedule of periods for formal meditation, sleep, meals, and so on, without falling into bad habits. Moreover, whether your practice is elaborate or unelaborate, do not let it be sporadic, but keep it even and regular, without leaving any room for the ordinary, even for an instant.

When in retreat, seal the entry of your cave with mud; or even if you do not seal it, do not meet face-to-face with others. Do not speak with others or be on the lookout for others. Completely calm all the wandering thoughts of your restless mind. Then, expel the stale breath and properly adopt the vital points of the posture. Your mind should rest in recollected awareness and remain firm, without wavering even for an instant, like a stake driven into the ground. All the signs and qualities of the practice will swiftly arise due to maintaining a strict outer, inner, and secret retreat. If you think, "Now it's important that I meet and speak with someone, but I shall keep to a strict retreat afterward," and thus erode your boundaries, over time the potency of your practice will decline, becoming slacker and slacker. So, from the very outset, if you make a firm resolve to remain in retreat, your practice will become stricter and stricter, and it will not be swept away by obstacles.

Although there are many ways of examining the characteristics of suitable places to practice, in general it is best to practice in a pleasant region that is blessed by *siddhas* of the past, [450] such as Guru Rinpoché, and not inhabited by people who have broken their samayas. It should be very secluded, where provisions are easily obtainable, and suited to your constitution. Due to the swift confluence of outer and inner fortuitous conditions in charnel grounds, haunted grounds, and other areas inhabited by malevolent local spirits, practicing in such places will enhance your meditation if you are up to it. But if you are not, you will have many obstacles. When your realization turns into the expanse, all unfavorable circumstances arise as aids. When that happens, it is especially helpful to engage in secret practices in places such as charnel grounds. Constantly reject all outer and inner busyness, for remaining in inactivity is true solitude.

As for the actual practice of purifying your mindstream, strive until you gain experience in each of the common practices of the four revolutions in outlook and the uncommon practices of refuge, bodhicitta, the purification of obscurations, and the amassing of the accumulations [of merit and knowledge], as they are taught in the meditation manuals. In particular, you should apply yourself to guru yoga as the life force of your practice. If you don't, progress in meditation will be slow, and even when there is a little development, obstacles will occur, and it will not be possible for genuine realizations to arise in your mindstream. Therefore, as a result of offering prayers of supplication with uncontrived, fervent admiration and reverence, after some time, the enlightened view from the guru's mindstream will be transferred to you, and extraordinary, inexpressible realizations will certainly emerge from within your own being. [451] Lama Zhang Rinpoché declared, "There are many who cultivate stillness, meditative experiences, *samādhi*, and so on. But rare are the realizations that are born from within due to the guru's blessings, which arise by the power of admiration and reverence."

Thus, the arising of the meaning of the Great Perfection in your mind-stream depends on the preliminary practices, which is why Jé Drigung declared,

> For other dharmas, the main practice is considered to be
> profound,
> but here we consider the preliminary practices to be profound.

And his enlightened perspective is true.

II. THE MAIN PRACTICE

Regarding the main practice—on how to cut through false superimpositions concerning the view, meditation, and conduct and then set out on the road of practice—I shall first address the view by which one knows the mode of being.

By establishing the actual nature of your own mind, the nature of existence of the ultimate character of reality, within pristine awareness that is free of all characteristics that are fabricated or modified by conventional cognition, pristine awareness dawns nakedly as self-emergent primordial consciousness.

Inexpressible with words, it cannot be indicated with analogies. It does not worsen in samsara, nor does it improve in nirvana. It has never been born and never ceases; it is never liberated, nor is it deluded; it has never existed, nor has it ever not existed; [452] it has never been delimited, nor does it fall to any extreme. In short, it has never been determined to exist as a substantial entity with elaborated characteristics, so its essential nature is originally pure, great, all-pervasive emptiness. With its empty inner glow unimpeded, the oceans of the realms of the phenomena of samsara and nirvana appear of their own accord, like the sun and its rays. Therefore, as it has never been sheer nothingness, or a blank vacuity, its manifest nature is the great, spontaneous actualization of primordial consciousness and its sublime qualities.

Thus, recognizing, just as it is, the pristine awareness that is the union of appearances and emptiness—the nature of the three kāyas, the mode of being of exactly this, the nature of existence of the primordial character of reality—is called "the cognition-transcending view of the Great Perfection." The great Ācārya [Padmasambhava] declared, "The *dharmakāya*, transcending cognition, is suchness."

How marvelous that we hold right here in our hands the enlightened view of Samantabhadra! This is the culmination of all the eighty-four thousand divisions of the Jina's teachings and the essence of the six million four hundred thousand tantras of the Great Perfection. There is not even a speck beyond this. The value of all dharmas should be determined upon this basis.

Now, once you have eliminated, from within, all doubts and false superimpositions regarding such a view, sustaining the continuity of this view is called "meditation." Apart from this, all meditations that have an object are conceptual meditations created by cognition, [453] so we do not practice that way. Within a state that has not lost the firm establishment of exactly the view that was set forth previously, let all your five sense consciousnesses settle in their natural state, loose and at ease. Do not purposefully meditate with the sense that "this is it," for if you are meditating, that is cognition, so there is nothing whatsoever on which to meditate.

Do not let yourself be distracted, even for an instant. If you are distracted from resting within your own nature, that is the real delusion, so do not be distracted. Whatever thoughts arise, let them arise. But do not follow after them, nor should you block them.

Well then, how shall we practice? Whatever appearances of objects arise, be like a child gazing at a temple. Without allowing grasping to encroach upon the appearing aspects, leave them fresh. Thus, all phenomena remain right where they are. So their features do not deteriorate, their colors do not change, and their luster does not fade away. Even though they appear, since they are not contaminated by thoughts of clinging and grasping, all appearances and modes of awareness nakedly arise as luminous, empty, primordial consciousness.

In general, people with lesser intelligence are puzzled by the great number of teachings that are said to be very profound and vast. So, to point a finger at the essential meaning that emerges out of all of them: During the interval when a past thought has ceased and the next thought has not yet arisen, isn't there a fresh consciousness of the present—a clear, naked awareness that has never changed, even by a hair's breadth? Oh, just that is how pristine awareness is present! [454] Then, insofar as you do not remain in just that state, doesn't a thought suddenly arise? That is a creative expression of pristine awareness itself. However, if you do not recognize it as soon as it arises, if a series of thoughts flows out, that is called the "chain of delusion," and it is the root of samsara. Simply recognizing thoughts as soon as they appear releases them in their own nature, such that they do not continue to proliferate, and if you relax and rest right there, then whatever thoughts arise, they are all uniformly released in the expanse of pristine awareness, the dharmakāya. Just this is the main practice in which the view and meditation of cutting through are united.

Garab Dorjé declared,

> Mindfulness of the instant that pristine awareness suddenly arises
> from the very nature of primordially pure, absolute space
> is like finding a jewel from the depths of the ocean.
> There is the dharmakāya, which has not been modified or created
>   by anyone.

You must persevere relentlessly in this and meditate without distraction day and night. So do not let emptiness remain as an object of understanding—bring it into pristine awareness!

Now, as for the way to enhance the meditation with conduct and set out on the road of practice: Most importantly, as stated before, without being separated even for an instant from the recognition that regards your guru as an actual buddha, pray from the depths of your heart. This is called the "universal panacea of admiration and reverence." This is superior to any other method for dispelling obstacles and enhancing your practice, and you will proceed along all the paths [455] with great momentum.

Regarding defects in the meditation, if laxity and dullness set in, arouse your awareness. When there is scattering and excitation, relax your consciousness from within. This should not be an enmeshed mindfulness in which you deliberately try to take the rapidly moving mindful awareness of the meditator and continuously thread it tight. Rather, with the mindfulness of simply not forgetting the consciousness of your own nature, continuously sustain this during all activities of eating, lying down, walking, and standing, both during meditative equipoise and the post-meditative state. Whatever joys, sorrows, afflictive thoughts, and so forth may arise, never react to them with either hope or fear, acceptance or rejection, and never counteract them with antidotes and so forth. Rather, whatever feelings of joy and sorrow are there, rest in their own essential nature: nakedly, vividly, and lucidly. For everything that occurs, there is nothing but this one crucial point, so don't confuse yourself with a lot of thinking!

There is no need to meditate separately on emptiness as an antidote for the thoughts and mental afflictions to be abandoned. As soon as you recognize with pristine awareness whatever is to be abandoned, it will release itself, like a snake unraveling its knots. It is common for people to know how to talk about this final, hidden meaning of the clear light vajra essence, but without knowing how to put it into practice, their words are like the squawking recitations of a parrot. We have such tremendous merit!

Still, there is more to consider carefully and understand. Since beginningless lifetimes until now, [456] the mortal enemy that has bound us in samsara is the duality of the apprehender and the apprehended. Now, by the kindness of the guru, you have been introduced to the indwelling dharmakāya, so those two disappear without a trace, like a feather consumed in fire. Doesn't that satisfy your heart? Now that you have received profound practical instructions on a swift path such as this, if you don't put it into practice, this will be like putting a wish-fulfilling jewel in the mouth of a corpse—what a waste! Practice without letting your heart rot!

Beginners will find that they get carried away from mindfulness by streams of negative thoughts, resulting in quite a few subtle thoughts suddenly slipping by unnoticed. After a while, when vivid mindfulness has returned, regret arises with the thought, "I was distracted." However, at that time, without doing anything such as cutting off the thoughts that have already entered or feeling regret about having been distracted, it is enough simply to sustain the stream of vivid mindfulness that has returned and settle naturally right there.

It is commonly said that you should not reject thoughts but regard them as the dharmakāya. However, until the power of vipaśyanā has fully manifested, if you rest in a vacuous śamatha while merely pretending that "it's the dharmakāya," there is the danger that you may slip into an ethically unspecified equanimity without being able to discern anything. So in the beginning stages, whatever thoughts arise, nakedly observe them without investigating, analyzing, or reflecting upon them at all. [457] Like an old man watching children at play, simply remain as the one who recognizes the thoughts, without evaluating them or attributing any importance to them. If you rest in that way, the increasing stillness of your naturally settled nonconceptuality will suddenly and spontaneously disintegrate, and in that very instant, naked, brilliant, primordial consciousness that transcends the mind will arise.

At the time of the path, even if such an experience does not come without being mingled with the meditative experiences of bliss, luminosity, or nonconceptuality, if you do not cling to them as supreme—and can settle without even a hair's breadth of craving, pride, hope, or fear toward them—that will prevent them from becoming grounds for leading you astray. It is important that you continuously abandon distraction and meditate with single-pointed mindfulness and determination. By straying into sporadic practice and intellectual understanding, you will feel special because of your smattering of śamatha; and, without bringing clear discernment to your experiences, your knowledge that consists of mere lip service will be of no benefit.

The Great Perfection teachings state, "Understanding is like a patch, for it comes off" and "Meditative experiences are like mist, for they vanish." This is how many meditators are deceived by even minor good or bad circumstances and get lost in them. Even though meditation has been planted in your mindstream, if you do not meditate continuously, the profound practical instructions will remain in your books; and with your stubborn, untamed mind that has become insensitive to the Dharma, your practice will become jaded, so that no authentic meditation will ever arise. Old meditators who are still novices at practice are in danger of dying with their heads encrusted in salt, so they should watch out!

By acquainting yourself with practice continuously in this way for a long time, [458] eventually, due to any one of the contributing conditions of admiration, reverence, and so forth, experiences will be elevated to realizations, and you will nakedly and vividly perceive pristine awareness. As if removing a veil from your head, you will feel wide open and perfectly balanced. This is called "the supreme seeing that does not see." From that time onward, thoughts will arise as meditation, and stillness and movement equally release themselves. At first, releasing thoughts by recognizing them is like meeting someone you already know. After a while, thoughts release themselves, just as a snake unravels its own knots. Finally, thoughts are released without causing benefit or harm, like a thief in an empty house. These three phases occur progressively, and a strong conviction arises from within that all phenomena are apparitions of your own pristine awareness alone. Emptiness is stirred by a whirlpool of compassion, any preference for nirvana or samsara is extinguished, and you will realize that there are no distinctions of good and bad regarding buddhas and sentient beings. Whatever you do, your joyous mind never wavers from the actual nature of reality, so you continuously rest day and night in an open expanse. As the Great Perfection teachings state, "Realization is like space—without change."

Accordingly, such yogins appear in ordinary human form, but their minds dwell in the effortless enlightened view of the dharmakāya, enabling them to progress without activity along the bodhisattva grounds and paths. Finally, both their cognition and phenomena are extinguished: like the space inside a broken pot, [459] their bodies dissolve into minute particles, and their minds dissolve into the actual nature of reality. This is called "dwelling as the youthful vase kāya, the inner luminosity of the primordial ground, absolute space." This is what will come to pass.

That is the culmination of the view, meditation, and conduct, so it is called "the actualization of the fruition where there is nothing to achieve." Moreover, these demarcations of meditative experiences and realizations may occur in a normative sequence, without prescribed order, or all at once, according to the specific capacities of different individuals. But at the time of the fruition, there are no differences.

III. Post-Meditative Practice

Regarding the post-meditative practice of keeping your samayas and vows and integrating all your activities of this life with Dharma, if you strive in the cultivation of the view, meditation, and conduct yet are not skilled in the methods of practice between sessions, your vows and samayas will degenerate. If that happens, in the short term there will be interferences and obstacles to progressing along the bodhisattva grounds and paths, and finally you will definitely fall into Avīci Hell. So it is of the utmost importance that, without ever being separated from the sentry of mindfulness and introspection, you are unmistaken in determining what is to be adopted and what is to be rejected. As the great Ācārya [Padmasambhava] declared,

> While my view is higher than the sky,
> my conduct regarding cause and effect is finer than barley flour.

Therefore, reject a casual, crude attitude, and behave with care in terms of cause and effect. Keep your samayas and precisely maintain your vows at subtler and subtler levels, [460] and you will not be contaminated by the stains of faults and downfalls. Although there are many kinds of Secret Mantra samayas, in brief, they are synthesized as the samayas of your root guru's enlightened body, speech, and mind. It is said that if you regard your guru as an ordinary person even for an instant, this will delay your accomplishment of *siddhis* by months and years. Why? This is because of the crucial point that the guru is a sacred field, as it is said,

> Because Vajradhara said that siddhis follow after the master.

Therefore, whoever you are, until you first accept someone as your guru, you are on your own. But from the moment that you devote yourself to a guru and become linked with him through empowerments and practical instructions, then you have no choice but to keep your samayas. At the conclusion of the four empowerments, you bowed in front of the guru as the principal deity of the maṇḍala and vowed to him,

> From now on, I offer myself
> to you as your servant.
> Please accept me as your disciple
> and make use of even the smallest part of me.

With that oath, however great and noble you may be, haven't you sworn your allegiance to the guru? Likewise, regarding the vow, "Whatever the principal deity commands, I shall do all that you say," from that time forward, do you have the right not to do whatever he says? If you do not fulfill your oath, you cannot be called anything but a "samaya-breaker," as disagreeable as that label may be. [461]

Furthermore, nowhere is it said that you must keep your samayas perfectly with great gurus who have many attendants and much wealth, power, and authority but not with minor gurus who accept a low status and live as beggars. Regardless of who it is, you should understand the crucial points of the advantages and risks of such a relationship, for it won't do to be like a dull-witted old nag. Therefore, as if you were preparing medicinal substances, settle your mind in its natural state and carefully consider whether the need to keep the samayas is for the guru's sake or for your own sake. If it is for the guru's sake, you may as well set them aside this very day. But if not, there is no point in throwing ashes on your own head!

In general, the samayas regarding your spiritual relatives and friends consist of looking charitably upon everyone who has entered the door of the Buddha's teachings and of cultivating pure perception of them. Avoid all bias and disparagement regarding philosophical schools. In particular, all those who have the same guru and are included within the same maṇḍala are vajra siblings and friends, so renounce such attitudes as contempt, competitiveness, envy, and deceitfulness, and hold them dear to your heart in mutual harmony.

Consider, "All sentient beings, without exception, have been our kind parents. How sad that they are tormented by the terrible miseries of endless samsara! If I do not protect them, [462] who will?" Unable to bear this thought, train your mind in the cultivation of compassion. By means of your body, speech, and mind, make whatever efforts you can to do only that which is beneficial, and dedicate all your virtue for the benefit of others.

At all times there are only three things to think about: the Dharma, the guru, and sentient beings. So do not let your intentions and actions deviate from those. Do not compete with those who bear the trappings and titles of realized adepts and monks. Rather, keep your mouth shut and control your own mind. This is of utmost importance, so don't be a fool.

If you fundamentally think of your own welfare solely in terms of future lifetimes, then you have good reason for the imperative to practice what we call "Dharma." But if you place your hopes in the roots of virtue that others may perform on your behalf after you are dead, it will be difficult to derive any benefit from them. So turn your mind within, keep it there, and with a heartfelt spirit of emergence, hold your ground by applying mindfulness, determination, and strong enthusiasm to saturate your entire life with spiritual practice. Strike the crucial points of the main practice of the profound view and meditation; between formal meditation sessions, keep your [Vajrayāna] samayas, [bodhisattva] training, and [Śrāvakayāna] vows; and don't behave in any way that is contrary to what should and should not be done according to your vows. As a result, virtuous qualities will inevitably arise from within, for the Great Perfection is a path that will forcefully bring to enlightenment even those who have committed very evil deeds.

By the power of the extraordinary profundity of the Great Perfection, there will also be obstacles, just as great profit often comes with great risk. This is because all the negative karma [463] you have accumulated in the past is catalyzed due to the potency of these practical instructions, and this manifests externally as the upheavals of demonic interferences and apparitions.

In the place where you practice, gods and demons may show their forms, call you by name, and take on the guise of your guru and make prophecies. Various terrifying apparitions may appear as meditative experiences or in your dreams, and it is possible that you may in fact be subject to beatings at the hands of others, theft, illness, and so on. All of these can arise in indeterminate ways.

Psychologically, you may inexplicably experience intense misery and sadness that will make you want to weep. You may experience strong mental afflictions, and your sense of admiration and reverence, bodhicitta, and compassion may decline. Thoughts may arise as your enemies, nearly driving you mad. You may misinterpret words intended to help you, and losing the desire to remain in retreat, you may consider abandoning your solemn commitment. You may experience false views regarding your guru, doubts about the Dharma, and so on. In addition, you may suffer false accusations and a bad reputation, your friends may arise as enemies, and so forth. Various outer and inner undesirable circumstances may well emerge.

Oh, these are all indications of upheavals, so recognize them! Here is the demarcation between profit and loss: If you embrace those obstacles by means of the crucial points of practice, they will turn into siddhis. If you fall under their influence, they will become hindrances. With pure samayas, admiration, reverence, [464] and unfaltering courage, entrust your heart and mind to your guru, and earnestly pray to him with confidence in whatever he may do. By taking unfavorable circumstances as something desirable, and by striving diligently in your practice, eventually the substantiality of those circumstances will naturally dissolve, and they will instead empower your practice.

Appearances will fade like mist, you will have even greater confidence in your guru and his practical instructions than you did before, and from now on you will find the fortitude to accept such upheavals with equanimity. Oh, this indicates that they are coming to an end, for by transforming such circumstances into the path, conditions for their termination are brought about. *A la la*, that is what we old fathers want! Don't behave like a fox sneaking up to a human corpse, with its haunches trembling in fear even as it longs to devour it. Make your mind strong.

Those with little merit, lax samayas and vows, flagrant false views, and a host of doubts, who make big commitments but whose practice is weak— such people, whose hearts stink like farts—request their guru's practical instructions only to leave them on their bookshelves. By fixating with a death grip on unfavorable conditions and then ruminating on them, they are easily snared by māras who lead them on the path to miserable states of existence. How very sad! Pray to your guru that this doesn't happen.

Moreover, although it may be relatively easy for unfavorable circumstances to arise as the path, it is very difficult for favorable conditions to do so. Therefore, if those who pride themselves on their supposedly high level of realization devote themselves solely to achieving high status in this life, [465] they are in danger of becoming servants of the māra of distraction, Devaputra. So you must be very careful. Understand that this is the test that determines the demarcation between meditators who go up or go down. Until the power of the qualities from your inner realizations is perfected, it is inappropriate to tell just anyone indiscriminately about your meditative experiences, so keep quiet. Furthermore, without boasting about how many months or years you have spent in retreat, devote yourself to practice for your whole life. Do not deceive yourself with your talk about emptiness, such that you dismiss the importance of virtuous deeds within the obscurative reality of cause and effect.

Do not linger in populated places for the sake of getting supplies by means of performing village rituals for subduing demons and so on. Keep pointless activities, unnecessary talking, and worthless thoughts to a minimum. Do not deceive others with what is incompatible with Dharma, such as pretense and guile. Do not engage in wrong livelihood by making indirect requests, flattery, and so on out of craving for desirable things. Do not associate with those whose views and conduct are incompatible with your own or with evil friends. Disclose your own faults, and do not speak of the hidden faults of others. All kinds of smoking are said to be tricks of demons that cause you to break your samayas, so earnestly avoid them. Although alcohol is to be relied upon as a samaya substance, do not carelessly drink it to the point of intoxication. Without discriminating, bring everyone along the path—including those with whom you have good and bad relations, those who faithfully serve you as well as those who distrust you, revile you, [466] and treat you badly—and look after them with pure prayers.

At all times, inwardly keep your spirits high, without losing heart, and outwardly keep your deeds discreet. Wear worn-out clothes. Uplift everyone: the good, bad, and middling. Live frugally and keep to mountain hermitages. Hold as your ideal the life of a beggar. Emulate the life stories of the siddhas of the past. Not blaming your past karma, practice Dharma as purely as you can. Not blaming transient circumstances, remain steadfast, no matter what happens. In short, with your own mind as your witness, unite your entire life with Dharma so that when you die, you have left nothing undone and you are not ashamed of yourself. The crucial point of all practices consists of this.

When it comes time for you to die, renounce all your worldly possessions without being attached even to a needle. In the face of death, the best practitioners feel elated, the middling have no apprehension about death, and the least experience no regret when they will die. If you experience the clear light of realization continuously, day and night, there will be no intermediate period, and only the encasing of the body will be destroyed. Otherwise, if you have confidence that you will be liberated in the intermediate period, whatever you do is fine. If you do not have such confidence, having already gained some experience in training in the transference of consciousness, perform the deed when the time comes, [467] and transfer your consciousness to the buddhafield of your choice. There you will progress along the remaining bodhisattva grounds and paths and achieve enlightenment.

Therefore, this precious lineage of ours is not just ancient history, for even these days there are individuals who come to the highest state of realization by following the paths of cutting through and the direct crossing over, and their material bodies dissolve into a mass of rainbow light.

This being the case, do not throw away this jewel and then seek some trinket. You are extremely fortunate to have encountered such profound practical instructions, which are like the heart blood of the *ḍākinī*s. Keep your spirits high and meditate with joy! Disciples, cherish this text as the jewel of your heart, and it is possible that great benefits will arise.

Colophon

With the primary cause being the mountain retreat practice of the meditators of Ogmin Pema Öling, and the contributing condition being the request of the diligent practitioner Rigzang Dorjé, who possesses the jewel of indivisible faith and reverence, this was spoken by Jigdral Yeshé Dorjé, as heartfelt and concise advice for practice. May this be a cause for the forceful emergence of the primordial consciousness of realization in the mindstreams of fortunate beings.

PART TWO

The Commentary

B. Alan Wallace

1. Introduction

Meaning of the Title

The translation of the title of the root text is *Extracting the Vital Essence of Accomplishment: Concise and Clear Advice for Practice in a Mountain Retreat.* "Extracting the vital essence" is called *chülen* in Tibetan. *Chü* is the vital, nutritive essence of earth, water, fire, air, and space and is that which actually nourishes your body. *Len* means "to extract." There are various types of vital essences; one such example is a flower vital essence. If you are an accomplished yogi, you would mix dried flower petals, along with some other herbs, together with ground, roasted barley flour called *tsampa* to give it substance, adding honey and butter to hold it all together, and then roll it into marble-sized balls. By the power of your samādhi, you then dissolve everything into emptiness, and from emptiness you turn your awareness to the dreamlike environment, drawing in the vital essences of the elements of earth, water, fire, air, and space, respectively. These are what sustain your body, while everything else is secondary. Then you channel these essences into the chülen pills. If you are able to accomplish that over a period of three weeks, during which you partake only of these pills without any coarse food—eating three pills a day, plus as much hot water as you want—then your whole metabolism may shift so that you can live on these pills indefinitely. Gen Jhampa Wangdü was the Tibetan yogi from whom I received the oral transmission of this, and he accomplished it when he was in retreat in Tibet, living on such flower essence pills for months on end.

The spirit of this "vital essence" is that simply by taking these pills, you get all the nutrition you need. Whereas, when you eat ordinary food, there is a lot of excess that is not needed and the body flushes it out. However, if you are taking only three pills like this, then your body assimilates all of it because that is exactly what you need, no more and no less. That is the connotation here of "extracting the vital essence." Likewise, by extracting the essence of all meditative accomplishment through the practice of Dzogchen, you draw forth the vital essence of consciousness itself. This is the ultimate aim of Dharma, and it is the central theme of this priceless text by Düdjom Rinpoché.

———

In their pursuit of happiness and freedom from suffering, most people devote their lives to seeking material gain and avoiding loss, pursuing sensual pleasures and avoiding displeasure, longing for praise and fearing blame, and trying to gain a good reputation and doing everything possible to avoid the dislike and disrespect of others. In Buddhism these are called the "eight mundane concerns," and they have never brought enduring satisfaction in the past and will never do so in the future. Yet, we pursue them at great cost: bearing the anxiety of not acquiring material gain, pleasure, praise, and respect—despite our best efforts—and then still facing anxiety once we do acquire them because we fear losing them, which we certainly will. It is a loser's game.

Due to the dominant influences of the metaphysical beliefs and values of scientific materialism, our modern society (more than any other in recorded history) has been brainwashed into looking outward for the causes of happiness as well as for the causes of our discontent and unhappiness. The unique potentials of human existence are ignored as we are taught to view ourselves as animals and nothing more—as if we have no inner resources to tap into that could actually provide us with the satisfaction and meaning that is our hearts' desire! So we are encouraged to run in circles in the human rat race in a futile search for happiness, but, as the comedienne Lily Tomlin quipped, "The trouble with the rat race is that even if you win, you're still a rat."

The fact that the pleasures we have experienced thus far are not sustainable may not bother us if we are convinced that life is short and it ends in oblivion. After all, if our consciousness terminates at death, then nothing we achieve is sustainable, so why not experience as many transient pleasures as possible during our brief existence? This whole way of viewing human existence is rooted in the blind faith that our consciousness emerges from matter during gestation and simply disappears at death. This view is taken to be a scientific fact and is secured by an uncritical faith in the primacy of matter in the universe. In reality, scientists have no knowledge of the necessary and sufficient causes that give rise to consciousness during the formation of a human fetus, so they are equally ignorant of what happens to consciousness at death.

Further, there is, in fact, no evidence that the brain itself is either conscious or intelligent. The mind is conscious and intelligent, it arises in dependence upon the brain, and it constantly interacts with the brain, but the configurations of chemicals and electricity in the brain—either individually or collectively—are no more conscious than the components of a computer. Historically, it is not mere ignorance but rather illusions of knowledge—like those promoted by neuro-mythology—that have proven to be the greatest obstacles to discoveries.

In scientific writings there is plenty of speculation about "how the brain produces consciousness," but this conjecture is nothing more than science fiction. The same is true of the nature of what is euphemistically called "artificial intelligence." Artificial sweeteners serve as substitutes for natural sweeteners, like sugar and honey. Artificial limbs perform the tasks of biological limbs. Conversely, computers and robots have no artificial intelligence; they have "imitation intelligence." That is, these programs respond *as if* they were intelligent, but this is a mere imitation of intelligence, for in reality they do not know or understand anything since they are not conscious of anything. Thus they cannot actually perform the function of intelligence. It is merely due to the conscious, intelligent programmers who design them in such a way that they function *as if* they were conscious and intelligent that enables the imitation of intelligence.

Presenting pseudoscience as science is fraudulent, and the editorial boards of such scientific journals as well as the popular media are culpable in perpetuating such nonsense. It is disturbing when the entertainment industry, too, suggests that there is a scientific basis for depicting robots and computer programs as conscious, sentient beings in movies, for example. For the same reason that scientists do not know how or when a human embryo becomes conscious—because the necessary and sufficient causes for consciousness are unknown to modern science—they do not know how or when a computer could possibly become conscious either. The assertion that it does is sheer speculation, and to present it as anything else is delusional. As propagandists know all too well, if you forcefully tell a lie often enough and with great confidence—no matter how groundless and far-fetched—many people will accept your words as truth, to the advantage of the propagandists but to the disadvantage of those they have knowingly or unknowingly duped.

The entertainment industry has lapped up the fiction that computers and robots are, or can be, conscious based on the assumption that if their algorithms are sufficiently complex, consciousness will pop out like a genie from a magical lamp. The unadorned reality is that the brain—consisting of complex configurations of protein, fat, water, and electricity—is no more magical or capable of producing consciousness than any other organ. We are not robots. We are conscious, but consciousness remains the last unexplored frontier for modern science. Most cognitive scientists acknowledge that it remains a mystery, but the fact that it is an unsolved mystery for scientists does not mean that no one else has fathomed it. It is high time for us to break out of our ethnocentric perspective and recognize that other "prescientific" cultures have made important, fundamental discoveries that modern Eurocentric societies have not replicated.

In his erudite, while nonetheless fundamentally Eurocentric, tome called *The Discoverers*, the eminent historian Daniel J. Boorstin writes, "The obstacles to discovery—the illusions of knowledge—are also part of our story. Only against the forgotten backdrop of the received common sense and myths of their time can we begin to sense the courage, the rashness, the heroic and imaginative thrusts of the great discoverers. They had to battle against the current 'facts' and dogmas of the learned." The fact that there has been no real revolution in the mind sciences since their inception 150 years ago is not due to ignorance but rather due to the ubiquitous illusions of knowledge rooted in the metaphysical beliefs of materialism. The adage "the mind is what the brain does" has become almost universally accepted in academia, but it falsely implies that the mind-body problem has been solved, whereas in reality no progress has been made in the past century to actually fathom how the mind and body interrelate.

Further, the corresponding, reductionist belief that all mental diseases are due to nothing more than chemical imbalances in the brain, and that they should be remedied as such, has been thoroughly discredited by copious clinical evidence. Despite billions spent on research and development, and many more billions made in profits by the sale of psychopharmaceutical drugs, the unhealthy alliance between the neuroscientific establishment and the pharmaceutical industry has not produced a single medication that cures any mental disease. Nevertheless, the persistent fiction that mental diseases are simply brain disorders continues to influence public opinion and the allocation of mental health research funding. Moreover, the psychiatric profession is equally culpable in this scandal, as they perpetuate the delusion by prescribing mental painkillers as if they were medications that actually heal mental diseases.

Dharma presents an alternative strategy to understanding consciousness and to cultivating genuine happiness and freedom from suffering. In particular, by extracting the vital essence of accomplishment along the path of the Great Perfection—through the achievement of śamatha, vipaśyanā, and cutting through to pristine awareness (*trekchö*)—the nature of consciousness can be thoroughly fathomed. By so doing, we can fulfill our innermost longing for genuine well-being and contentment, no longer needing to "feed on the coarse food" of mundane pleasures through the pursuit of wealth, power, and fame. Once we are able to live on the "food" of samādhi, we will no longer need or be attracted to mundane pleasures.

In his classic work *The Ocean of Definitive Meaning*, the Ninth Karmapa, Wangchuk Dorjé, was referring to the achievement of a high level of samādhi when he wrote, "Thus, due to the experiences of bliss, luminosity, and nonconceptuality, craving for the allures of the desire realm subsides, there is no need to eat food, and the movements of the respiration are not sensed. Great joy arises with the thought, 'Now *this* is what the Buddha had in mind.'"[7]

Rather than looking in vain to the outer world for a sustainable sense of well-being, fruitlessly pursuing it in all directions, the wise look inward and cultivate their own minds. By tapping into their inner resources, they find what they have always been looking for. The true source of genuine well-being is our own pristine awareness, and Düdjom Rinpoché points us directly to this hidden treasure.

Returning to the title of the root text, the term *mar tri* is translated as "direct" or "concise." Literally *mar tri* means "red guidance," which means "concise" and "right to the point" so that it is "directly applicable." This is a teaching method in which the subject is explained using practical examples, and it is analogous to a physician who cuts open a cadaver and points directly to the various internal organs. As for "clear," the term is *go der jöpa*, which means "easy to understand." This guidance is easy to understand, though it may be difficult to practice. The word *labja* simply means "advice." *Ri chö* is "mountain Dharma."

So, this is "Concise and Clear Advice for Practice in a Mountain Retreat," given by the mind emanation of Düdjom Lingpa—Düdjom Rinpoché, Jigdral Yeshé Dorjé.

2. The Structure of the Root Text

Düdjom Rinpoché begins the text with homage, reverence, and humility, writing,

> **I reverently bow and take refuge at the feet of the sublime and glorious guru, whose kindness is beyond compare. Bless me and my disciples so that unmistaken realizations of the profound path may swiftly arise in our mindstreams and that we may take hold of the primordial citadel in this very lifetime.**

We receive kindness from many people in our lives, for which we then seek to repay this kindness. However, the kindness that sentient beings can grant us is embedded within the fleeting comforts of samsara, as the great crushing machine of aging, sickness, and death comes along and whatever kindness, benefits, advice, counsel, and help we have received from sentient beings turns into nothing. This is not an exclusivism or triumphalism with regard to Buddhism over any other spiritual tradition; but rather, simply with a focus on Buddhadharma, we recognize that the incomparable guidance, advice, and kindness offered by the guru is the only guidance that can be of benefit in this and all future lifetimes. It is "beyond compare" with any kindness that can be given to us by ordinary sentient beings alone.

Düdjom Rinpoché then calls upon his own guru: "Bless me and my disciples so that unmistaken realizations of the profound path may swiftly arise in our mindstreams and that we may take hold of the primordial citadel in this very lifetime." The term *path* is utterly central to the practice and to understanding the view. We can receive much advice from others in order to become more virtuous, calmer, and kinder, and although the advice can be very helpful, will any of it lead to a path that carries us through this lifetime, through death, through the *bardo*, into the next lifetime, and, continuing in an unbroken fashion, all the way to enlightenment? How many people can give that kind of guidance and are even striving to reach the path? This instruction, time and again, puts repeated emphasis on reaching the path and progressing all the way through to enlightenment.

When Düdjom Rinpoché writes in the text, "Bless me and my disciples so that . . . we may take hold of the primordial citadel in this very lifetime," the words "primordial citadel" are referring to *rigpa*, or pristine awareness. He is urging us to take hold of it, live in it, dwell in it, and abide in it—to identify it and sustain taking hold of it so that we are able to remain there. However, this "taking hold" does not mean grasping onto it like an object, which is completely contradictory to fathoming pristine awareness.

Düdjom Rinpoché then writes,

> There are three general topics in this concise and clear presentation of advice for the practice of the very secret Great Perfection, consisting of training in the crucial points for a mountain retreat.

In order to receive these Dzogchen pith instructions, it is necessary to come to a certain view. In the Dzogchen context, look upon the guru and other practitioners with pure vision, seeing into the purity and depths of each one. Recognize that any impure appearances are like a simulation. Although there is causality in the simulation, do not take it to be inherently real. Gyatrul Rinpoché said many times of himself, with a sense of humor, that he is an empty lama sitting upon an empty box. Taking these simulations to be real catalyzes a deluge of emotional upheavals. Rather, as the Buddha guided Bāhiya in his pith instructions, "In the seen, let there be only the seen; in the heard, let there be only the heard; in the tactilely sensed, let there be only the tactilely sensed; and in the mentally perceived, let there be only the mentally perceived." Without superimposing anything upon the sense fields, view everything as dreamlike, as simulations generated by karma and *kleśa*, or mental afflictions. With insight into the emptiness of inherent nature of all phenomena, you are not caught in the drama of the simulations. Therefore, if you are living at home, take care not to get tangled in the simulations of the people around you who are viewing everything as if it is really there. Instead, rest attentively in the serenity and stillness of your own awareness with an open heart, and act like an illusory being who sees everything as dreamlike.

Regarding "very secret," here is a bit of context. There are nine *yāna*s, or successive vehicles, on the path to enlightenment, and the ninth one is the highest one and is the *atiyoga*, which is Dzogchen. Atiyoga has three different classes: the mind class, the expanse class, and the pith instruction class. Each of these classes is very extensive and includes a broad body of teachings, practices, and so forth. Within the three classes of Dzogchen teachings—mind, expanse, and pith instructions—this root text belongs to the most profound class: these are pith instructions. Then within the class of pith instructions, there is the outer, the inner, the secret, and the ultrasecret. This text is the ultrasecret, or the "very secret." This classification is true as well, without exception, for all of the visionary teachings on Dzogchen that Düdjom Lingpa transmitted—they are all pith instructions and are all very secret. These are intended for people who have the faith, confidence, determination, and vision to put these teachings into practice and achieve rainbow body in the near future. They are not intended for people who will receive the teachings in this lifetime but will not have time to put them into practice, simply hoping to find this wish-fulfilling jewel again in the next lifetime when they hope to have more leisure and not to have so many things to do that they consider to be more important. If you place your priorities only on mundane things now, how do you expect to find better circumstances in a future life, the conditions for which will be ripening from the karma you are creating now? If you cast aside the wish-fulfilling jewel of the most sublime Dharma now, how do you expect to find another such jewel in the future?

He continues, saying,

> **This provides an entrance for those fortunate individuals in whom previous prayers and pure, residual karma are united; for those who have heartfelt trust in the profound, secret Dharma of the Great Perfection and in the guru who reveals it; and for those who are intent on pursuing this practice to its culmination.**

For those who have made prayers in past lives, this is the thread, like connecting beads on a *mālā*. Right now we can be threading the beads of this and future lifetimes with the power of our pure, deep, bodhicitta-inspired prayers to see that every bead, every lifetime—whether it is one lifetime, a thousand lifetimes, or three countless eons of lifetimes—is meaningfully connected to the previous ones, and it is not just a bunch of beads on the floor. There is a clear coherence as we proceed into the endless future, which is called a *path*. The first thing we can do to create continuity is dedicate merit. In conjunction with our prayers of dedication is residual karma, *lé tro*, which consists of the things we set out to do in past lifetimes but did not quite finish, such as achieving enlightenment in one lifetime. The prayers and aspirations were there, yet through the direction of our mundane desires—for temporary achievements, financial security, influence, reputation, and so forth—coupled with our residual karma, we remained in samsara. In other words, our merit will go wherever we desire it to go, such that our mundane desires can keep us stuck in samsara, never quite fulfilled.

Bodhicitta and the four immeasurables—loving-kindness, compassion, empathetic joy, and impartiality—are undoubtedly desires and aspirations, and so, they too can bring us back to samsara. The aspiration that all sentient beings may find happiness and the causes of happiness, and the resolve that we shall lead them to such happiness means our work will not be finished until all sentient beings are free from samsara. However, that does not mean we must stay bound in samsara ourselves until everyone else has achieved awakening. Rather, it does mean that our quintessential work is not finished, which is a kind of residual karma, or unfulfilled task. As Śāntideva wrote in his *Guide to the Bodhisattva Way of Life*, "For as long as space remains, for as long as sentient beings remain, so long shall I remain for the alleviation of suffering of the world." Our prayers of dedication are the reins that direct our residual karma, threading it from lifetime to lifetime.

When Düdjom Rinpoché says, "for those fortunate individuals in whom previous prayers and pure, residual karma are united," he is identifying a very specific group of people. Further, "for those who have heartfelt trust in the profound, secret Dharma of the Great Perfection and in the guru who reveals it" means placing trust in both the Dharma and the guru, whereby the guru must not behave in such a way that betrays that trust. Further, the primary practice to support all other practices of Dzogchen is guru yoga. On the Dzogchen path, if you do no other preliminary practices except for guru yoga, that may be enough. Guru yoga will hold everything—the four immeasurables, bodhicitta, and so forth—but without it, you are not really practicing Dzogchen. It is core, central, and indispensable. This text is intended for those who have this heartfelt trust and who reverently practice guru yoga.

Finally, it is "for those who are intent on pursuing this practice to its culmination." Everything you need to know in order to realize the Great Perfection, to view reality from the perspective of the Great Perfection, and to engage in the full path is here in this text. Düdjom Rinpoché is extracting this vital essence for people who have the faith, determination, and self-confidence that this is the path they are choosing to follow and that they will follow to its culmination.

In this context, he continues,

> These are the three general topics to be understood: (1) the preparation: how to cut the ties of attachment and clinging, direct your mind to Dharma, and purify your mindstream; (2) the main practice: how to cut through false superimpositions regarding the view, meditation, and conduct and then set out on the road of practice; and (3) the post-meditative practice: how to keep your samayas and vows and how to incorporate all your activities of this life into the Dharma.

Regarding the first topic on the preparation, "how to cut the ties of attachment and clinging, direct your mind to Dharma, and purify your mindstream," recall the pith instructions of Dromtönpa, the foremost disciple of Atiśa: "Give up all attachment to this life"—that is, cut the ties of attachment and clinging to the eight mundane concerns. Then, "direct your mind to Dharma" by letting your mind become Dharma, never wavering from it. Finally, "purify your mindstream." This is the preparation.

Next, the main practice is "how to cut through false superimpositions regarding the view, meditation, and conduct and then set out on the road of practice." Here, they can be superimpositions or preconceptions that you project upon reality. The nectar of the Dzogchen that is being presented and then filtered through your mind can be easily contaminated, so that it becomes muddied with your own ideas, preferences, and preconceptions to the point that what was taught is unrecognizable with respect to its original form. It is necessary to cut through those projections and make your understanding leaner, with none of the fat that you project upon it. In this way, the main practice is how to cut through, or eliminate, such superimposed misconceptions regarding view, meditation, and conduct and then "set out on the road of practice." Once you have gained understanding, all of that is preparation, with the whole of your being, to set out on the road. This highlights something that is central to all of Buddhadharma, beginning with the four ārya realities (widely known as the four noble truths). People who do not practice any kind of authentic Dharma do not have a path to liberation—they only have a spinning merry-go-round to more samsara; only it is not so merry—more like a "misery-go-round." But that is not a path. All of Dharma is about path; it is about a road where you are heading in a particular direction instead of going around in circles. You begin by floundering in the ocean of samsara, and then you become increasingly free until you are no longer floundering at all—that is a path.

The third general topic addressing post-meditative practice is "how to keep your samayas and vows and how to incorporate all your activities of this life into the Dharma." Many of you may not be living in a mountain retreat, but there are two types of solitude. One is the outer simplicity that occurs when living in solitude, surrounded by the beauties of nature, with very few things to do. The other is inner solitude, which is overwhelmingly more important. You may be alone, but your mind could be totally trafficking in all the affairs of the world. In that case, outer solitude would be a mere semblance of real solitude. In principle, however, outer solitude is for the sake of cultivating and sustaining inner solitude. For a great being like Düdjom Rinpoché, he was married twice and had eleven children, but he never absconded to solitary retreat for long periods of time. He brought such enormous momentum into this life from being an emanation of Düdjom Lingpa that there was no need for him to adopt the outer veneer of leaving his wife and children in order to go off into the mountains on extended retreats. Rather, he was always in retreat—abiding constantly in rigpa, in which one's physical location does not matter because one sees everything as displays of pristine awareness.

If you take these teachings very personally, as if Guru Rinpoché himself is giving this advice right now for you to be able to transform your present circumstance, then you will derive the greatest possible benefit.

3. The Preparation

Düdjom Rinpoché begins the first preparatory stage by writing,

> **Now I will say a little about the first topic. Alas! From the very first, the vivid, clear, swift knowing of this so-called mind of ours has emerged simultaneously with Samantabhadra.**

Choosing his words carefully, he does not say, "this mind of ours" but rather says, "this so-called mind of ours." It is "so-called" because it is simply a way of talking about the mind, which has only a nominal existence. In the Prajñāpāramitā sūtras, it is written, "The mind is not the mind; the nature of the mind is clear light." This point is also seen in the Pāli canon: "Monks, this mind is luminous, but it is obscured by adventitious defilements. Monks, this mind is luminous, but it is free from adventitious defilements."[1]

Even so, we have thoughts, emotions, laxity, excitation, and many other mental fabrications, about which the nun Vajirā said of her own identity, "This is a heap of sheer constructions: Here no being is found. Just as, with an assemblage of parts, the word *chariot* is used, so, when the aggregates are present, there's the convention *a being*." If you look for the car, or the chariot, you do not find it. A chariot never actually came into existence by any nature of its own. There was never a point in time when first there was no chariot and then suddenly there is a chariot, all from its own side. The same holds true for tectonic plates, mountains, planets, and so forth. There was never a point when, objectively, any of it actually came into existence. The earth will not always be here, but there will never be a time when it stops existing from its own side either. So this is what the nun Vajirā says: As for the chariot, so for you, me, and everything else.

When Düdjom Rinpoché writes that "the vivid, clear, swift knowing of this so-called mind of ours"—in other words, the mind with its fundamental characteristics of luminosity and cognizance—"has emerged simultaneously with Samantabhadra," this means that our samsaric minds and Samantabhadra are coemergent in every moment, and neither one has a beginning. The mind is not really there; if you look for its origin, location, destination, and if you look for that which is looking, what do you find? It is a simulation of mind.

Tsokyé Dorjé, the Lake-Born Vajra, offers a powerful vaccine toward the beginning of *The Vajra Essence*.[2] He says that before you take this so-called mind, the impure mind, as the path in the practice of śamatha, know that it is not really there—it has no origin, no location, and no destination. From that point on, when your mind torments you with outer, inner, and secret upheavals, then you will know that all these *nyam*, or meditative experiences, are simply simulations all the way through. As such, they are free to come and go without the mind's habit of reification making them seem real and substantial. If you know that, and you are lucid with respect to your mind, then there is nothing your mind can do to harm you or discourage you, for your mind is not even there—it is just an array of empty appearances.

It is possible to see for yourself that it is a "so-called mind" if and only if you are not caught in its grip. On the other hand, if you are entangled in your emotions, desires, feelings, anxieties, fears, and so forth, then simply saying that your mind is just a conceptual imputation and has no existence from its own side is not going to be very persuasive. However, where your mind is, there is Samantabhadra; where Samantabhadra is, there is your mind. Samantabhadra is the embodiment of your own pristine awareness, which is indwelling and always present. Since your mind in samsara and Samantabhadra are coemergent, this means you always have a choice: You have a choice whether to view people and all mental and physical phenomena according to their impure, manifest forms, which are arising from karma and mental afflictions, or to look straight through those appearances to their emptiness, to their pure ground. If you can recognize the primordial purity of your own mind as Samantabhadra, from which only pure appearances emerge, then you can begin to view everything from the perspective of Samantabhadra, your own pristine awareness, which means that appearances will arise as pure displays of primordial consciousness. And even before this takes place spontaneously, you can choose to view appearances from your approximation of that perspective, and this practice can instantly loosen your grip on things as being real in the way they first presented themselves to your ordinary mind.

Düdjom Rinpoché continues,

> But Samantabhadra is free because he knows his own nature, while we sentient beings endlessly wander in samsara because we do not. We have become embodied countless times among the six types of existence, and everything we have done has turned out to be meaningless. Now, for once out of a hundred times, on this occasion when have taken human form, if we fail to achieve the means to avoid taking rebirth in samsara and the miserable realms, after we die, there is no certainty as to where we will be reborn. Wherever we take birth among the six types of beings, there is nothing but suffering. It is not enough to have acquired this human form, and since the time of death is unknown, we must practice authentic Dharma right now.

Habitually, we are engrossed in the simulation, and that simulation has a reality to it—it is not nothing. The simulation of who you think you are, where you think you are, who you think your teacher is, and so forth certainly has a lot of clout and power to it with its causal efficacy. Nonetheless, it completely obscures a deeper reality, which is Samantabhadra. The difference between sentient beings and buddhas is that buddhas know who they are, whereas we sentient beings do not because we are so caught in the grip of hoping and fearing everything about the illusory phenomena that we take to be real.

He asserts that "we have become embodied countless times among the six types of existence, and everything we have done has turned out to be meaningless." What do we have to show for all the striving we have done for countless lifetimes, always with the same motivation of wanting to be free from the sufferings of samsara and yearning to find happiness? Are we less angry, less selfish, and less arrogant than the people around us who have not encountered Dharma? A life without Dharma is a life that is meaningless. In this case "Dharma" does not refer solely to the Buddhadharma, for there are those in other spiritual traditions with authentic understandings and practices that then become their Dharma. If you do not have Dharma, then you do not have anything of value at all, and "everything we have done has turned out to be meaningless." Further, there is a clear demarcation between genuine Dharma and mundane dharmas. In terms of mundane activities, they always prove to be meaningless. When all is said and done, the culmination of such mundane dharmas is that we get older and our health inevitably declines. There are no enduring effects that lead to liberation from such cyclic existence when motivation is rooted in the mundane dharmas.

He continues, "Now, for once out of a hundred times, on this occasion when we have taken human form, if we fail to achieve the means to avoid taking rebirth in samsara and the miserable realms, after we die, there is no certainty as to where we will be reborn." For all practical purposes, this is the most important discovery ever made about the mind, and it has been replicated countless times. The mind does not emerge from matter. Any knowledgeable physicist would agree that something so intangible, immaterial, and nonphysical as the mind cannot, in principle, emerge from chemicals or electricity, for example. There is no branch of physics in which nonphysical phenomena have been shown to emerge from physical things. Rather, if contemporary scientists could come to recognize, through replicable contemplative experiments, that the human mind has emerged from a subtle continuum of consciousness and dissolves back into that continuum at death, this would bring about a scientific revolution of even greater magnitude than those inaugurated by Galileo, Darwin, or Einstein.

The continuity of consciousness from lifetime to lifetime is, according to Buddhist epistemology, a "hidden phenomenon"—namely, one that is not immediately evident, but can be discovered by means of direct experience and logic. The continuity of an individual, subtle stream of consciousness after death and the emergence of a configured mind from that consciousness at the beginning of gestation in a new lifetime is not something that can be detected with the physical instruments of material technology, but it can be observed with the contemplative technology of a mind fully trained in samādhi. This is something to investigate as thoroughly as possible until its truth is discovered firsthand, and it will be one of the most important discoveries you ever make.

Further, "Wherever we take birth among the six types of beings, there is nothing but suffering. It is not enough to have acquired this human form, and since the time of death is unknown, we must practice authentic Dharma right now." How do we come to know whether or not the Dharma we are following is authentic? Ask yourself: Does it alleviate your mental afflictions? Does it nurture virtue? Does it give rise to genuine well-being and peace of mind? Does it open the heart to compassion and loving-kindness? Does it give rise to insight that transforms and frees the one who gains such insight? These are all signs of authentic Dharma and are undoubtedly not confined to Buddhism alone, for, as mentioned, these fruits can be found in the practices of other spiritual traditions as well.

Düdjom Rinpoché then advises,

> So that we do not feel remorse in the face of death and are not ashamed of ourselves, we must be like the venerable Milarepa, who declared,

> > In my Milarepa Dharma tradition,
> > we are not ashamed of ourselves.

Now with a sense of urgency, we must practice authentic Dharma "so that we do not feel remorse in the face of death and are not ashamed of ourselves." Would you not feel embarrassed if, upon receiving valuable teachings from authentic lamas, you procrastinated and prioritized mundane pursuits instead? Perhaps you feel that full-time practice can wait until your life shifts, as other things seem more important. But before you know it, death comes sooner than you thought, and then you feel ashamed of yourself for having received these profound teachings, but postponed practicing them. His Holiness the Dalai Lama once told me that the more you have been given in terms of understanding, knowledge, and insight, the greater responsibility you have. Like His Holiness the Dalai Lama, Dilgo Khyentsé Rinpoché, Düdjom Rinpoché, Archbishop Desmond Tutu, and many other great beings, you must take full responsibility for the preciousness, authenticity, and power of the teachings and practices you have received. You must not squander this opportunity that is given to you.

The line "In my Milarepa Dharma tradition, we are not ashamed of ourselves" means that you know what you have received and are doing your absolute best to put it into practice so that when you die, there is no shame.

THE CRITERION FOR AUTHENTIC DHARMA

Düdjom Rinpoché states,

> So that our Dharma practice leads to the path, it is not enough to maintain an outer facade of Dharma. Rather, we must set aside all activities that are concerned with this life and cut all ties to the allures of the desire realm.

Myriad sentient beings have engaged in virtue throughout history. No species, nor any ethnicity, religion, and so forth, has a monopoly on virtue. However, simply practicing virtue does not constitute Dharma. For example, a wealthy entrepreneur may want to donate a large sum of money to start a new wing in a prestigious hospital, though he or she may desire an eponymous label for the new wing. Donating money to serve a hospital is virtue indeed and people derive benefit from that, but when the altruistic intention is combined with the intention to gain a good reputation by having one's name on the hospital wing, this makes it, in Buddhist terminology, "tainted virtue." In all such cases, take care to not pretend it is Dharma. In dialectical terms, if there is virtue, there is not necessarily Dharma; but if there is Dharma, then there is necessarily virtue. The distinction is that the simple enactment of virtue of body, speech, and mind may result in happiness, but then it is gone after it ripens into its result, whether in one's next lifetime or a later one. Whether or not virtue actually leads to the path of irreversible transformation, however, depends on whether it is dedicated to a path of total liberation and omniscience, and whether the intention is deep enough that there will be continuity from lifetime to lifetime. Virtue becomes Dharma with pure intention and sustained, genuine practice.

There is virtue, there is Dharma, and then there is path. Ultimately, the whole of Buddhadharma is about path—everything else is just a prelude. Among the four ārya realities, the first three would have no traction if there were no path, which is the fourth. Teaching the first, the reality of suffering, is beneficial only if the causes are findable. The causes, which constitute the second reality, are worth knowing only if they can be eradicated. Then there is the third reality, the cessation of suffering, but knowing about the cessation of suffering is only worthwhile if there is a path that leads to the end of suffering. This is the fourth reality, which is to be practiced. This Dzogchen path is the straightest, most unelaborated path found anywhere in Buddhism, and it can lead you to rainbow body in this very lifetime.

When Düdjom Rinpoché writes, "it is not enough to maintain an outer facade of Dharma," he challenges us to look deeply at whether there is a difference between what our practice merely looks like on the outside and what it actually means to practice authentic Dharma. You could be meditating many hours a day and performing a plethora of practices, but if the motivation is not completely in accord with authentic Dharma, then this only consists of "an outer facade." But how can we know, from our innermost being, whether we are practicing genuine Dharma?

Düdjom Rinpoché tells us the criterion: "We must set aside all activities that are concerned with this life and cut all ties to the allures of the desire realm." All aspirations, desires, goals, and so forth that are limited to this lifetime alone are not Dharma. If our sights are set within this lifetime, then of course, we become disappointed when we do not achieve our goals and temporarily elated when we do. But this approach has a short half-life. People will go to tremendous lengths to achieve what they feel to be meaningful in this lifetime, only to lose it all at death. Even as such, do not cut all ties to activities that are necessary in the short term because they enable you to work toward your goals far beyond this lifetime. This is what makes them meaningful. So, if your teeth need work, go to a dentist. If you need a new pair of glasses, go to an optometrist. Within the context of one life, many things can become meaningful when set within the scope of goals and aspirations that actually lead to the path.

Thinking back to my childhood in the 1950s, the vision of a good life, success, and the life that was idealized was very materialistic. Finding the right person to marry, having a good job, owning a house and a car, having kids, getting a good pension and benefits, going on fun vacations, owning nice things, growing old, being in a comfortable retirement home, and having a fine funeral really embodied the American Dream. That is still as much as many people can imagine for "the good life," and Düdjom Rinpoché is saying that it is nothing at all and certainly not an "achievement." It is just an insubstantial simulation—not a meaningful human life. Instead, what matters in the face of death is that you have cultivated virtue and firmly avoided nonvirtue, with an understanding that this is what carries through from lifetime to lifetime. On this basis, then, you can follow a path—the fourth ārya reality—that leads to complete liberation from samsara.

For those who live a socially engaged way of life that involves activities and responsibilities—for example, taking care of loved ones, seeing grandchildren, looking after parents, and so on—know that these can be valuable pursuits that are also a part of Dharma practice. Düdjom Rinpoché is not saying that as soon as we are exposed to these teachings we should divest ourselves of all activities and pleasures. Rather, to "cut all ties to the allures of the desire realm" means to cut all ties of *attachment* to those activities and pleasures that have meaning only within the context of this life but that, beyond this life, are irrelevant and void. Therefore, do what is needed within the context of this life, but cut all ties and become completely disillusioned with respect to hopes and fears about things that have significance and value only in this lifetime.

This disillusionment leaves nothing behind so that there is a definite emergence, or *ngenjung*, from the orbit of samsara. As we gain the escape velocity with which to emerge from this powerful orbit, we must have a clear goal toward which we can then orient our desires, aspirations, intentions, and resolve. This revolution in outlook, which takes place in the face of our inevitable death, entails a fundamental shift in our priorities and values. What is our vision of the good life? This preparatory phase addresses how to direct our minds to Dharma so that our aspirations, ideals, visions, joy, and enthusiasm are all focused on that one domain. Then when we are viewing our entire life in that way, our choices and actions have a chance of fulfilling our eternal longing.

REMAINING FIRM

Düdjom Rinpoché continues,

> Without cutting them, even though we enter the gateway of Dharma, if we enter with a merely wishy-washy attitude while being attached to our homeland, possessions, relatives, friends, loved ones, and so on, then with the conjunction of that mind of attachment acting as the primary cause and those objects of attachment acting as the cooperative conditions, māras will create obstacles, we will mix again with worldly people, and the outcome of our deeds will go awry.

When Düdjom Rinpoché says, "Without cutting them," he is referring to cutting the ties of attachment. Entering "the gateway of Dharma" means that we have found authentic Dharma and entered through the door. However, by entering "with a merely wishy-washy attitude," we may encounter authentic Dharma but still be invested in and attached to the mundane activities and pleasures of life. As Alfred North Whitehead, the great English mathematician and philosopher, wrote in his insightful work *Science and the Modern World*, "Religion is tending to degenerate into a decent formula wherewith to embellish a comfortable life."[3] Secularized yoga, popularized Zen, transcendental meditation, popularized vipassanā, mindfulness meditation, and secular Buddhism in general have all gone that route: with no reference to rebirth, karma, nirvana, or taking refuge, they all provide methods for alleviating stress and unhappiness in this life alone, which serve only to make this one life a bit more comfortable. But as Mañjuśrī, the embodiment of enlightened wisdom, said in a vision to Sachen Künga Nyingpo, the founder of the Sakya order of Tibetan Buddhism, "If you cling to this life, you are not a Dharma practitioner."

Dzogchen can easily be diluted in the same way. It is common nowadays for people with no background in Buddhism to receive pointing-out instructions from lamas on the nature of the mind, for example. This may entail hearing teachings on the luminous and cognizant qualities of awareness, which are the defining characteristics of consciousness. When putting this into practice, one may experience an inner stillness from which one can observe the movements of the mind—thoughts, images, desires, emotions, and so on. This is invaluable, for in so doing, one establishes an "observatory" for objectively examining mental processes without being caught in their grip. One is experiencing the stream of mental consciousness of a sentient being, which arises from moment to moment in dependence upon and conditioned by a wide range of material and immaterial phenomena. The Buddha said of this mental consciousness, "Monks, I know of no other single process so quick to change as is this mind."[4] Just as a hummingbird is sometimes still and then darts from one flower to another to drink their nectar, so does the mind ever so rapidly move from here to there, merging with one mental process and its object after another. Relatively speaking, the essential nature of the mind is luminous, but it swiftly shifts from a state that is relatively pure (though still subject to dualistic grasping) to one that is obscured by adventitious defilements, such as attachment and hostility.

While this is a very valuable insight, it must not be mistaken for a realization of pristine awareness, or rigpa, which is unconditioned and transcends all conceptual categories of existence and nonexistence, arising and passing, coming and going, unity and multiplicity. If this fleeting experience is mistaken for a realization of pristine awareness, then the practice has become diluted and muddied.

When Düdjom Rinpoché writes, "if we enter with a merely wishy-washy attitude while being attached to our homeland, possessions, relatives, friends, loved ones, and so on," he is saying that you may be engaged in many Dharma practices while still being enmeshed in a whole network of attachments. Furthermore, "with the conjunction of that mind of attachment acting as the primary cause and those objects of attachment acting as the cooperative conditions," then the fruition—or the consequence, the result—will definitely arise. The primary cause, which you actually have the capacity to cut, is the mind of attachment. The contributing conditions are the objects of attachment. If there are objects of attachment to which you are not attached, then it is like having a fertile field that is moist and well-tilled but where no seeds have been planted for anything to grow. Therefore, you only need to cut one thing—not the object of attachment but rather the attachment itself.

But if the primary cause of attachment is not cut, then when it encounters the contributing, cooperative conditions of all the things to which you so easily become attached, then "māras will create obstacles." You have created a fertile field for māras to arise and create obstacles, and if you let them, they will throw you off course. The whole raison d'être of māras is to prevent you from reaching the path. If you do try to reach the path, then they try to bump you off by instilling discouragement and loss of confidence in yourself, in the Dharma, and in your teachers so that you abandon the Dharma and recommit to samsara.

Māras will create inner, outer, and secret obstacles to your practice. Inner obstacles entail the challenges that arise in the space of the body, making you think that you cannot practice Dharma because your body is unwell. Outer obstacles occur in terms of people and situations that may threaten your practice. Secret obstacles are where the māras enter in from the back door, so to speak. You are at the front door of the mind, which has the things you can see, hear, remember, and so on. When māras enter through the back door, they sneakily make you think that they are you and that their voice is your voice. So "secret upheavals" are psychological and are so called because no one else can perceive them except you. They are private.

If you venture into Dharma, obstacles will arise. If they arose for Buddha Śākyamuni and for myriad other great beings in the past, then they will certainly arise for you as well. Complaining about and ruminating on the obstacles you encounter is futile. Contrarily, knowing how to apply the wisdom of the Dharma to whatever arises is the way through the obstacles in order to transform or dissolve them.

So, if we "enter the gateway of Dharma" with a "wishy-washy attitude" and are constrained by attachments, then "māras will create obstacles" and "we will mix again with worldly people, and the outcome of our deeds will go awry." We may temporarily withdraw from people immersed in their worldly priorities and worldviews, but if māras influence us by causing us to abandon our practice, then we will fall right back into a mix of people who are focused single-pointedly on the prioritization of the eight mundane concerns, leading us away from a contemplative way of life until we forget there even was such a thing as a path to irreversible transformation and liberation from suffering.

Mixing again with worldly people, "the outcome of our deeds will go awry." That is, you understood the Dharma and saw the path with all of its possibilities but then were overcome by obstacles and fell into the mindsets and activities of worldly people.

THE REAL BOUNDARIES FOR RETREAT: A CONATIVE REVOLUTION

Düdjom Rinpoché continues,

> Therefore, sacrificing our concern for food, clothing, and conversation, and relinquishing attachment to the eight mundane concerns, we should apply our minds single-pointedly to Dharma, like Gyalwa Yang Gönpa, who declared,
>
>> In solitude, where awareness of death penetrates one's heart,
>> the adept, who utterly renounces clinging,
>> draws the boundaries of retreat by renouncing concerns of this life.
>> Thus one does not encounter people
>> whose minds are filled with the eight mundane concerns.

These are your retreat boundaries—not something you draw in the sand outside of your retreat cabin. The real retreat boundaries establish a line within your mind so that the eight mundane concerns are "over there" and you are "in here," as if to say, "I know them, but I am not mingling with them." The eight mundane concerns that you separate yourself from consist of four pairs of related attachments and aversions: (1) attachment to obtaining material goods and wealth, and aversion to losing them; (2) attachment to mundane, stimulus-driven pleasures and aversion to discomfort and stimulus-driven dissatisfaction; (3) attachment to praise and aversion to abuse; and (4) attachment to having a good reputation, garnering admiration and respect from others, and the aversion to losing your reputation, becoming disgraced, and being looked down upon by others.

As an example to elucidate this mental boundary, imagine a very wise and compassionate psychotherapist in an institution for people who are mentally ill. Such a psychotherapist engages with but does not slip into their patients' psychoses or identify with them so much that he or she would totally embrace their patients' worldviews, thoughts, and so forth. Instead, the psychotherapist would be totally present with their patients, recognizing mental imbalances as mental imbalances and, therefore, attending to their patients with compassion but without being captured by their mental states. Once we have recognized the eight mundane concerns to be merely distractions from our highest goals—goals that transcend this life and even samsara itself—then we will find it as easy to draw an invisible boundary between our mind and any appearances of those concerns that arise in the mind, as it is for the wise psychotherapist not to be drawn into a patient's psychosis.

Moreover, we must recognize the extremely contagious quality of mental afflictions—not only the obvious ones such as hatred and racism but attachments of all kinds, those of ego and competitiveness, as well as attachment to the eight mundane concerns. These mental afflictions are more contagious than any biological virus or bacteria. If you engage with people who are caught up in the world and you are not well-vaccinated with Dharma before doing so, then they will draw you back into samsara because they outnumber you. What they are saying makes perfectly good sense to them, and what you are doing makes very little, if any, sense to them. Therefore, if you get disillusioned with, disappointed in, or lose your confidence in the Dharma, then they will be right there to welcome you back into the fold. They are not spiritual friends.

CULTIVATING CONATIVE INTELLIGENCE: THE FOUR REVOLUTIONS IN OUTLOOK

Düdjom Rinpoché continues,

> Otherwise, Dharma that is mixed with those eight concerns is like consuming food mixed with poison, and this is extremely dangerous.

As sad as it is to admit, there are those who may engage in any kind of spiritual practice—meditation, prayers, and so forth—with the mundane wish to make an impression and earn people's admiration and respect. Some may even aspire to be a Dharma teacher and then work to gain credibility so that people will respect them as such. You may be able to create a good facsimile or simulation, thereby fooling others into thinking you are practicing pure Dharma, but it will be nothing more than an imitation, and you will die an ordinary death without any realization or liberation to carry through into your next life.

In order to completely revolutionize the way you view your life and thus create a stable foundation for genuine Dharma practice, it is imperative to investigate how deeply you have thoroughly assimilated the four revolutions in outlook, each one of which is more transformative than the one that comes before. The four revolutions in outlook are insights into (1) the rarity and preciousness of a human life imbued with the leisure and opportunity to devote oneself to the practice of the Buddhadharma, which can result in lasting benefits in all of one's future lifetimes until one is enlightened; (2) death and impermanence, in which one realizes that one's impending death is certain, the time of one's death is utterly uncertain, and the only thing of value in the face of one's death is Dharma; (3) the ubiquitous, unsatisfying nature of the whole of samsara, in which no lasting sense of well-being is ever found; and (4) the infallible causal relationships between one's actions in this life and their consequences in future lives, with nonvirtuous behavior leading to misery and virtuous behavior leading to good fortune. The Tibetan term *lo dok* means "reversing the direction of the mind"—that is, "a revolution" or a one hundred and eighty degree "turning away from" the views, priorities, and way of life that one held previously.

When we look at past scientific revolutions in physics and biology, we may acknowledge that it can be helpful to discover more about the physical world and not be burdened by false beliefs, but we must ask: Have these scientific revolutions made any real impact on our lives at all? Have our mental afflictions decreased and virtues increased? Are we finding greater genuine happiness and well-being? Are we less violent and more ethical? These revolutions in science were never designed to transform our minds in such ways. The inner revolutions that can take place as a result of understanding these four core teachings of Dharma, however, can radically transform our lives here and now and not just at some distant time.

If one is truly going to devote oneself to Dharma, but one has not cut the ties of attachment and clinging, one's Dharma practice is going to be like a rocket that has liftoff but then promptly crashes to Earth in a flaming explosion. At best, what remains after the crash might be a bit of Dharma to make life a little more meaningful, a smidgen more comfortable, and a tad more peaceful, but it will have no real lasting effect.

Cutting the ties of attachment and turning the mind to Dharma is a conative revolution. Conation refers to the entire class of our volitional states of mind: our desires and vision of what the good life actually consists of, along with our aspirations, goals, values, and criteria of success. It addresses what we really want. There is great emphasis in the Indian and Tibetan Buddhist traditions on motivation, which is the springboard for all practices. If we do not have an authentic Dharma motivation, then we are merely going through pointless motions that slightly resemble Dharma.

Düdjom Rinpoché explains,

> Those eight concerns can be understood succinctly in terms of hope and fear, which basically refer to attachment and aversion. Inner attachment and aversion take on the guise of outer male and female demons. As long as your mind is not freed from attachment and aversion, you will never be free of those demons, and there will be no end to obstacles. So you must repeatedly examine your own minds to see if, in your innermost thoughts, there is any conceited clinging to the eight concerns of this life, and if it arises, you must take care to get rid of it.

Attachment tells us that the source of my happiness is over there—it is that person, job, place, house, and so on. Aversion's message is that I am unhappy because of something outside of myself. Inner attachment and aversion are qualities of your mind. If you ever wonder what makes you happy, it is your own mind. If you ever wonder what makes you upset, it is your own mind. Attachment and aversion are mental afflictions, or kleśas.

When he says that inner attachment and aversion appear as "outer male and female demons," he means that you take your mental afflictions and objectify them as another person. Outer male demons are, for example, all of those "bad men" who make you angry and upset. On the other hand, sometimes you are really happy, feel loved and respected, and you think it is because of "her." She is the female demon who is drawing you away from the Dharma. Of course, this applies vice versa as well. Essentially males and females can act as external projections of inner mental states of aversion and attachment. Every time you point your finger outward to someone or something outside of yourself as being the cause of your happiness or unhappiness, you disempower yourself.

Further, "As long as your mind is not freed from attachment and aversion, you will never be free of those demons, and there will be no end to obstacles." The demons are all creations of your own mind; they have no inherent, objective existence from their own side. He continues, "So you must repeatedly examine your own minds to see if, in your innermost thoughts, there is any conceited clinging to the eight concerns of this life, and if it arises, you must take care to get rid of it." When he says "in your innermost thoughts," he is referring to those quiet, secret, private thoughts that you do not share with others. Moreover, upon examination, if "there is any conceited clinging to the eight concerns of this life . . . you must take care to get rid of it." Going through the motions of receiving teachings, meditating, doing good works, teaching Dharma, and so forth with a motivation rooted in the eight mundane concerns is fraudulent, and you must "take care to get rid of it." Do not try to do a sullied hybrid of being a samsaric being and a Dharma practitioner. It will not lead you to the path.

Setting Forth into True Solitude

Düdjom Rinpoché then asserts,

> If these eight concerns hold you in their grip while you fabricate a facsimile of Dharma, even your acquisition of goods will constitute wrong livelihood because they were obtained through deceit. In accordance with the aphorism, "By leaving your homeland behind, half the Dharma is accomplished," turn your back on your homeland and wander among unfamiliar lands.

This is especially a caution to anyone who takes on the responsibility of teaching Dharma. Even if there are no offerings or honoraria, if one is doing it for a mundane motivation, such as wanting respect as a Dharma teacher, then it is still deceitful. It is like a doctor who is seeing clients for his own sake because it makes him feel good to be a doctor, he likes the reputation, and so forth.

In my own case, when I was twenty, there was no Dharma that I could relate to where I lived, so I had to wander in "unfamiliar lands." Initially I went to Germany and met my first lama, followed by more lamas. Then when I saw that Buddhism was my path, I went from Germany to India, where the conditions for learning and practicing Dharma were superb. There is a lot to be said for going to unfamiliar lands, leaving behind your homeland and all of your supposed security. I did so because I felt I had no choice. The choice it seemed I had was not a feasible one: I could either have security and no Dharma, or insecurity and Dharma—but then what is the security? Aging, sickness, and death were no security to me. The alternative was to find Dharma.

Düdjom Rinpoché then counsels,

> Amicably part ways from your friends and relatives, and do not listen to those who seek to dissuade you from practicing Dharma. Give away your wealth and possessions, and rely on whatever alms come your way. Recognize all desirable things to be obstacles linked with bad habits, and arouse disinclination for them. If you are not satisfied with just a little of such things as material possessions, then if you get one thing, you will want two; and for as long as that goes on, you will easily be possessed by the devious māras of the allures of the desire realm.

He is speaking to people who are going into full-time, serious retreat—not people who are doing an hour of practice a day, living with their family, going on vacations, and so forth. He says to "amicably part ways from your friends and relatives." The word "amicably" implies that there are two ways of parting from friends and relatives: There is the very literal way of traveling a far distance, but that is not necessarily the best, most skillful route for everyone—i.e., not to see your loved ones again, or for a long time. The other way is more subtle yet more challenging. That is, even while amicably remaining in contact with friends and relatives, cut all ties of attachment. Outwardly, you are as friendly, loving, and caring as you ever were, and inwardly, you are cultivating impartiality. This abiding in impartiality is free of attachment to those who are near (people with whom you are emotionally close), and free of aversion to those who are far (people with whom you are not emotionally close). While in the midst of friends and family, cultivating impartiality means that there is no diminishment of your care, affection, love, and compassion. As such, they will not know that anything is different—while internally you are cultivating nonattachment. This route is much more challenging because you cannot simply separate yourself from them through physical distance and must have a firm foundation in impartiality lest you get drawn back into familiar attachments and emotional patterns.

Likewise, as with relatives and friends, so it is with wealth and possessions. Düdjom Rinpoché states, "Give away your wealth and possessions, and rely on whatever alms come your way." This is essentially what I did when I left in search of the Dharma, but is it necessary in every case to "give away your wealth and possessions," such that all you have is the clothes on your back, and you fully "rely on whatever alms come your way"? In traditional Tibet, if you set out to be a yogi, you would unquestionably find people who would want to support you. For much of the history of India, there were *sannyasis*, wandering ascetics who lived on alms. However, in our modern civilization where we are contemplatively backward, that is likely more difficult. There is no need to empty your bank account and have only one set of clothes. What *is* necessary is to give up all *attachment* to your wealth and possessions. As with your family and friends, there is no need to throw it all away, but the attachment must go.

Therefore, "Recognize all desirable things to be obstacles linked with bad habits, and arouse disinclination for them." Regarding "all desirable things," these are all the allures of the desire realm that would draw you out in pursuit of them. This is a fundamental revolution in priorities. Earlier in your life, the Dharma had no meaning, allure, or value, but there was always value placed in the eight mundane concerns. It is a radical shift to redirect all the value you placed in the eight mundane concerns toward the Dharma instead. That is *lo dok*, a complete reversal, or revolution, in priorities. This is a purely conative transformation—it is your intention and desire that determine the outcome.

Regarding desirable things in samsara, he says, "If you are not satisfied with just a little of such things as material possessions, then if you get one thing, you will want two; and for as long as that goes on, you will easily be possessed by the devious māras of the allures of the desire realm." The māras, of course, are not "out there." It is because you have attachment to these things that they become māras for you. You could be a bodhisattva king or queen with a tremendous amount of wealth at your disposal yet have no attachment. It depends wholly on the state of your mind and not on how much wealth or possessions you have access to.

Düdjom Rinpoché then addresses reputation:

> **Whatever good or bad things people say, do not take them to be true or respond to them with hope or fear, affirmation or denial. Rather, let them say what they will, as if they were speaking about someone who is dead and gone.**

Even the Buddha could not control what people said about him, nor could Jesus. If they could not control the things people say about them, then there is no hope you can either. If someone falsely criticizes you, do not defend yourself. Likewise, if the remarks about you are in the form of praise, then simply let it be. In this way, do not "respond to them with hope or fear, affirmation or denial."

Moreover, "Let them say what they will, as if they were speaking about someone who is dead and gone." People are going to say what they want, so you may as well release resistance to this. Like letting the rain fall, you do not have any control over it. Allowing them to say what they will, as if you were "dead and gone," is supported by your practice as an illusory being who is viewing all phenomena as dreamlike.

On Whom Should You Rely?

Düdjom Rinpoché then strikingly states,

> **No one but a qualified guru—not even your parents—can give you sound advice, so hold your own ground, and do not let anyone else take hold of your nose rope. Remaining outwardly good-natured, know how to engage harmoniously with others without "burning anyone's noses." If anyone—strong or weak—actually becomes an obstacle to your practice, you must not be moved by that individual, as if you were an iron boulder pulled by a silk scarf. It won't do to be of a weak character,**

bending your head in whatever direction the wind blows, like grass on a mountain pass.

If you are turning your mind to Dharma with the intention to reach the path, it is imperative that you find a qualified guru. There are many lamas who will give you a wealth of teachings, mantras, visualizations, rituals, and meditations, which are all virtuous, but there are not many who will make it a central point to help you reach the path. In addition, "not even your parents . . . can give you sound advice." Sound advice refers to the wisdom from genuine Dharma teachings in the context of a path to total enlightenment, such as those given here. As previously mentioned, many people give good advice that will make you a bit happier for a little while in samsara, but that is all. Since no one apart from a qualified guru can give you sound advice, "hold your own ground, and do not let anyone else take hold of your nose rope." If you had a ring through your nose with a rope attached to it, as a cow or a yak does, then it would be very easy to lead you around by your nose rope. Do not fall under the domination of those who are not qualified to lead you to the path. Do not give up your autonomy in this way.

He continues, "Remaining outwardly good-natured, know how to engage harmoniously with others without 'burning anyone's noses.'" That is to say, we should engage harmoniously and show gratitude for advice from others so that we do not upset them.

However, "If anyone—strong or weak—actually becomes an obstacle to your practice, you must not be moved by that individual, as if you were an iron boulder pulled by a silk scarf." Some people may really want to entirely derail you from your practice. In this case, turn around, get out, and do something entirely different! If you succumb to their pressure, you will become like the person who is exerting the pressure. Instead, in this case, do not worry about burning their noses. If anyone becomes an obstacle in this way, do not budge, "as if you were an iron boulder pulled by a silk scarf." When tugging against something as steady and solid as an iron boulder, the flimsy silk scarf is inevitably going to rip.

Düdjom Rinpoché elaborates, "It won't do to be of a weak character, bending your head in whatever direction the wind blows, like grass on a mountain pass." Do not go with the flow of what other people expect, demand, or want of you. Many people have agendas for others, but their agendas are probably not aimed at how you can reach the path of the Great Perfection in this lifetime. Discerning this difference is the way to cultivate conative intelligence.

MOVING FROM CONATIVE INTELLIGENCE TO ETHICAL INTELLIGENCE

Having begun with conative intelligence, we now turn to the cultivation of ethical intelligence. We know what we want and what our aspirations and goals are, but now what do we do? Which behaviors can we engage in that will support us in pursuing those ideals, and which behaviors will act as obstacles to derail us? We must develop ethical intelligence about which kinds of behaviors to adopt and which kinds to reject so that we can fulfill our own aspirations, for motivation alone is not enough. As stated by the old aphorism, "The road to hell is paved with good intentions." A good intention may be there, but if you do not have skillful means—that is, if you do not know what to do—and your behavior is deplorable, then your motivation will fail to come into fruition.

Focusing on ethical intelligence, Düdjom Rinpoché writes,

> For any practice, from the time you begin until you come to its culmination—whether thunderbolts fall from above, a lake springs up from below, or boulders cave in from all sides—carry through to the end, keeping your promise to act in accordance with your samayas, even at the cost of your life.

Whether you are practicing śamatha, cultivating the four revolutions in outlook, the four immeasurables, the four applications of mindfulness, or any other virtuous practice, "from the time you begin until you come to its culmination—whether thunderbolts fall from above, a lake springs up from below, or boulders cave in from all sides—carry through to the end, keeping your promise to act in accordance with your samayas, even at the cost of your life." The great Indian paṇḍita and bodhisattva Śāntideva advises in his *Guide to the Bodhisattva Way of Life*, "After first examining one's means, one should either begin or not begin. Surely, it is better not to begin than to turn back once one has begun. This habit continues even in another life; and due to that sin, suffering increases. Another opportunity for action is lost, and the task is not accomplished."[5] If you determine that something is definitely worthwhile, especially in the context of Dharma, then cut through all afflictive uncertainty. As both Śāntideva and Düdjom Rinpoché assert, when you have made a commitment to yourself—for example, to achieve śamatha—then unwaveringly persevere until you have achieved your goal. Do not give up, "even at the cost of your life."

Düdjom Rinpoché continues,

> From the very beginning, gradually establish your schedule of periods for formal meditation, sleep, meals, and so on, without falling into bad habits. Moreover, whether your practice is elaborate or unelaborate, do not let it be sporadic, but keep it even and regular, without leaving any room for the ordinary, even for an instant.

Whether or not you are in full-time retreat, start out modestly. Do not start out with an intensive schedule only to find it is not sustainable, thereby failing almost as soon as you begin. Rather, whether you are seeking to integrate Dharma into a relatively active way of life with some hours of irreplaceable formal meditation each day or you are embarking on strict, full-time retreat, proceed modestly at the beginning: do shorter sessions and fewer hours than you think you are capable of so that you establish a sustainable routine with confidence. Then, as your abilities increase, so does your familiarization. In time, and perhaps in consultation with your lama, you may then start increasing the duration—perhaps adding more hours and augmenting your retreat with supporting practices. Start developing the momentum and let that momentum carry you all the way to the path and beyond. Therefore, it is crucial to choose wisely what to do and what not to do, taking care not to overextend yourself and burn out.

Also, consider how much sleep you need. For example, some people need eight or nine hours a night, while others need only four or five. This is simply a matter of your own physical constitution, so do not be embarrassed by your particular body's needs. Get the sleep you need, so that when you awake, you feel refreshed and full of vitality for the path! Exceptional yogis have given the advice to get to bed early in order to get up early. For instance, it is best if you can go to bed by 8:00 p.m. and awake by 4:00 a.m. That is an example of "yogi time," in which it is most important to center your sleep around midnight.

As for meals, find the diet and nutrition that work best for your body. You can do this through trial and error, consulting a nutritionist, or learning about various healing modalities that include food, such as Ayurvedic recommendations. Whatever you decide, your meals are essential for your health, so do not create bad habits.

He further instructs that "whether your practice is elaborate or unelaborate, do not let it be sporadic, but keep it even and regular, without leaving any room for the ordinary, even for an instant." Do not succumb to fair-weather Dharma, such that you practice only when you feel good and not when you feel subpar. Let practice be unwavering and steady, "without leaving any room for the ordinary, even for an instant." Of course, all of this takes place in the context of Dzogchen. In the course of Düdjom Rinpoché's text, he gives a comprehensive layout of the view, meditation, conduct, and post-meditative practice on the Dzogchen path. If you follow his instructions here, you will find that there is not even a second for the ordinary, or the mundane.

To elaborate on this point just briefly here, consider that Dzogchen is the pinnacle, the ninth yāna, for a reason. It is difficult to practice Dzogchen every single moment—viewing every thought that arises, whether on and off the cushion, from the perspective of pristine awareness realizing the emptiness of all phenomena. Knowing that this is the deepest view within the context of the three inner tantras—mahāyoga, anuyoga, and atiyoga, or Dzogchen—means that sometimes you may need extra assistance. To receive any extensive Dzogchen teachings, it is important to receive a Vajrayāna empowerment, in which one is authorized to engage in the cultivation of "divine pride," wherein you dissolve your ordinary sense of identity into emptiness, and out of emptiness visualize yourself as the deity, while shifting the locus of your identity to that of an enlightened being. The whole point of Vajrayāna practice is to see through impure appearances and concepts to the divine nature of your environment, guru, other sentient beings, and yourself. The cultivation of pure vision and divine pride in Vajrayāna practice is an important step toward directly seeing your own face as the dharmakāya, which is characteristic of Dzogchen practice. In the whole of the Tibetan tradition, Dzogchen is never practiced in a way that would be completely decontextualized from Vajrayāna, Mahāyāna, and the four ārya realities.

Dzogchen is like high-altitude climbing. So if, on occasion, you find the air is too thin and that you are simply not able to rest in rigpa continuously, to see all phenomena as empty of inherent nature, equally of one taste, and as displays of pristine awareness, then you have a fallback. That is, you fall back not into the ordinary sense of your identity—the ordinary "I am" and ordinary impure vision—because this would be like falling from the hundredth story of a skyscraper down to the ground. Instead, fall just one story: fall back to sustaining divine identity and pure vision in the context of mahāyoga. By never regressing to the ordinary—even at the times when you are not explicitly resting in awareness and you are activating a sense of "I am"—then at the very least you are seeing with pure vision that "I am Padmasambhava. I am Samantabhadra. I am Buddha." Likewise, you see your guru and all others with pure vision, as being buddhas, *vīras*, and ḍākinīs. In this way, all appearances arise as *nirmāṇakāya*, all sounds are *sambhogakāya*, and all mental states are dharmakāya. Then when you are ready, return to Dzogchen, but leave no room for the ordinary.

Additionally, Düdjom Rinpoché advises, with regard to the extremely subtle ethics of retreat practice:

> When in retreat, seal the entry of your cave with mud; or even if you do not seal it, do not meet face-to-face with others. Do not speak with others or be on the lookout for others.

Of course, we do not need to take that literally by sealing the entry to our retreat cabin, which may not be very practical. Nonetheless, if you are in a strict retreat within the Dzogchen context, then do not meet face-to-face with others, unless, of course, it is in a retreat center where there is a shared view, meditation, and way of life among fellow retreatants. Similarly, meeting face-to-face with your guru is permissible, of course. In essence, you do not want to engage with people whose view is limited to ordinary vision, who do not understand what you are doing in retreat, and who may dissuade you from practicing the Dharma, for they are going to pour their impure vision and mundane concerns onto you. Even if you are viewing them with pure vision, it is not reciprocated. Further, when he says, "Do not speak with others or be on the lookout for others," this points to cultivating a deep solitude. This concludes the crucial guidance on the ethics of body and speech in the context of a strict retreat.

MOVING FROM ETHICAL INTELLIGENCE TO ATTENTIONAL INTELLIGENCE

We start with conative intelligence, proceed to ethical intelligence, and then continue to attentional intelligence. Düdjom Rinpoché advises,

> Completely calm all the wandering thoughts of your restless mind. Then, expel the stale breath and properly adopt the vital points of the posture. Your mind should rest in recollected awareness and remain firm, without wavering even for an instant, like a stake driven into the ground. All the signs and qualities of the practice will swiftly arise due to maintaining a strict outer, inner, and secret retreat.

Once you are behaving appropriately—avoiding nonvirtuous behaviors and embracing virtuous behaviors of body, speech, and mind—the next step is to turn inward. Can you stay focused, or are you getting distracted or bored? Are you going to lose clarity, falling into laxity and dullness? As Jé Tsongkhapa teaches, based on the works of Asaṅga and Kamalaśīla: "Completely abandon all conceptualization involving desires and so on." This is not only to be upheld on the cushion, but it should permeate the entirety of your days and nights. This is an expression of attentional intelligence and is a prerequisite for developing the single-pointedness of śamatha.

Then, Düdjom Rinpoché says to "expel the stale breath and properly adopt the vital points of the posture." You can expel the stale breath through either the threefold or the ninefold expulsion of stale *prāṇa*. The "vital points of the posture" can be attained by sitting with the seven points of Vairocana. By adopting this posture, over time, the channels become relatively clear. However, it is of utmost importance to let your body be as comfortable as possible. If you are not comfortable in vajrāsana, or the full lotus posture, then find a way to be comfortable—whether in half-lotus, in the sattva posture with both legs crossed and lying flat on the ground, supine, or sitting in a comfortable chair.

Returning to the mind, Düdjom Rinpoché writes, "Your mind should rest in recollected awareness and remain firm, without wavering even for an instant, like a stake driven into the ground." This is pure śamatha. He did not say to try or to do your best, but rather this is what you *should* do. If you are setting out on this royal path of the view, meditation, and conduct of Dzogchen, it is imperative that you have a serviceable mind. This sentence synopsizes the whole of Phase One of a tantra revealed by Düdjom Lingpa, called *The Vajra Essence*—on how to take the impure mind as the path and dissolve that mind into the substrate consciousness. It is only then that you completely fulfill the instructions here and achieve śamatha. Further, at the beginning of Atiśa's renowned *lojong* text, *The Seven-Point Mind Training*, the second point states, "Once stability has been achieved, let the mystery be revealed."[6] The "mystery" refers to the mystery of the actual nature of your mind. First and foremost, though, you have to achieve stability. This is a crucial point that is often overlooked, marginalized, and misinterpreted across the Theravādin, Zen, and Tibetan traditions of Buddhism.

He continues, "All the signs and qualities of the practice will swiftly arise due to maintaining a strict outer, inner, and secret retreat." The outer retreat is your environment, the inner retreat is your conduct, and the secret, or private, retreat is completely withdrawing from the eight mundane concerns. The final one of these is the most challenging. Hibernating animals go into retreat every winter. Misanthropes go into retreat because they do not like people. It is easy simply to seclude yourself in privacy. However, the inner retreat of maintaining proper conduct and the secret, or private, retreat of withdrawing from all mundane concerns are not so easy. Yet that is exactly what is necessary.

Further, he states,

> If you think, "Now it's important that I meet and speak with someone, but I shall keep to a strict retreat afterward," and thus erode your boundaries, over time the potency of your practice will decline, becoming slacker and slacker. So, from the very outset, if you make a firm resolve to remain in retreat, your practice will become stricter and stricter, and it will not be swept away by obstacles.

The word *retreat* in Tibetan is *tsam*, which means "a boundary." If you keep breaking your retreat boundary, thinking that you have to meet with this person, have to do that, and so forth, then "over time the potency of your practice will decline, becoming slacker and slacker." On the other hand, once you "make a firm resolve to remain in retreat," you will naturally not want to do anything else. Outwardly, it may look like a very strict retreat, yet, inwardly, you are simply doing what gives you the greatest satisfaction, joy, and fulfillment. Your confidence and enthusiasm increase as your resolve to remain in retreat without becoming slack or eroding your boundaries is upheld. In this way, you "will not be swept away by obstacles." This completes Düdjom Rinpoché's highly condensed teaching on cultivating attentional intelligence by way of training in samādhi, mindfulness, and introspection.

INTEGRATING EARTH AND SKY: AN INTRODUCTION TO A ŚAMATHA MEDITATION

If Dzogchen, the ninth, culminating yāna, is like the sky, then the Śrāvaka teachings of the first yāna taught in the first turning of the wheel of Dharma in the Pāli canon are like the earth. Returning to the Buddha's pith instructions to Bāhiya, he said, "In the seen, let there be only the seen; in the heard, let there be only the heard; in the tactilely sensed, let there be only the tactilely sensed; and in the mentally perceived, let there be only the mentally perceived." Continuously, discerningly, and vividly, be totally present with whatever appearances are arising, but without habitually reifying and projecting conceptual associations and preferences.

As Yangthang Rinpoché writes in his root text, *A Summary of the View, Meditation, and Conduct,* "Thus, whatever good and bad thoughts arise, do not fixate on them, but let them arise and be released by themselves." Similarly, in *Cutting the Root of Suffering and Equalizing Excitation and Laxity,* when Dromtönpa, Atiśa's foremost disciple, asks him, "Master, what is the enemy?" Atiśa responds, "Drom, it is conceptualization." Drom then asks Atiśa how one should destroy conceptualization, and Atiśa counsels to "destroy it the moment it surfaces."[7]

This does not mean that no thoughts arise. Even after you have achieved śamatha, thoughts bubble up here and there. As you will see later in this text, even after achieving śamatha and vipaśyanā and once you have identified and are resting in rigpa, you may still have not yet fully achieved śamatha in rigpa. Maybe you have achieved it in your ordinary mind but not in rigpa, which means thoughts will continue to emerge. As you are seeking to rest in rigpa, they may divert you away from it. So, do not expect thoughts to stop—because they are not going to. As Dūdjom Rinpoché wrote in his own commentary to a treasure he had revealed, *The Illumination of Primordial Wisdom,* "As all appearances will manifestly release themselves, thoughts will arise as aids to meditation."[8] This means that, at this point, as thoughts arise while you are dwelling in pristine awareness, you see them not as distractions but as creative displays of dharmakāya, which itself is absolutely nonconceptual and inconceivable. Thus, "thoughts will arise as aids to meditation."

Your relationship with conceptualization has persisted through countless past lives into your current life. It can be seen as an addiction to conceptualization, whereby you may tend to think that latching onto "just one more thought" won't be a problem, but, as with any addiction, it always leads to more. If you are the kind of person who still has this habitual craving for conceptualization—and it's not just that you cannot get thoughts to stop manifesting, it is that you cannot stop *thinking* them—then it may be helpful to go back to the ground, to the earth, of the Pāli canon. The Buddha said that among five different personality types, one consists of individuals who are strongly prone to obsessive, compulsive conceptualization. For those who keep falling back into the cycle of conceptualization, just having a little spin with "one more thought" here and there, he taught mindfulness of breathing as the optimal method of śamatha.

Ārya Asaṅga taught mindfulness of breathing according to the way it had already been practiced for more than eight hundred years in the Buddhist tradition, and in particular he emphasized noting the experience of the breath throughout both the coarse and subtle cavities of the body. The coarse cavities are the mouth and nose, while the subtle cavities consist of the pores spread out over the entire body. Thus, at a certain stage, Asaṅga described the object of mindfulness as follows: "When one is intent upon and focuses on the passage of inhalations and exhalations through the minute cavities of the pores of the body, one authentically experiences the entire body; and when a breath is inhaled, one practices by noting that 'I authentically experience the entire body and the breath is inhaled.' When one is authentically experiencing the entire body and the breath is exhaled, one practices by noting that 'I authentically experience the entire body and the breath is exhaled.'"[9]

This meditation is intended to so completely fill the flow of your nonconceptual mental awareness with an equally nonconceptual object that there is no room for conceptuality to catch hold. The object here consists of the ongoing flow, the undulations, or fluctuations, of prāṇa throughout the body that arise in tandem with your breathing. In this meditation, then, you lay the nonconceptual flow of your mindfulness onto the bed of the equally nonconceptual tactile sensations arising throughout your body that correspond to the rhythm of the respiration. But this nonconceptual flow of mindfulness is replete with discerning intelligence and is infused with introspection, stability, clarity, and vividness. Thus, just like two hands pressed together, where each one fully covers the other, your mindfulness now covers the bed of the ebb and flow, the rhythm, of the tactile sensations corresponding with the respiration throughout the entire body so that there is no space for intruding thoughts, just as there is no space between my hands pressed together. It's "full-court press," if you are a basketball fan. It's complete engagement. You are descending your awareness into the field of the body so that you are fully face-to-face with the tactile sensations, like a stake driven into the ground.

A classic śamatha metaphor depicts the wild elephant of your mind that is restrained with the rope of mindfulness to a stake in the ground. In this practice, you do have an object. It is not the thoughts; in this case, the fewer the better, because thoughts are supposed to subside the more closely you maintain mindfulness on the selected object of attention. The object here consists of the tactile sensations associated with the fluctuations of prāṇa correlated with the rhythm of the respiration. It is, in a gentle way, like the horse-whisperer approach to taming a horse. You entice the conceptual mind to calm down so that you can completely calm all the wandering thoughts of your restless mind, such that this becomes a default mode, your new resting mode. This is a preparation for engaging in the meditative and post-meditative conduct of Dzogchen, where you continuously sustain a flow of mindfulness without ever getting entangled in thoughts.

MEDITATION: A FRESH TAKE ON ASAṄGA'S METHOD OF MINDFULNESS OF BREATHING

Find a comfortable position where you can be the most relaxed—be it cross-legged, supine, or in a chair. The context of this entire teaching is set within the act of taking existential refuge in the Buddha, Dharma, and Sangha and in the ultimate source of refuge that is your own pristine awareness. Now take a few minutes to arouse bodhicitta as your motivation for practice so that this meditation may be of the highest benefit for all sentient beings.

Now thoroughly imbued with this motivation, let your faculty of nonconceptual mindfulness—the faculty of bearing in mind continuously—come to rest, face-to-face, with the non-conceptual, image-free appearances of the fluctuations of prāṇa throughout the whole body. There are all kinds of fluctuations, but now selectively focus on those fluctuations throughout the body corresponding to the in-and-out breath. And let your mindful engagement with these fluctuations, this rhythm, be as continuous as possible, with no room for the ordinary habit of falling back into rumination.

Relax deeply with every out-breath, being aware of the whole field of tactile sensations throughout the body. With every out-breath, release at subtler and subtler levels. Release the muscles in your face, your shoulders, your jaw, your arms, your chest, wherever you detect constriction or tightness as you breathe out.

With every in-breath, gently arouse and focus this nonconceptual but discerning flow of mindfulness, single-pointedly on a field, not a point—namely, on the sensations throughout the body correlated with the breath.

Now, this is straight śamatha. It's simply a placing of the flow of your attention, sustaining it with mindfulness. We know that Asaṅga was a great teacher of this method, and he also taught the Cittamātra, or Mind Only, view. From that perspective, there are only appearances to the mind but no external physical world independent of consciousness. This implies there is no real body independent of appearances at all. Beyond perceptual appearances, there are simply conceptual constructs: cells, electricity, and chemicals. All that we directly perceive are appearances, and they are not the appearances *of* something else—for example, of a physical body existing objectively. And so, when Yogācarins in Asaṅga's lineage are doing this practice, I think we can be quite confident they are not experiencing these appearances, these tactical sensations, while thinking "these are sensations of *my* body," as if it were something objectively physical, made of atoms, molecules. They are not thinking that. The evidence does not support that. So let us follow in the footsteps of Asaṅga here:

In the tactilely sensed, let there be just the tactilely sensed and nothing more—no imagery of your body, no mental imagery that you are projecting upon the tactile field. There are just the bare, raw, unmediated sensations of what we'll call "fluctuations of prāṇa," but they are nothing more than appearances. No imagery, no thought that "this is my body"—abandon such thoughts.

If the body is conceptually designated, it comes into existence by the power of conceptual designation. Stop it. Terminate it. Cut it. Abandon any notion of body.

In the midst of these sensations, these fluctuations, for some of us there is an ongoing feeling of physical discomfort: our bodies are defective. What can you do? We are not practicing *vedanā satipaṭṭhāna*; we're not closely applying mindfulness to feelings. They are not of interest. Whatever feelings arise—pleasant, unpleasant, or neutral—we're not focusing on them. They are not of interest, and, moreover, they do not exist objectively. Feelings are a subjective way of experiencing objective appearances, but they are not in the appearances themselves.

So, focused on the tactile sensations themselves, let there be just tactile sensations—no body, no interest in feelings. And to the best of your ability, while maintaining this continuous flow of nonconceptual mindfulness of nonconceptual sensations, which are arising in the space of awareness—where else?—let your focus on these sensations be so continuous that it is hard for a thought to intrude. You're fully occupied. Leave no temporal space, no intervals for the dry rot of conceptualization to creep in and contaminate the flow of your mindfulness, no time for anything other than a continuous flow of nonconceptual mindfulness of nonconceptual sensations correlated with the rhythm of the respiration, relaxing and arousing.

What is the first sign that you are making progress along this path of *ānāpānasati samādhi*, or single-pointed concentration by way of mindfulness of breathing? The first indication is that your breath settles in its natural rhythm. The body, presumably, has already settled in its natural state—relaxed, still, and vigilant—but then, next is the respiration. When has your respiration settled in its natural rhythm? According to Tertön Lerab Lingpa, it is when it has become so subtle, so shallow, that you don't hear it: you don't hear yourself breathing, and the fluctuations are so subtle, you really have to pay close attention to perceive that ongoing rhythm.[10] Outwardly, somebody looking at your body might find your breath to be imperceptible.

Take as a working hypothesis—I invite you—the respiration settling into a rhythm of fifteen cycles per minute: two seconds for each inhalation, two seconds for each exhalation. This is not something that occurs by forcing it, but occurs over time as a natural result of authentic practice.

At the beginning, the in- and out-breaths are bound to be long. Your body needs more oxygen. But as you calm the wandering mind—the conceptualization—your body will need less air. Breathing in short, you know "I breathe in short;" breathing out short, you know "I breathe out short."[11]

When you know that your breathing has settled in its natural rhythm—and this is not difficult to recognize with certainty once it happens—then continue following the Buddha's pith instructions: Attending to the whole body, I breathe in; attending to the whole body, I breathe out.[12] Asaṅga takes that literally. Don't get bored; don't get distracted. Take a keen interest in the practice of maintaining a continuous flow of the "whole body" of the in-and-out breath, and the whole body in its entirety, without the notion of "body," just sensation.

If you were to embrace this method as your primary technique for achieving śamatha, then you would find over time that the frequency remains constant. The amplitude—the magnitude of the fluctuations of prāṇa in the body—becomes subtler and subtler and subtler, while your awareness becomes more and more and more vivid, clear, luminous, and bright. In the concluding phase of the stage of generation, the entire maṇḍala dissolves into the seed syllable, and the seed syllable dissolves from the bottom up to the *tiglé* and to the *nāda*, to its vanishingly small point, and then dissolves into emptiness. Likewise, with increasing vividness, you will eventually reach the eighth stage, then the ninth stage of śamatha, attending to these vanishingly subtle sensations, until you release them, leaving only the *ālaya*, the substrate. You rest for a little while in that mindfulness devoid of mindfulness, dwelling simply in the brilliance of your awareness illuminating the sheer vacuum. Then you invert your awareness in upon itself, and by crossing the threshold from the desire realm to the form realm, you fully achieve śamatha. Your mind has settled in its natural state.

Bring this meditative session to a close and dedicate the merit of this practice to the realization of your highest aspiration so that you may be a most suitable vessel to help all others achieve their own perfect awakening.

THE POWER OF BODHISATTVAS THAT ARISES FROM ŚAMATHA AND BEYOND

The great Fourth Paṇchen Lama, Lozang Chökyi Gyaltsen (1570–1662), who was the tutor of the Fifth Dalai Lama, wrote in his autocommentary to his root text on Mahāmudrā, *The Highway of the Jinas: A Root Text on Mahāmudrā of the Precious Geden and Kagyü Lineages,*

By sustaining the practice in that way, the essential nature of meditative equipoise, not being obscured by anything, is lucid and very clear. Not being determined in any way as a physical entity, it is a clear vacuity like space. Moreover, a meditative experience arises in which whatever good or bad objects of the five senses may emerge, they appear clearly and vividly, as if they were reflections in a lucid mirror, and one is free from the identification of anything as "this is this" or "this is not that." Such samādhi, however stable—if not imbued with the bliss of mental and physical pliancy—is said to be single-pointedness of the mind of the desire realm. On the other hand, samādhi that is so imbued [with mental and physical pliancy] is said to be śamatha.

The Sanskrit term for *pliancy* is *praśrabdhi*, which means "suppleness, buoyancy, and malleability," both mental and physical. So the distinction that Paṇchen Rinpoché is making here is between a flawless meditation of the ninth attentional state and the full achievement of śamatha, which transcends the desire realm. So, the emergence of mental and physical pliancy and the bliss that follows from that is absolutely critical. You are getting a fundamental tune-up, a refinement, an upgrade of your physical energy system and of your mind. This is what occurs when you release the object of your meditation and invert your awareness in upon itself.

Paṇchen Rinpoché continues, writing that such śamatha "is the source of many positive attributes, such as extrasensory perception, paranormal abilities, and so forth. In particular, the ārya paths of all three yānas are attained in dependence upon this [achievement of śamatha]." Your mind's psychological immune system is bolstered tremendously, so that even if an afflictive thought arises between sessions, it does not gain traction or dominate your mind. Moreover, mental afflictions arise less frequently and with less power, even off the cushion.

Why is it so important to achieve extrasensory perception and paranormal abilities? The extrasensory perception that you can achieve just from śamatha—as the Fourth Paṇchen Lama indicates here—includes knowing other people's minds, remote viewing, and so on. "Paranormal abilities" refers to capacities of the mind that are often regarded as miracles, such as the "mind-over-matter" ability to transform the elements. These are known as *siddhi*s, but in Buddhism these are not regarded as supernatural but rather as natural potentials of the mind that are unveiled through the achievement of samādhi. Take lasers as a modern analogy, for they may appear to the ignorant as miraculous, or supernatural, but they simply demonstrate the power of light that is unveiled through advanced technology. As the science fiction author Arthur C. Clarke wrote, "Any sufficiently advanced technology is indistinguishable from magic."[13]

It is natural to feel overwhelming sadness as we look at the brutal invasions, civil wars, and sheer violence based in hatred that have dominated our world for so long and seem only to be increasing. But why should the powers of evil be so triumphant? Why should the Dharma appear weak? We know that among the bodhisattva's enlightened activities, there are those that are peaceful. We often associate peaceful activity with the saints, who in general are thought to be gentle, calming, soothing, and healing. But that is often where our Western imagination stops when we think of saintliness. However, that is not always enough. If people are hungry, they do not want gentle words—they want food. If they have no place to live, they want shelter. If they are unprotected from the elements, they need clothing. Historically, it has always been part of the saints' and bodhisattvas' enriching enlightened activity to offer material aid to those who are impoverished, to refugees, and so on. But that, too, is where, for the Western imagination, the concept of saintly behavior often stops. Yet, this is not where a true saint's or bodhisattva's work ends.

In Buddhism, according to the bodhisattva's vows and the trainings of the Mahāyāna path, siddhis—supernormal abilities or achievements—must be accomplished. Padmasambhava's powerful siddhis overcame demonic obstacles in the early dissemination of the Buddhadharma in Tibet so that it could flourish for twelve hundred years. He had greater power than the obstructive forces, demons, and so forth that were threatening the flourishing of the Dharma in Tibet, and he effectively subdued them. It is important for those of us who are devoted to the bodhisattva path to develop siddhis precisely in order to enact deeds of power for the benefit of others. That's our technology. Atiśa said that you cannot help other people reach the path if you do not have extrasensory perception, *abhijñā* in Sanskrit. If you cannot perceive others' minds but are limited to ordinary, sensory perceptions of them, you are like a doctor with no stethoscope and no diagnostic tests. How is a doctor supposed to diagnose others if he or she is limited to seeing only the surface of their bodies?

In the last resort, when even the siddhis involving sheer power are not sufficient, where the opposing forces are so violent that they can be stopped only with compassionate ferocity, with wrath: Can this be done without hatred but only with pure benevolence? The wrathful deities of Vajrayāna Buddhism—Mahākāla, Yamāntaka, and Vajrakīlaya—as well as the mahāsiddha Padmasambhava himself, show that there is a place for wrath. There is a place for ferocity—to protect the Dharma and to protect sentient beings. But this has to come from the depths of pristine awareness and the wisdom realizing emptiness—ultimate compassion—or else it will be contaminated and derailed by more of the same kinds of mental afflictions that incited the evil in the first place. So only advanced bodhisattvas are prepared to enact siddhis of ferocity with total purity while remaining untainted by mental afflictions.

Right here on the path of śamatha, vipaśyanā, and trekchö, as taught by Düdjom Rinpoché, we are on a straight path, absolutely unelaborated, on which we do not need to do anything more, or engage in any separate techniques, in order to develop these siddhis. Here we know that pristine awareness is the wellspring of all the maṇḍalas, all the empowerments, all the siddhis, and all the kinds of abhijñā—heightened awareness, clairvoyance, and so on. We see here the benefits of śamatha, not to mention the siddhis and the modes of extrasensory perception, or "yogic perception," that arise from the union of śamatha and vipaśyanā, which are on a whole other dimension altogether. But if, moreover, we can cut through the conditioned mind to the siddhis that arise from the realization of rigpa—as did Padmasambhava and many of the other great mahāsiddhas of India and Tibet— then we can be of benefit even in the most overwhelming of circumstances.

There is a time when pernicious ferocity needs to be overcome by a more powerful, benevolent, enlightened ferocity, not with the intention to harm any sentient being—never—but rather to quell the fires of evil ferocity, which manifest as violence, hatred, cruelty. When people's minds are heavily oppressed by mental afflictions, the advanced bodhisattva needs ferocity to conquer those demons. This is not a matter of conquering sentient beings—for no sentient being is a demon—but of conquering the demons of mental afflictions, because the ferocity of rigpa is rooted in reality, while the ferocity of tyrants and despots is rooted in delusion.

On this path, none of us needs to feel powerless. For teachings like these are empowering—not to the ego but with the power that comes from pristine awareness. The power of Dharma is greater than the power of the violence, hatred, and cruelty of those deluded by attachment to their own side and aversion to the other side.

So, arouse great compassion, *mahākaruṇā* in Sanskrit, first with the question, "Why couldn't all sentient beings be free from suffering and the causes of suffering?" Then, when you see that their mental afflictions do not get into their core, which is pristine awareness, you see they could be free, and then you arouse the aspiration, "May we all be free of suffering and its inner causes." Then you make it personal. With the basis of designation of "I am" being your own pristine awareness, you arouse great compassion with the determination, "I shall free us all." Not just this group, or that group, not just human beings—*all* sentient beings. Finally, to conclude this liturgy, call on the blessings of the enlightened ones: "May my gurus and personal deity bless me so that I am able to do so!"

There is no Dzogchen without great compassion. There is no bodhicitta without great compassion. We need to take full responsibility for having the opportunity to understand, to meditate upon, and to gain realization of this path. The rarity is almost inconceivable, the preciousness inconceivable. Every one of us has the potential to reach the Mahāyāna path in this lifetime by developing the uncontrived and unshakable resolve to achieve enlightenment for the sake of all sentient beings. Everyone has the capacity to put these teachings into full practice and reap the harvest, achieving enlightenment as swiftly as possible. Be aware of the Dharma wish-fulfilling jewel in the palm of your hands, and make full use of it.

CHOOSING A CONDUCIVE RETREAT SPACE

Düdjom Rinpoché continues in his root text, elaborating on how to choose a suitable place to practice. He writes,

> Although there are many ways of examining the characteristics of suitable places to practice, in general it is best to practice in a pleasant region that is blessed by siddhas of the past, such as Guru Rinpoché, and not inhabited by people who have broken their samayas. It should be very secluded, where provisions are easily obtainable, and suited to your constitution.

This significantly narrows down suitable places to practice, as not every place is equally blessed. But there are many blessed sites for practice around the world, and one only needs to do some research to discover who the sublime beings may be who have blessed a particular area of land with their sincere practice and prayers. When Düdjom Rinpoché says that "it should be very secluded, where provisions are easily obtainable, and suited to your constitution," this refers to the constitution of your body, mind, and behavior. In the context of finding a suitable location, for example, some may like it cold and dry; others may prefer a climate that is warm with plenty of humidity; and others may favor warm, dry weather. Choosing a location that is suitable for your constitution will bring about greater balance to your health, which will in turn support your practice. Nevertheless, even if the outer environment in which you are able to practice in retreat is not perfectly suited to your personal constitution, there are other ways that you can compensate, especially through diet and exercise, to approximate the ideal balance of outer conditions for your constitution.

He then advises,

> Due to the swift confluence of outer and inner fortuitous conditions in charnel grounds, haunted grounds, and other areas inhabited by malevolent local spirits, practicing in such places will enhance your meditation if you are up to it. But if you are not, you will have many obstacles. When your realization

turns into the expanse, all unfavorable circumstances arise as aids. When that happens, it is especially helpful to engage in secret practices in places such as charnel grounds. Constantly reject all outer and inner busyness, for remaining in inactivity is true solitude.

Do not rush into practicing in "charnel grounds, haunted grounds, and other areas inhabited by malevolent local spirits." Go slowly, because if you are not ready for these conditions, "you will have many obstacles." You must take seriously that human beings and animals are not the only beings with whom we share this earth, or else you may take lightly the implications of practicing in such areas before you are ready. But when you are ready and your realization of pristine awareness has become such that it is with you all the time, with no real distinction between sessions of meditation and post-meditative sessions, then it is said that your realization has turned into the expanse, and you are at the point where "all unfavorable circumstances arise as aids." At that point in your spiritual development, it will become extremely powerful for you to practice in such dangerous and potent places as charnel grounds.

Finally, he says, "Constantly reject all outer and inner busyness, for remaining in inactivity is true solitude." As previously mentioned, there is outer solitude and inner solitude. In the foundational Mahāyāna teachings, inner solitude means that you separate yourself from the eight mundane concerns. If you do not do this, then it doesn't matter how far away you are from others, you're not in real solitude because you're bringing with you the company of the eight mundane concerns—and all the people they make you think about. Here, however, Düdjom Rinpoché is going even deeper than that. Inner solitude occurs gradually as you follow this path step by step—preparing with the common and uncommon preliminary practices, developing śamatha, gaining insight into emptiness, cutting through to pristine awareness, and then utterly deactivating your body, speech, and mind as a sentient being. Then you have found the most authentic solitude, or isolation, because you have separated yourself from your very identity as a sentient being.

Deactivating your body, speech, and mind as a sentient being does not mean you never move, but rather there is only an appearance of movement as your illusory body manifests in different places and appears to be engaging in a variety of activities—in fact, though, you do not have the sense of doing anything *as a sentient being* with your ordinary sense of personal identity. This is akin to experiencing thoughts that you were not thinking but that just appear. Likewise, your body may be set into motion, and you are witnessing it, but you do not have a sense of there actually being a body or it moving through space. There is no sense of being in charge of the body, as the body simply does what needs to be done. Then you may also find that sometimes your speech is altogether spontaneous and appropriate—that is, nothing is premeditated and the words simply flow in a way that is wholly appropriate for any given situation.

ARRIVING PREPARED FOR THE MAIN PRACTICE

In the context of the preliminary practices, it is necessary to prepare your mindstream by accumulating merit and purifying negative karma and obscurations. This is a preparation that is similar to bathing your body and brushing your teeth before going out in public. Here we are heading out on a major endeavor, the main practice, and you want to show up clean and well-bathed mentally.

Regarding this purification, Düdjom Rinpoché writes,

> As for the actual practice of purifying your mindstream, strive until you gain experience in each of the common practices of the four revolutions in outlook and the uncommon practices of refuge, bodhicitta, the purification of obscurations, and the amassing of the accumulations [of merit and knowledge], as they are taught in the meditation manuals.

In order to purify your mindstream and fathom the unique and profound nature of the Buddhadharma, begin by studying and meditating on the four ārya realities, the foundational teaching that provides the structure for every other Buddhist teaching you will ever receive. Once you start to fathom them, then proceed to the cultivation of the spirit of definite emergence and bodhicitta. The spirit of definite emergence is the aspiration to emerge *from* samsara and *toward* nirvana with a definite conviction to do so. Bodhicitta is the resolve to achieve perfect enlightenment for the sake of all beings. As you read and listen to the teachings, do not just do so intellectually, but reflect on them and put them into practice. This is the only way you will come to experience firsthand whether the medicine of the Dharma works.

It is imperative that you know this for yourself and not simply accept it with blind faith, for it is only by experientially knowing with certainty how the practices transform your own mind that genuine practice can be sustained.

Further, you may have witnessed people who show up to Dharma teachings with a rush of inspiration and enthusiasm, but then after some time, their interest strays to something else. What often happens is that they find something else they deem to be more worthwhile or interesting than Dharma, something that provides them with greater immediate gratification, such as engaging in a new hobby, getting a better job, finding a new girlfriend or boyfriend, raising a family, and so on. Whenever people find something so inexpressibly precious as authentic Dharma and then do not take full advantage of it, it always traces back to the fact that they never truly fathomed the four revolutions in outlook. Without realizing the implications of these four revolutions at their depths, without shifting your entire perspective on your own life and your place in the scope of the whole of reality, you are never going to have a sustainable motivation to carry you through to the achievement of śamatha, much less to full awakening. There is nothing as important, to begin, as realizing the rarity and preciousness of having a perfect human rebirth endowed with the leisure and opportunity to achieve enlightenment in one lifetime.

You begin to assimilate the first revolution in outlook when you see for yourself that in your hands you hold the deep authenticity of the Śrāvakayāna, the majesty of the Mahāyāna, the incandescent power, wisdom, and compassion of the Vajrayāna, and the breathtaking simplicity and profundity of the pinnacle of all yānas, Dzogchen. With this in mind, then the notion of the rarity and preciousness of such a life is something you can never forsake. This first revolution in outlook is then augmented with the second revolution, which is a deep awareness of the reality of death and impermanence—that things are in a state of constant flux and one day you will die, no matter how invincible and unchanging your life may seem. The third revolution comes when you understand the depth and breadth of suffering and are able to identify its true causes, for it is only then that you can begin to take the steps to become free from such misery. The fourth and final revolution is a recognition that the reality of actions and their consequences, or karma, is such that all nonvirtue and suffering arise from mental afflictions, which are all created from ignorance of the actual nature of reality. Further realization of this fourth revolution encompasses the fact that individual consciousness continues from lifetime to lifetime, each one karmically crafted by your mental and physical conduct in previous life-times. The experiential evidence supporting this assertion is overwhelming, but facing this reality can be daunting. These shifts in perspective are truly revolutionary and effect real change if you thoroughly integrate them into your worldview, values, and actions. Then, as a result, the way forward is clear: Give your whole life to Dharma because nothing else has the revolutionary power to free you from the cyclic bondage of samsara and to help every other sentient being to do the same.

Düdjom Rinpoché then writes,

> In particular, you should apply yourself to guru yoga as the life force of your practice. If you don't, progress in meditation will be slow, and even when there is a little development, obstacles will occur, and it will not be possible for genuine realizations to arise in your mindstream. Therefore, as a result of offering prayers of supplication with uncontrived, fervent admiration and reverence, after some time, the enlightened view from the guru's mindstream will be transferred to you, and extraordinary, inexpressible realizations will certainly emerge from within your own being.

When he says that "you should apply yourself to guru yoga as the life force of your practice," this means that without it, your practice is lifeless. But with its powerful stream of blessings, you have the vigor, vitality, strength, courage, and stamina to proceed along the path. If you do not apply yourself to guru yoga, then "progress in meditation will be slow." You will instead need to move forward with sheer grit, effort, and intelligence, and will likely find that endeavoring in this way is not enough to ensure success in your practice. Moreover, "even when there is a little development, obstacles will occur." As you are devoting yourself seriously to practice and are progressing, you are concurrently churning the depths of your psyche, which is when nyam—meditative experiences and upheavals—are aroused. The deeper and more advanced your practice becomes, the more powerful are the nyam.

If you do not have a guru to tell you that nyam are a normal part of the practice and that they will inevitably enable you to emerge stronger and more resilient than before, then when these upheavals occur, you may conclude that they are too much for you and subsequently abandon practice. You need the guru's encouragement, guidance, and wisdom to keep going.

Drawing not only from the guru's experience but from a hundred generations of yogis before, the blessings of the guru can help you see that what appears to be adversity can actually strengthen your resolve, wisdom, compassion, and renunciation.

In addition, if you do not apply yourself to guru yoga, "it will not be possible for genuine realizations to arise in your mindstream. Therefore, as a result of offering prayers of supplication with uncontrived, fervent admiration and reverence, after some time, the enlightened view from the guru's mindstream will be transferred to you, and extraordinary, inexpressible realizations will certainly emerge from within your own being." As stated in *The Vajra Essence*, on this path of Dzogchen as revealed by the Lake-Born Vajra, if there is profound and authentic realization of pristine awareness upon the firm foundation of śamatha and vipaśyanā, then it is not necessary for every individual on this path to practice either the stage of generation or completion. It will be your choice once you have enough understanding to discern your own path properly.

However, along the ascent to the ninth yāna, if you do not establish your "base camps" with practices of the stages of generation and completion, which are higher than śamatha and vipaśyanā alone, then the realizations and transformations that are meant to come about through those practices of the stages of generation and completion must be made manifest in some other way. These practices of sādhana and the subtle body are not redundant or superfluous; they are crucially important. For many practitioners of Vajrayāna, that is the totality of their practice, for they do not practice Mahāmudrā or Dzogchen. When practiced upon the firm foundation of the Sūtrayāna, the stages of generation and completion themselves have the potential to take you all the way to buddhahood in one lifetime. So, if you decide not to practice those two stages while seeking to follow the unelaborated path of Dzogchen, then something powerful enough must act as a substitute to do all the work of those otherwise essential Vajrayāna practices. The inner transformations brought about by the stages of generation and completion must be accomplished through the practices of cutting through and the direct crossing over, both rooted in the thorough accomplishment of śamatha, vipaśyanā, and guru yoga.

What is it that will actualize the transformation that needs to take place in any case, even if you do not explicitly engage in the Vajrayāna practices of sādhana and the subtle body, which involve a tremendous amount of visualization, recitation, and effortful control of the breath, channels, and subtle energies of the body? Over the centuries, the actual choice of yogis in the lineages of Mahāmudrā and Dzogchen has usually been to engage in the elaborated practices of Vajrayāna in order to augment, complement, and empower the unelaborated practices of śamatha, vipaśyanā, and trekchö. However, if one chooses not to engage in elaborate sādhanas or practices of the subtle body, then, within the Dzogchen and Mahāmudrā traditions, it is the profound practice of guru yoga that can accomplish the work of the entirety of the stages of generation and completion—if one is able to engage in it properly and with full understanding.

A Brief Introduction to the Four Empowerments

The four empowerments are rooted in the cultivation of admiration and reverence—but for whom or for what? Ultimately, we need to seek the core of all refuge, all wisdom, and all purity—namely, the dharmakāya that is the ground of all samsara and nirvana, which is personified in this tradition as Samantabhadra. Then Samantabhadra manifests to us in myriad forms such as Amitābha, Avalokiteśvara, Tārā, Guru Rinpoché, Düdjom Lingpa, the sublime blessings flowing straight through to great beings in our recent living memory, such as Düdjom Rinpoché, Yangthang Rinpoché, and Gyatrul Rinpoché.

When Düdjom Rinpoché writes, "the enlightened view from the guru's mindstream will be transferred to you," you may recall the Buddha's words, "Buddhas do not wash away sins with water, nor do they remove the sufferings of beings with their hands, neither do they transfer their own realization into others. Teaching the actual nature of reality, they liberate beings." If the buddhas cannot transfer their realizations to others, then how can the enlightened view of the guru be transferred to you?

When we take the four empowerments in the spirit of reverence and devotion, we do not need to call the guru from afar; he or she does not have to travel to us from a distant pure land on a beam of light. That kind of visualization is a skillful means that can be useful for those who, at some level, still believe the guru dwells far away and needs to be invited in order to be present in our midst. In reality, though, the guru's body, speech, and mind are always and everywhere present. As the Dzogchen aphorism states, "Do not look outside yourself for the Buddha." The guru, indivisible from Samantabhadra, primordially dwells within our own mindstreams. To transfer his or her enlightened view to us means to make manifest the pristine awareness that has always already been present within us. It is a transference from the unmanifest to the manifest, so that we may realize the actual nature of our own minds to be none other than the enlightened mind of Samantabhadra.

Meditation: Taking the Four Empowerments

Find a comfortable position, preferably seated and upright for this meditation. Then settle body, speech, and mind in their natural states.

As you turn your attention to the guru, begin this session by focusing upon the one who first turned the wheel of Dharma in this historical era and made possible all the Dharma that has flowed since then—the Buddha Śākyamuni, who by his life and his teachings has blessed this world and continues to do so as a living presence. Reflect upon the life and teachings of this perfectly enlightened one.

Just as the torch of his enlightened wisdom was carried from one generation to another, then bring to mind Kāśyapa, Ānanda, Śāriputra, Maudgalyāyana, Subhūti, and the Buddha's eight great sons in the Mahāyāna tradition, and see how the blessings flow like a powerful current from one generation to the next. Likewise, consider the lives and teachings of the great Nāgārjuna, Asaṅga, Padmasambhava, Atiśa, Sakya Paṇḍita, Jé Tsongkhapa, His Holiness the Dalai Lama, and the myriad other great paṇḍitas, mahāsiddhas, and bodhisattvas throughout history. Reflect upon the reality that you have received the guidance and blessings of these great beings, spanning more than two millennia. You have held out your begging bowls, and they have been filled with the ambrosia of the Śrāvakayāna, Bodhisattvayāna, Vajrayāna, all the way through to the Atiyogayāna, the pinnacle of Dzogchen.

Then focus specifically on that manifestation of Guru Rinpoché, who has revealed the path presented in *The Vajra Essence* and other visionary teachings received by the great vidyādhara Düdjom Lingpa. Allow your reverence and admiration to flow to the individuals who have shared this Dharma and to the teachings themselves.

Visualize in the space of awareness in front of you an image in the form of Guru Rinpoché in whatever manifestation most deeply touches your heart and arouses your faith and reverence. Imagine Guru Rinpoché facing you and surrounded by a host of ḍākinīs, vidyādharas, and bodhisattvas. Invoke not only the visualization but the actual presence of Guru Rinpoché in the space of awareness in front of you. He is already there, so attend to him.

Now offer your supplications:

> Grant me the blessings of your body, speech, and mind to transmute my own body, speech, and mind that is generated by karma and kleśa, purifying utterly my very identity as a sentient being. Purify me so that I may transcend the confines of a sentient being's body, speech, and mind. Grant me your blessings.

In the spirit of reverence, imagine as clearly as possible the intimate presence of Guru Rinpoché, who is gazing upon you with the great compassion of all the buddhas. Now recite "The Seven-Line Supplication":

> HŪṂ
> In the northwest frontier of Oḍḍiyāna,
> in the heart of a lotus,
> sits the one renowned as Padmasambhava,
> who achieved the wondrous supreme siddhi
> and is surrounded by a host of many ḍākinīs.
> Following in your footsteps, I devote myself to practice.
> Please come forth and bestow your blessings.
> GURU PADMA SIDDHI HŪṂ

In order to take the first empowerment—the self-empowerment of the body, or the vase empowerment—visualize the seed syllable *oṃ* at the crown of Guru Rinpoché's head in the space in front of you. From there, a cascading white light of blessings flows into the *oṃ* at the crown of your head, filling this insubstantial space of your body, which consists only of a matrix of appearances, devoid of any objective, inherent existence. Imagine this light flowing into this translucent space and utterly purifying all obscurations, illnesses, diseases, demonic influences, negative karmic imprints, and habitual propensities associated with the body. Imagine this white light completely purifying and perfecting your body, sowing the seeds of the nirmāṇakāya. It is "perfecting" the body because each sentient being's body has a profusion of harmful influences and contamination from karma and mental afflictions. In your mind's eye, purify it entirely so that by the time you come to the end of receiving this first empowerment, you are able to imagine a perfected body, as you have utterly transcended your body as a sentient being. Effectively, by the time you have completed this empowerment, from your perspective, you no longer have an impure body generated by karma and kleśa. It has been purified, which means it has been dissolved into emptiness, you have vacated the space occupied by your physical body, and it is gone. Where it once was, there is now a sheer, luminous emptiness, and from that emptiness arises a primordially pure vajra body. In so doing, you receive the vase empowerment, fully blessed with the blessings of the vajra body of Guru Rinpoché himself.

Once again, in the spirit of supplication, request the second, secret empowerment, which sows the seeds for the sambhogakāya and the purification of all defilements and obscurations pertaining to speech. From a ruby-red *āḥ* syllable at Guru Rinpoché's throat flows a fountain of incandescent, radiant, ruby-red light. This red light flows into the *āḥ* at your throat *cakra*, permeating your being and purifying all of the negative karma you have accumulated by way of speech, any obscurations pertaining to speech, any harm done by way of speech. This ruby-red light from the *āḥ* syllable purifies the energies of speech entirely so that by the time the second empowerment is received, your speech as a sentient being has been purified to the point of being transcended. In its place there is a luminous vacuity of the emptiness of speech, and your speech has been transferred to the guru's speech vajra. Speech now rests in its natural state of effortless silence.

Then make supplication to receive the wisdom-primordial-consciousness empowerment, which encompasses the blessings of the enlightened mind of Guru Rinpoché. This third empowerment causes you to experience a complete dissolution of your ordinary mind, which awakens in your mindstream the spiritual capacity to manifest the dharmakāya. Visualize an indigo-blue *hūṃ* syllable at Guru Rinpoché's heart. From this *hūṃ*, an indigo-blue light streams into your heart, purifying all the obscurations—afflictive and cognitive—in the entire space of the mind, thus perfecting and transcending the mind. You realize the absence of the mind of a sentient being, its emptiness. Your mind—with your personal history, strengths, weaknesses, virtues, nonvirtues, mental afflictions, and so forth—is vaporized in this high-frequency indigo-blue light, and there is no mind to be found anywhere. In that luminous, empty space, the realizations of the guru's mindstream are transferred to your mindstream. Where there was a mind, there is a sheer vacuity, but now filled with the light of the blessings of Guru Rinpoché.

Then to complete this empowerment, turn to the fourth empowerment—the word empowerment—which plants the seed for realizing the *svabhāvakāya*. This is like the seal for acquiring full confidence that the preceding empowerments are complete, purifying anything that remains. Here you simultaneously and respectively merge the powerful threefold currents of body, speech, and mind from the *oṃ*, *āḥ*, *hūṃ* syllables at the crown, throat, and heart cakras, dispelling the last vestiges of anything that has escaped the purification process thus far, purifying even the habitual propensities for the afflictive and cognitive obscurations, such that there is no remnant of any sentient being's body, speech, and mind at all. There is now a vajra body, vajra speech, and vajra mind, indivisible within the empty nature of all three. Receiving this empowerment is a threefold assault on your presumed status as a sentient being. The nirmāṇakāya, sambhogakāya, and dharmakāya are now all simultaneously united in the svabhāvakāya, which is their empty, essential nature.

Then, at your invitation, Guru Rinpoché's entourage and the seat formed of a lotus, sun, and moon dissolve into him, and, gradually diminishing in size, he comes to the crown of your head, where he instantaneously faces in the same direction as you. Then make the supplication, "Please become indivisible with me." Bliss-fully, he then dissolves into light that flows down through your *avadhūtī*—the central channel, which runs vertically in front of your spine—until his form reappears at your heart cakra. His mind merges indivisibly with your mind, his speech with your speech, and his body with your body. Thus, your body, speech, and mind have now been merged with the body-speech-mind vajra of the guru, actualizing your own mind as the mind of the Buddha. In this way, the guru's realizations are transferred to you, but not from outside, as the visualization has all taken place within the space of your awareness and nowhere else.

Now imagine a radiant white Avalokiteśvara on the crown of your head, a ruby-red Amitābha at your throat cakra, Guru Rin-poché at your heart cakra, and in his heart cakra is Samantabhadra in union with his divine partner Samantabhadrī. Then imagine your outer, purified form dissolving into the Guru Rinpoché at your heart; he dissolves into Samantabhadra and Samantabhadrī, and they dissolve into the indigo-blue syllable *hūṃ*. The *hūṃ* then melts from the bottom to the top of the syllable into emptiness. Rest there with no object.

Then, instantly and effortlessly, out of that emptiness, imagine yourself emerging—not as a sentient being but in an illusory form where you are appearing to be a sentient being but are not actually there. You are manifesting as a living-being nirmāṇakāya.

Bring this meditation to a close by dedicating the merit of this practice so that you may swiftly actualize your true identity as the Lake-Born Vajra and bring every sentient being without exception to this very state of perfect awakening.

A Deeper Understanding of Guru Yoga

Do not look outside yourself for the Buddha. The actual Guru Rinpoché is not in front of you, hovering in space somewhere out there, though it can be a very skillful means to imagine this. Guru Rinpoché is always primordially here, and through guru yoga you are now simply acknowledging that which has always been true. In so doing, you realize the inseparability and the non-duality of your own pristine awareness and Guru Rinpoché's enlightened awareness. Lo and behold, the transference of realization has taken place! But it never passed from one individual to another. One vanished, and in the place of that illusory sentient being, there already was and there is now manifestly a buddha. Where, then, did the transference of those realizations actually come from? From your own pristine awareness into your waking manifest awareness—that was the transference.

Yet without the guru, how would you do that? How would this be anything more than a light show, sheer imagination, or pretending? The fact that your guru appears to be a human being—such as Düdjom Rinpoché, Gyatrul Rinpoché, Yangthang Rinpoché, and so forth—is very helpful for a simple reason: You appear to yourself to be a sentient being, and you take that all too seriously. So, if you can learn to see through your guru's ordinary appearance as a human being, and to see that Guru Rinpoché is actually present where the guru is, then you can learn to see through your own ordinary appearance as a human being and see why it is even possible for Guru Rinpoché to be actually present right where you are. But if you cannot see that where the guru is, there is the Buddha, then you do not stand a chance for being able to realize that authentically within yourself. Do you think you are a buddha and your guru is not? As we will see, Düdjom Rinpoché writes later in the text that if you linger even for a moment thinking that your guru is actually a sentient being, then you close all the valves of blessings. For how can one sentient being give another sentient being blessings? From authentic guru yoga, though, blessings can be both transferred and received. So, through this quintessential guru yoga—all that would have needed to be done by means of the quintessential stage of generation and completion practices, had you followed that route—is done by means of this practice, within the simple, unelaborated path of Dzogchen. That is why guru yoga is so enormously important.

Düdjom Rinpoché then writes,

> Lama Zhang Rinpoché declared, "There are many who culti-
> vate stillness, meditative experiences, samādhi, and so on. But
> rare are the realizations that are born from within due to the
> guru's blessings, which arise by the power of admiration and
> reverence."

Many people strive with sheer grit and determination, and they have a wide variety of meditative experiences. Yet, experiences come and go like mist. Even samādhi, from lifetime to lifetime, comes and goes. With samādhi all by itself, not one hair's breadth of progress is made in reaching and proceeding along the path. Of course, we are not striving for samādhi alone. There are many who do that, "but rare are the realizations that are born from within"—that is, that are not achieved, acquired, or accomplished through striving. If they are born from within, then they are manifesting more in the manner of grace, a gift, or a sheer, spontaneous display, or effulgence, of pristine awareness. Then, they are "due to the guru's blessings." The guru begins as someone with whom you have an I-thou relationship. You can speak to the guru, ask questions, receive instructions, blessings, and so on. This "I-thou" relationship begins there and ends with the deep realization of the inseparability of yourself from the guru.

Yet, what are blessings, actually? Blessings are what bring about beneficial transformation in one's mind at a level that would not have been possible based upon one's karmic maturation alone at any given moment. The source of all blessings is the dharmakāya. They may flow by way of one's lama and spiritual friends, by way of sacred places, statues, and paintings, as well as sacred texts, stūpas, and relics. Or they may flow directly from one's own pristine awareness. When receiving teachings from a lama, one is receiving not only knowledge but tangible blessings from the lama if one's mind is transformed in meaningful ways and turns to virtue as a result of being in the presence of that lama and listening to his or her teachings.

As for the realizations, they arise by the power of your faith, reverence, and admiration. They are not something to be achieved, thereby making them susceptible to being lost. By receiving the four empowerments, you open the wellspring of your pristine awareness, and realizations emerge from there. There is nothing more sustainable than that. An adage from the teachings on renunciation says that whatever you acquire, you will lose—whether it be friends, money, wealth, reputation, body, health, and so on—whereas you cannot lose what is already there at the very ground of your being. You cannot lose your buddha nature, though it is either veiled or unveiled. Therefore, when realizations emerge by the power of faith, blessings, reverence, admiration, supplications, or the four empowerments, then they are deeply sustainable since they are not acquired from somewhere else. Bear in mind also that the foremost of all the preliminaries to the view, meditation, and conduct of the Great Perfection is guru yoga, without which you may gain some degree of insight or wisdom, but if it is unsupported by the guru yoga that is the source of all blessings, such insights are unlikely to bring about profound and irreversible transformations in your mind.

Moreover, guru yoga provides the approach to Guru Padmasambhava. From there arises the actualization of the guru, and then your own body, speech, and mind merge with the vajra body, speech, and mind of Padmasambhava. Düdjom Lingpa and Düdjom Rinpoché provide perfect examples of that type of guru yoga within their own lives. In one of Düdjom Lingpa's previous incarnations, about twelve hundred years ago, he was Drokben Khyeuchung Lotsāwa, the youthful interpreter, one of Guru Padmasambhava's twenty-five close disciples in Tibet. Khyeuchung Lotsāwa approached Padmasambhava throughout the stream of his practice and sat in his presence, receiving blessings, empowerments, and teachings. Then, when this mindstream manifested centuries later as Düdjom Lingpa, he experienced many visionary encounters with Padmasambhava in the form of the Lake-Born Vajra. This once again actualized the utter merging, the indivisibility of the enlightened mind of Padmasambhava and the mind of Düdjom Lingpa, which then became the mind of Düdjom Rinpoché. So, it is said that Düdjom Rinpoché was both an incarnation of Düdjom Lingpa and all his previous incarnations—encompassing that stream of an individual from lifetime to lifetime—and also an emanation of Guru Padmasambhava, for their minds, their awareness, had become of one nature. As we attend to the words of Düdjom Rinpoché, we are listening of course to Düdjom Rinpoché, the mind emanation of Düdjom Lingpa, but we are also listening to Padmasambhava himself.

Having Conviction in the Teachings and Finding a Qualified Guru

In order to make any substantial progress in approaching, reaching, and then proceeding along the path, your admiration and reverence for the teachings and the teacher must be backed by strong conviction based in discerning intelligence and not be coming from mere blind faith. Conviction can arise from a deep understanding of the teachings of the three turnings of the wheel of Dharma or perhaps even from a strong intuition wherein, by going into the depths of your being, which is permeated by dharmakāya, you can discover whether or not you intuitively affirm the teachings you have received.

However it may come, the foundation for authentic guru yoga arises from a conviction concerning three principles taught by Maitreya in the *Uttaratantra*: "Because the perfect Buddhakāya emanates everywhere, because it is inseparable from suchness, and because all embodied beings have the lineage, they always possess buddha nature."[14] That is, you must come to a firm conviction that the following are simultaneously true: (1) The dharmakāya is ubiquitous, permeating all phenomena. (2) All phenomena are empty of inherent nature, which is why it is true that the very distinction between your own mindstream and the dharmakāya is also empty of inherent nature. That is, your own mindstream and the dharmakāya are not two inherently separate realities, but rather they are of the same essential nature—emptiness. (3) You are imbued with buddha nature and have the potential to become a perfectly enlightened buddha.

If and only if you have a firm conviction in these three principles, are you ready to practice guru yoga at the level of Vajrayāna and Dzogchen as described previously. Now, you may have the good fortune to have found a lama who is qualified to lead you to the culmination of this path of Dzogchen. But in order to determine—beyond a mere intuition or blind faith—whether or not someone who is appearing to you as a lama is actually a qualified lama, ask yourself these empirical questions: (1) Are the lama's teachings authentic and in accord with the lineage that he or she is representing? (2) Is the lama's conduct in accordance with those teachings? Finally, (3) when the lama grants empowerments, transmissions, and spiritual guidance, do you find them deeply beneficial and transformative for you personally? In this way, the lama is like a physician and the Dharma he or she imparts is like the sole medicine that heals the afflictions of your mind. When you find a qualified lama whose teachings are authentic, whose conduct is authentic, and from whom you find the teaching and guidance to be actually beneficial, then you have found a qualified spiritual mentor.

Yet, in most cases, from the perspective of the spiritual mentor, he or she is still experiencing himself or herself as a sentient being who is teaching authentically, behaving in accordance with the teachings, and whose teachings, presence, empowerments, and pith instructions are helpful. In the role of disciple, however, we must recognize that it is utterly inappropriate to give infinite admiration and reverence to a human being with finite virtues.

Therefore, you may recognize and admire the virtues of the guru whom you perceive as a human being, but it is then crucial to dissolve your perceptions of this individual into emptiness—down to the ground of their own buddha nature, indivisible from dharmakāya—and then only out of that emptiness, to view him or her with pure vision and boundless devotion. To view your guru with pure vision is to see that in reality the guru is none other than your own appearance and a reflection of your own pristine awareness.

The Guru-Disciple Relationship

Our gurus are our spiritual friends, or *kalyāṇamitra*. Buddha Śākyamuni was called the Great Kalyāṇamitra (Tib. *Gewé Shé Nyen Chenpo*), the Great Spiritual Friend, or the Great Virtuous Friend. Similarly, Jesus is also regarded as a spiritual friend, which suggests a type of intimacy and warmth, while implying a divine and sacred relationship. Likewise, our gurus are our spiritual friends, but they are not our buddies. For the most part, friendships apart from authentic spiritual friendships are at some level rooted in attachment.

This was searingly brought to my attention many years ago when I was a monk in Switzerland and was speaking one-on-one with my lama Geshé Rabten. I casually referred to someone as being my friend, and he turned to me very sternly and said something like, "You shouldn't speak of some particular person as being your friend!" I knew exactly what he meant: That is, as soon as I point to someone and say, "This is my friend," this implies that there are other people whom I do not regard as my friends. If everybody is equally my friend, I would not say "my friend" because it would be like saying, "my human being."

Further, a principal reason for leaving your home and entering a monastery to become a monk or nun is to cut the ties of attachment to friends and family so that you can view all beings equally with loving-kindness and compassion. So, on the one hand, you could say that you now have no friends, in the sense that there is no one for whom you feel a congenial attachment, and no family, in the sense that there are no individuals for whom you feel the attachment of a familial relationship. You have now become homeless, without family or friends. When you choose friends, it is typically done so on the basis of finding them appealing, friendly, virtuous, helpful, and so on. Likewise, for people you regard as not being your friend, you might see them as unappealing, unfriendly, nonvirtuous, and antagonistic.

The whole distinction between friend, enemy, and a neutral person pertains to the first meditation Geshé Rabten ever taught me, which was on immeasurable impartiality. He commented at the time that all discord in the world stems from attachment to those with whom one feels close and aversion to those for whom one feels no affinity. The ideal of becoming a monastic is to cut all ties of attachment so that the loving-kindness and compassion one feels for others is not tainted by self-centeredness. But this approach need not be reserved strictly for monastics—it is wholly possible as a layperson who is practicing authentically.

Moreover, do not choose your spiritual mentor, or lama, because you like him or her, because they are nice to you, or because they have psychic powers or clairvoyance. In those cases, the relationship would then be rooted in attachment. The Tibetan word *geshé* means "spiritual friend." Your guru is your spiritual friend, and there is only one reason for the relationship: The guru is there to guide you, inspire you, instruct you, and do all he or she can to help you on your spiritual path—nothing more.

His Holiness the Dalai Lama spoke many years ago on the meaning of the "root guru." He said that you may study, train with, or receive empowerment or transmission from many gurus, but the one who has most deeply benefited you, inspired you, transformed you, and effectively guided you on the path is your root guru. Then, within Mahāyāna, especially in the Vajrayāna context, you should regard all your other gurus as emanations of your root guru. For me, I recognized His Holiness the Dalai Lama as my root guru the first time I received personal guidance from him in 1971. Almost twenty years later, when I was ripe to receive guidance on the path of Dzogchen, I saw that His Holiness, Avalokiteśvara, was manifesting as Gyatrul Rinpoché—that is, an emanation of Avalokiteśvara manifesting as Padmasambhava. Then, years later, I met Yangthang Rinpoché, once again Avalokiteśvara, but now manifesting as Vimalamitra.

It is significant that religious people in the cultures of Tibet, India, and Southeast Asia never refer to their lama or guru by their personal name but instead address them by their title as "teacher" in various ways: Geshé-la, Khandro-la, Rinpoché, Khenpo-la, Lama-la, or if your teacher, who may be your root lama, does not have a title, is not a tulku, a geshé, or a khenpo, then you would simply say "Gen-la," meaning "Teacher," and the "la" is simply an honorific. This is similar to the way that religious people in the West respectfully address their spiritual mentors as Reverend, Father, Rabbi, and so forth. It is proper to invoke a tone of formality in order to honor the gravity of a relationship that is unlike any other friendship you will ever have.

Ideally, the relationship between guru and disciple is one of total freedom from attachment, which in no way implies any decrease or withdrawal of kindness, affection, warmth, love, care, or compassion. All of those qualities are other-centered, whereas attachment, by nature and definition, is always self-centered and self-serving. So, in the Dzogchen context, as you look upon your guru with admiration and reverence, there may be faith, affection, devotion, worship, and appreciation, but optimally there is not attachment.

Three months before Buddha Śākyamuni passed into *parinirvana*, he let his followers know that he would soon pass away. Those touched by his teachings then went to see him and receive final teachings from him. When he knew that his work in that lifetime was complete, the Buddha lay down on his right side and passed into samādhi, passing through all the *dhyāna*s and *samāpatti*s. He was surrounded by his loving disciples who knew they would never see him again or receive any further guidance from him. At this time, many of them wept. For them, it was as if the sun, moon, stars, and planets were vanishing all at once.

However, among all the disciples around him—those who were ordinary beings, stream-enterers, āryas, *arhat*s, and so on—there was one group of his disciples who did not shed a tear and showed no sign of distress. Their beloved teacher was passing away, the *Samyaksambuddha*, or the perfectly awakened Buddha bearing all the thirty-two signs and eighty symbols of perfect enlightenment. They even knew it would be a long time until Maitreya, the next Samyaksambuddha, would appear again and freshly turn the wheel of Dharma. But it was only the arhats who witnessed his passing and showed no distress. They adored and worshipped the Buddha, but their reverence was with no attachment and, therefore, no sorrow.

Shortly before his passing, the Buddha said, "Therefore . . . be islands unto yourselves, refuges unto yourselves, seeking no external refuge, with the [Dharma] as your island, the [Dharma] as your refuge, seeking no other refuge." In this way, the ideal of the guru-disciple relationship is one in which the disciples have no attachment toward the guru and, likewise, the guru has no attachment toward the disciples. Your guru as a buddha has infinite, vast, immeasurable, and transcendent loving-kindness, compassion, empathetic joy, and impartiality—but not one iota of attachment.

THE PROFUNDITY OF THE PRELIMINARY PRACTICES

Düdjom Rinpoché completes the preparatory stage, writing,

> Thus, the arising of the meaning of the Great Perfection in your mindstream depends on the preliminary practices, which is why Jé Drigung declared,
>
> > For other dharmas, the main practice is considered to be profound,
> > but here we consider the preliminary practices to be profound.
>
> And his enlightened perspective is true.

If the term "Great Perfection" is like a finger, then the referent is what it is pointing to, which is "the meaning of the Great Perfection." The meaning is not simply a definition using more words; in fact, it is an utter transcendence of words. The referent of the Great Perfection is inexpressible, ineffable, and transcends all words, examples, metaphors, and so on. The arising of the referent of "the Great Perfection in your mindstream depends on the preliminary practices."

Thus, the great founder of the Drigung Kagyü lineage, Jé Drigung Kyobpa Jikten Sumgön (1143–1217) declared, "For other dharmas, the main practice is considered to be profound, but here we consider the preliminary practices to be profound." Düdjom Rinpoché then adds, "And his enlightened perspective is true." The preliminary practices may seem like the warm-up for the main event, but they are not to be taken lightly or as something to "get through." They serve as an indispensable foundation for the main practice and should not be skipped or minimized in any way. The preliminary practices include refuge, cultivating the spirit of definite emergence, bodhicitta, śamatha, and vipaśyanā, and they will pave the way for the main practice of the view, meditation, and conduct of the Great Perfection.

4. The Main Practice: View

Having covered the preliminaries, we now turn to the main body of the practice, which consists of the view, meditation, and conduct.

With respect to the main practice, Düdjom Rinpoché begins by presenting the view:

> Regarding the main practice—on how to cut through false superimpositions concerning the view, meditation, and conduct and then set out on the road of practice—I shall first address the view by which one knows the mode of being.

> By establishing the actual nature of your own mind, the nature of existence of the ultimate character of reality, within pristine awareness that is free of all characteristics that are fabricated or modified by conventional cognition, pristine awareness dawns nakedly as self-emergent primordial consciousness.

To "cut through false superimpositions" is to cut through conceptual projections by which we impute things onto reality that are not actually there. We are seeking here the view of the Great Perfection by which "one knows the mode of being," "the actual nature of your own mind," the way that phenomena actually exist.

Please attend now to this very concise but complete introduction to the view of the Great Perfection and attend to each phrase as pointing-out instructions, regarding your own mind here and now as Düdjom Rinpoché points out the actual nature of our own mind, that which is already here as you are reading these lines. This is quintessentially characteristic of Dzogchen: that, fundamentally, the awareness with which you are receiving these teachings on the view of the Great Perfection *is* the Great Perfection.

Düdjom Rinpoché points it out directly: "By establishing the actual nature of your own mind, the nature of existence of the ultimate character of reality, within pristine awareness that is free of all characteristics that are fabricated or modified by conventional cognition, pristine awareness dawns nakedly as self-emergent primordial consciousness." The view is that by which one understands the actual nature of the whole of reality. Here, Düdjom Rinpoché draws no distinction between the nature of emptiness, which is the mode of being, the nature of existence of the ultimate, fundamental "character" of reality, and pristine awareness. Thus, in this presentation, he highlights from the very beginning the primordial indivisibility of the two, which is beyond the dualistic confines of subject and object. This indicates that it is by the sheer fact of identifying the actual nature of your own mind within, or from the perspective of, pristine awareness that this awareness itself manifests as self-emergent primordial consciousness, whereby you view all reality from the perspective of pristine awareness. By so doing, the nature of emptiness becomes manifest—which is "the mode of being" of all phenomena.

Here there is no prelude consisting of classic vipaśyanā teachings on the nature of apprehended objects and the apprehending mind, indicating the emptiness of inherent nature of both. Instead, Düdjom Rinpoché turns directly to pristine awareness, indicating that with the realization of that one reality, the primordial ground, the nature of emptiness will naturally be revealed. Then, for the quintessential pointing-out instructions, as he points to that which is beyond words and concepts, and even beyond analogies and parallels, he will point it out with phrase after phrase, wherein each phrase removes a veil and what is left is not a sheer vacuity or a sheer absence. What remains when all of the veils have been lifted is the self-emergent, already present and now manifest, primordial consciousness.

Düdjom Rinpoché's quintessential pointing-out instructions are as follows:

> Inexpressible with words, it cannot be indicated with analogies. It does not worsen in samsara, nor does it improve in nirvana. It has never been born and never ceases; it is never liberated, nor is it deluded; it has never existed, nor has it ever not existed; it has never been delimited, nor does it fall to any extreme. In short, it has never been determined to exist as a substantial entity with elaborated characteristics, so its

essential nature is originally pure, great, all-pervasive emptiness. With its empty inner glow unimpeded, the oceans of the
realms of the phenomena of samsara and nirvana appear of
their own accord, like the sun and its rays. Therefore, as it has
never been sheer nothingness, or a blank vacuity, its manifest
nature is the great, spontaneous actualization of primordial
consciousness and its sublime qualities.

Let these words come to you and speak to your own pristine awareness, and
let them immediately point to the referent of each word as you look within
and see if you can identify that which is already present, already knowing,
some dimension of your awareness here and now that does not fluctuate.
Identify that which does not worsen in samsara or improve in nirvana, a
dimension of your awareness here and now of which it can be said, "It has
never been born and never ceases." Conditioned consciousness does arise
and cease, of course. It arises and passes moment to moment to moment.
We know this. It is everywhere in the Buddhist teachings. It is evident; we
don't have to imagine it. This flow of mental awareness moves, it shifts, it
fluctuates. It becomes dull and then clear. Can you detect something deeper,
something vaster, more encompassing, a quality of awareness that "has never
been born and never ceases"? Can you identify this awareness, here and now,
that is as vast as space?

This pristine awareness "has never been determined to exist as a substantial entity with elaborated characteristics, so its essential nature is originally
pure, great, all-pervasive emptiness. With its empty inner glow unimpeded,
the oceans of the realms of the phenomena of samsara and nirvana appear
of their own accord, like the sun and its rays. Therefore, as it has never been
sheer nothingness, or a blank vacuity, its manifest nature is the great, spontaneous actualization of primordial consciousness and its sublime qualities."

To continue,

> Thus, recognizing, just as it is, the pristine awareness that is
> the union of appearances and emptiness—the nature of the
> three kāyas, the mode of being of exactly this, the nature of
> existence of the primordial character of reality—is called "the
> cognition-transcending view of the Great Perfection." The
> great Ācārya [Padmasambhava] declared, "The dharmakāya,
> transcending cognition, is suchness."

When Düdjom Rinpoché says "the nature of the three kāyas," he is referring to the empty, essential nature of dharmakāya; the manifest, luminous nature of sambhogakāya; and the all-pervasive, spontaneous compassion of nirmāṇakāya. Pristine awareness encompasses all three of these. Thus, the recognition of pristine awareness as "the mode of being of exactly this, the nature of existence of the primordial character of reality—is called 'the cognition-transcending view of the Great Perfection.'" This explains the statement by the great Ācārya, Padmasambhava, "The dharmakāya, transcending cognition, is suchness." "Suchness" here refers to the actual nature of reality.

Düdjom Rinpoché concludes,

> How marvelous that we hold right here in our hands the enlightened view of Samantabhadra! This is the culmination of all the eighty-four thousand divisions of the Jina's teachings and the essence of the six million four hundred thousand tantras of the Great Perfection. There is not even a speck beyond this. The value of all dharmas should be determined upon this basis.

A Meditation: Śamatha without a Sign, Imbued with the Dzogchen View

> Find a comfortable position and settle your body, speech, and mind in their natural states.
>
> In order for there to be an indivisibility of the teaching and the meditation, now merge the teachings with experience in the space of your awareness.
>
> As we lay down our weary minds, exhausted by so many lifetimes in samsara, lay the mind down to rest on the bed of awareness, and let the bed of awareness hold your mind as the Dharma holds us. The very meaning of Dharma is "to uphold," "to uplift," "to hold." From that sense of ease, that stillness, that clarity of awareness, invoke Guru Rinpoché, as if from afar, as if from the Glorious Copper-Colored Mountain. Invoke him into your immediate presence, wherever you are, and recite "The Seven-Line Supplication." Have a sense that it is not simply that you are visualizing

him or imagining him coming to you, but that by the power of your imagination, your yearning, your aspiration, your faith, you are unveiling his presence with you that is, in fact, already there. It is like an empowerment, where you have a red ribbon that covers your eyes, and then you lift the ribbon from your eyes and see what is already there.

Now take and receive the four empowerments, supplicating Guru Rinpoché first to bless you and then to merge with your purified body, speech, and mind so that they become inseparable from his body, speech, and mind vajras.

Entering into this practice of śamatha without a sign, recognize that awareness is already resting in its own place at this very moment. Where else would it rest? It is already effortlessly illuminating its own manifest nature and knowing its own essential nature—that indivisibility of luminosity and cognizance; it *already knows*. So, in this practice of śamatha without a sign, there is no withdrawal, nor is there a flowing outward. The sovereign remains upon the throne. Awareness rests where it already is. It does not withdraw. It simply does not venture out—while in the context of this śamatha practice. It does not venture out into any of the six domains of appearances. It is content, effortlessly, to rest right where it is, with no interest in any appearances, no cogitation, no conceptualization, nondually and nonconceptually knowing itself.

Your eyes are open. All of the senses are open, but no light is deliberately flowing out to them to illuminate them. All the light remains right where it is—in this inner glow of this self-illuminating awareness. It is so simple, so unelaborated, so unadorned. It is the sheer luminosity and the sheer cognizance, without any additives.

It is awareness that is free of the mind—the encumbrances, the constriction, the entanglements, the veils, the vacillations of the mind. It is free. It rests right where it is without venturing out into the mind or the five sensory domains.

It is into this pure mountain stream of awareness that your mind will dissolve when you die. Become familiar with it now; this does not die. It will never be extinguished.

It is this sheer luminosity and sheer cognizance that you have in common with the mind of the Buddha, which is also luminous and cognizant. This is your common ground with dharmakāya. It is your entry to the dharmakāya.

In that which is aware, can you see that that which is aware, the subject, is unborn? It never comes into existence—neither in the past nor in the present—moment by moment. It is unborn, empty of origin.

In the vastness of objectless space, it is nowhere to be found; it has no location.

It never departs; it has nowhere to go, no destination. It eludes the conceptual mind; it slips through all the categories. It cannot be pinned down to "exist" or to "not exist."

Now let us throw off the constraints of śamatha, in which awareness is directed inward. Let the inner glow of awareness, this unborn, unceasing awareness, be unobstructed. Open all of the six doors of perception. Let the light of your awareness flow forth effortlessly and unimpededly in all directions, not directed, utterly transcending the mind. Let your awareness rest in primordial stillness, in which there is never any movement. Illuminate all appearances, all these empty appearances, all of them equally creative expressions of this primordial consciousness—and rest in that open presence, free of all activities of the mind.

Now bring this session to a close. Take a moment to dedicate the merit of this meditation session to the realization of the Great Perfection so that you may help guide all others to make manifest their own dharmakāya.

5. The Main Practice: Meditation

The Authentic Practice of Dzogchen Meditation

With the foundation of the view, we turn seamlessly to the teachings on meditation within the triad of view, meditation, and conduct. Düdjom Rinpoché continues,

> Now, once you have eliminated, from within, all doubts and false superimpositions regarding such a view, sustaining the continuity of this view is called "meditation." Apart from this, all meditations that have an object are conceptual meditations created by cognition, so we do not practice that way. Within a state that has not lost the firm establishment of exactly the view that was set forth previously, let all your five sense consciousnesses settle in their natural state, loose and at ease. Do not purposefully meditate with the sense that "this is it," for if you are meditating, that is cognition, so there is nothing whatsoever on which to meditate.

When it comes to Dzogchen meditation, this ultimate lojong, or mind training, entails a continuous, seamless flow: from establishing the view to sustaining it in meditation and carrying that view from meditation into conduct, or your way of life. The term *lo* means "cognition," and *jong* means both "to train," such as training your mind, and also "to purify." The meaning of the word *cognition* may not be clear, but it is not mysterious at all. This *lo*, or *cognition*, is a term for which the referent is the whole range of activities of the mind. Translating it as "intellect" is too small because intellect is just one activity of the mind and there are many others. In this way, *lo* refers not just to the intellect, which is something you can put down and pick up. Rather, it is referring to *all* the dualistic activities of the mind, both conscious and subconscious.

Thus, this view, meditation, and conduct is the ultimate lojong, or the transcendence of mind training, just as the *prajñāpāramitā* is the perfection, or transcendence, of wisdom. That is, the perfection of generosity is the transcendence of generosity, such that there is no longer any sense of being generous. It is beyond the very notion of generosity, like the right hand giving something to the left hand. Generosity is transcended not by turning away from it but by perfecting it, by becoming more and more and more generous until you are not generous at all because the very category of generosity—wherein there is a duality of self and other—has been left behind. So, although you may still outwardly appear to be generous, inwardly there is no sense of engaging in acts of generosity toward sentient beings seen as really "other." The conception of there being an inherently existent self, other, and act of giving has been transcended. Likewise for the other *pāramitā*s as well.

By this same principle, the view, meditation, and conduct of Dzogchen is the perfection of mind training. If you aspire to the Dzogchen path, you begin by training and purifying your mind with the Śrāvakayāna teachings, with the Mahāyāna teachings of the second and third turnings of the wheel of Dharma, and with the stages of generation and completion in Vajrayāna, if you are so inclined. All the paths of Buddhism, from the Śrāvakayāna through the Mahāyāna, Vajrayāna, and Dzogchen, accept a structure of five paths leading to perfect enlightenment. Though explained somewhat differently in the various yānas, all of these paths begin with the path of accumulation and then move to the path of preparation, the path of seeing, the path of meditation, and finally culminate in the fifth path, known as the path of no more training. In the Mahāyāna, having so beautifully, magnificently, and completely trained the mind throughout the first four paths, you perfect the training with "no more training." That is the fifth and final path where all the work is complete and you simply rest in that ultimate and perfect "not doing," which is the culmination of the path in authentic and complete buddhahood itself.

In Dzogchen, an approximation of this resultant state of perfect effortlessness is taken as the path even while one is entering its early stages as a practitioner. Here, we may begin to learn about the Dzogchen view, meditation, and conduct even before we have entered the Mahāyāna path of accumulation—for we are still developing bodhicitta in a contrived way.

That is, prior to entering the Mahāyāna path of accumulation, bodhicitta is not yet arising in an uncontrived, continuous, and spontaneous way within our mindstreams. Nonetheless, in our wholehearted efforts to establish enthusiastic perseverance on the bodhisattva path, we can still approximate Dzogchen practice, which transcends the mode of effortful training, even as it requires undistracted mindfulness. Thus sustaining the continuity of the view of the Great Perfection that one has previously ascertained—at all times, both on and off the cushion—is called Dzogchen meditation.

When Düdjom Rinpoché says, "all meditations that have an object," this refers to meditations that are ensnared in dualistic grasping involving a subject and an object. These meditations "are conceptual meditations created by cognition," or created by the activities of the mind, and Dzogchen practitioners are not to "practice that way." Those who are truly ready to venture fully into practice of the Great Perfection—having already stabilized their minds with śamatha and ascertained the view through vipaśyanā and identification of pristine awareness, and whose hearts are replete with bodhicitta—should no longer engage in dualistic, conceptual meditations. Nevertheless, until one has reached that point of preparation, alternation with other types of meditations and practices will be essential to maintain a well-rounded Dharma practice. But here within the authentic practice of Dzogchen view and meditation, as Düdjom Rinpoché was teaching it to fully committed practitioners entering into long-term Dzogchen retreat, one does not "practice that way"—that is, with a dualistic object—anymore.

Nevertheless, one can still learn how to practice Dzogchen meditation properly, even when alternating with other types of practice. Here is the quintessential instruction: "Within a state that has not lost the firm establishment of exactly the view that was set forth previously, let all your five sense consciousnesses settle in their natural state, loose and at ease. Do not purposefully meditate with the sense that 'this is it.'" That is, do not meditate with conceptions such as, "Now I'm getting it right!" or "Now I'm making progress!" You are not meditating with a purpose outside of the meditation itself, for to rest in dharmakāya is to be there already. It is without a referent; it is without a purpose. You are not doing it for something else or as a means to an end. Thinking that you are trying to achieve something defeats the point since you are already there and there is nothing to achieve. So, do not meditate "with the sense that 'this is it,' for if you are meditating, that is cognition"—in other words, you are using your dualistic mind to accomplish a task—"so there is nothing whatsoever on which to meditate."

When he writes that "there is nothing whatsoever on which to meditate," this does not mean that the preliminary practices are all for naught. Bearing in mind the context of this statement, he is saying that there is nothing whatsoever on which to meditate *once you have identified the view and are resting in the view*—that is, when the time has come for the meditation of open presence.

Continuing in that spirit of *via negativa*, in this case, what to do is to be sure *not* to do anything *with* the mind. Düdjom Rinpoché elaborates,

> **Do not let yourself be distracted, even for an instant. If you are distracted from resting within your own nature, that is the real delusion, so do not be distracted. Whatever thoughts arise, let them arise. But do not follow after them, nor should you block them.**

When he says not to "let yourself be distracted," this points to releasing any activity of the mind. Distraction is one of the fifty-one mental factors according to classic Indian Buddhist psychology. So, do not slip into distraction, but allow yourself to rest your awareness effortlessly right where it is. Further, "If you are distracted from resting within your own nature, that is the real delusion, so do not be distracted." What is your own nature? It is rigpa. That is your own nature; that is your own face. That is who you are. Do not be distracted from that, and do not dismount from the throne of your pristine awareness because when you do, "that is the real delusion"— that is when samsara begins. So, do not be distracted.

At the same time, "Whatever thoughts arise, let them arise." Imagine this: the mind of Padmasambhava, or the dharmakāya, is aware of every thought that arises in you right now. Thoughts do not cease just because you have someone monitoring them, being aware of your thoughts. They will continue chattering away. Gyatrul Rinpoché once told me not to expect my thoughts to stop—because they will not. But the dharmakāya that is aware of your thoughts is not somebody else peering in or eavesdropping on your experience. Dharmakāya is not coming in from someplace else, but the dharmakāya that is your own pristine awareness that is witnessing your thoughts—Buddha-mind—does not suppress them. It does not modify them. It is perfectly, discerningly aware of them. It knows each one but does not interfere or try to fix them. "Whatever thoughts arise, let them arise." That is what the dharmakāya would do, so you have to be just like the dharmakāya; do not act contrary to the dharmakāya. In essence, this means not to act at all, which is the supreme "not doing."

However, "do not follow after them, nor should you block them." That is exactly what dharmakāya does: it is never distracted and never follows after thoughts, nor does it block them either. That is nonabiding nirvana. The dharmakāya is the actual nature of your mind. It is aware of everything that is going on in your mind but never departs from nirvana, never departs from that primordial stillness of pristine awareness. So, don't do anything the dharmakāya wouldn't do.

Düdjom Rinpoché then guides us to what we shall do instead:

> Well then, how shall we practice? Whatever appearances of objects arise, be like a child gazing at a temple. Without allowing grasping to encroach upon the appearing aspects, leave them fresh. Thus, all phenomena remain right where they are. So their features do not deteriorate, their colors do not change, and their luster does not fade away. Even though they appear, since they are not contaminated by thoughts of clinging and grasping, all appearances and modes of awareness nakedly arise as luminous, empty, primordial consciousness.

When he writes, "Whatever appearances of objects arise," this is referring to all objects appearing by way of the six doors of perception. When these appearances arise, to "be like a child gazing at a temple" does not involve a departure or a venturing out to examine stimuli. It is neither deliberately turning inward upon awareness itself nor deliberately causing that awareness to flow outward. Nevertheless, to accurately discover this sublime middle way in which awareness is neither directed inward nor outward, you must have experienced the dissolution of the coarse mind into the substrate consciousness first. Otherwise, you will not have the capacity to prevent awareness from straying without exerting continuous effort—but this very effort is what is contrary to the practice of open presence. So, you must have achieved effortlessness through the progressive stages of śamatha meditation, and it must have become effortless and habitual for your coarse mind to be able to withdraw so completely from appearances—when you wish to—that the coarse mind and its sensory appearances dissolve into the substrate and substrate consciousness. In this way, the direct route to the culmination of the path of śamatha, by way of śamatha without a sign, is the substrate consciousness. Experiencing the substrate directly is analogous to falling asleep lucidly, but with the radiance of your awareness becoming increasingly brilliant until you come to the mother lode of conditioned consciousness, which is the self-illuminating substrate consciousness. The substrate consciousness is incandescently lucid, but upon having fully achieved śamatha, it illuminates only itself in the space of the substrate and nothing else. Because the five senses have imploded, awareness is directed inward, and its creative power is impeded. Nevertheless, it is necessary to come to that temporary base camp if you are to embark authentically on the path of the Great Perfection.

For example, in *The Vajra Essence*, when the bodhisattva Boundless Great Emptiness asks the Lake-Born Vajra whether or not one really needs to endure the myriad and often unpleasant upheavals, meditative experiences, and so forth that arise on the path of śamatha, the Lake-Born Vajra responds that the achievement of śamatha is indeed necessary. Many Dzogchen practitioners nowadays skip this crucial path of purifying the mind, thinking they need only to become accustomed to just enough samādhi to be able to feel a sense of continuity. They may think they are following Düdjom Rinpoché's instructions by sitting without distraction and without wavering, but if one does not know better, that might just mean that out of the nine stages of śamatha, one has only achieved the first four. But, with that alone, your mental continuum will not dissolve into the substrate consciousness on stage four out of nine. It must become progressively subtler than that, passing through stages five, six, seven, eight, and nine until it dissolves into the substrate consciousness. There is no shortcut for this to occur.

Padmasambhava in his manifestation as the Lake-Born Vajra said in *The Vajra Essence* that "among unrefined people in this degenerate era, very few appear to achieve more than fleeting stability."[1] The reason is that almost everyone is in a hurry, eager to get on to the "more profound" meditative practices without lingering in what may seem to be a beginner's practice: the simple cultivation of śamatha. Why should we dawdle with śamatha when we could be developing bodhicitta or meditating on emptiness, practicing the stage of generation, or devoting ourselves to bona fide Mahāmudrā or Dzogchen meditation? Many aspiring yogis nowadays (as in the past, even for centuries in Tibet) think it is enough to achieve just a modicum of śamatha and then move on to the main practice. However, even apart from the importance of śamatha for Vajrayāna practice, the great seventeenth-century master of Mahāmudrā and Dzogchen, Karma Chagmé wrote,

"Once you have cultivated śamatha by itself, then the greater the śamatha, the greater the creative power and fine qualities of vipaśyanā. If śamatha is weak, the power of vipaśyanā will be weak, just as little rain falls from a small cloud or a small flame burns from a small piece of wood."[2]

Since hardly anyone in this modern age is seeking to accomplish śamatha in a conducive environment and with skilled guidance, virtually no one is achieving it, and consequently, the achievement of siddhis and extrasensory perception is equally rare. As Atiśa wrote in his classic, *A Lamp for the Path to Enlightenment*, "Without the achievement of śamatha, extrasensory perception will not arise. Therefore, make repeated efforts to accomplish śamatha." This message is not new but has been largely ignored. The transcendence of the mind *must* be preceded by the purification of the mind. You cannot skip śamatha any more than you can skip the foundational teachings and ethical commitments of the Sūtrayāna, the samayas and vows as the bedrock of Vajrayāna, the transformational practices of guru yoga, and so forth. It is with the full achievement of śamatha that your mind is purified of the five obscurations and richly endowed with the five dhyāna factors.[3] It is not that the obscurations are eradicated but that they become dormant and no longer disrupt you. When those five obscurations are dormant, then you have gained a mind that is serviceable for all the other higher practices in which you wish to engage.

The destination for everyone who follows the path of śamatha without a sign to its culmination is that your coarse mind dissolves into the subtle mind of the substrate consciousness. You thereby achieve the transcendence of the coarse mind—in that it has been purified and dissolves—and what remains is a highly functional subtle mind, imbued with all five dhyāna factors. This is crucially important, and it shows us why passively resting in open presence is not a path of śamatha. This is because in open presence you are simply letting awareness be, without directing it either inward or outward, in which case it would not naturally dissolve within. This would be a bit like lying in bed with your eyes wide open, attentive to anything that comes to your awareness, with the lights on, music playing, incense burning, thoughts arising, and at the same time trying to fall asleep. You could not fall asleep—that is, allow your coarse mind to dissolve into the substrate— while the senses are so stimulated because for that you would have to withdraw from the visual, auditory, tactile, and so forth. For someone who is still engaging with objects dualistically, you can actively take an interest in appearances arising in your five sense fields or you can actively withdraw your awareness from your physical environment, focusing it inwardly upon the mind. But it is extremely difficult to do both at the same time. In a similar way, for a beginner, open presence is not a path that entails a withdrawal of your awareness into the substrate consciousness, with the purification that that entails, for it is not designed for that. In authentic open presence, one is resting in pristine awareness, without deliberately directing the awareness either outward or inward. By not doing anything with one's awareness, one does not trigger subject-object grasping. But this is impossible if one has not identified pristine awareness, and that realization is not easy to sustain if one has not yet traversed all nine stages on the path of śamatha.

Nevertheless, for exceptionally gifted individuals it may be possible to achieve śamatha *for the first time* right there in the realization of rigpa. Such people are exceedingly rare, especially in such a degenerate era as ours. For this to be possible, however, the crucial point is that such an extraordinary individual must still have authentically identified pristine awareness by way of the view before he or she could rest in that flow of realizing pristine awareness and possibly achieving śamatha there in that flow. It is certainly not enough to rest in the flow of one's ordinary mental consciousness and think that that is somehow going to naturally dissolve into rigpa. If that were the case, then the ordinary śamatha practice of awareness of awareness, without any ontological inquiry or introduction to the view of Dzogchen, would be sufficient to realize the dharmakāya. Clearly, this is not so.

"Well then, how shall we practice?" In this open presence, having identified pristine awareness, and now continuing to meditate in the manner of nonmeditation, Düdjom Rinpoché tells us, "Whatever appearances of objects arise, be like a child gazing at a temple." Envision the magnificent imagery of a Tibetan temple or a European cathedral, and imagine that you are a prelingual child who does not yet have a command of language but is not unintelligent. You are taking in all aspects of the temple, moment by moment, in awe—nonreactively and nonconceptually.

As though simply gazing at the grandeur of this temple, "without allowing grasping to encroach upon the appearing aspects, leave them fresh." Ordinary people, with no philosophical training, conflate the name of something with its referent. The tulku known as Yangthang Rinpoché commented that he was identified and given the title of Yangthang Tulku at the age of nine. He was not born as "Yangthang Tulku," and he emphasized that he was not Yangthang Tulku, for that was just what they called him. It is not as if he became someone else when he was given this name. He and his title were entirely different, but people commonly conflate names and their referents and then reify them as being identical. The name is just a sound made through a created system of language and is not a person or thing. It is completely empty of a person or thing, as the person or thing is completely empty of all names. In this classic analogy, the child gazing at the temple is gazing "nakedly" at the murals in the temple, without falling into the conceptual confusion of conflating appearances with the labels that language users impute upon them.

"Grasping" includes the actions of verbalizing and conceptualizing, so "without allowing grasping to encroach upon the appearing aspects, leave them fresh." In order to "leave them fresh," you must let appearing aspects remain unadorned, unelaborated, and uncloaked by any grasping to conceptual elaborations such as names, labels, and associations.

In this way, "all phenomena remain right where they are. So their features do not deteriorate, their colors do not change, and their luster does not fade away. Even though they appear, since they are not contaminated by thoughts of clinging and grasping, all appearances and modes of awareness nakedly arise as luminous, empty, primordial consciousness." All the way through, it is *via negativa* by knowing what not to do—not activating the mind, conceptualization, verbalization, naming, and so on. That is the practice.

SIMPLE INSTRUCTIONS FOR CONTINUOUS PRACTICE

Düdjom Rinpoché then explains,

> In general, people with lesser intelligence are puzzled by the great number of teachings that are said to be very profound and vast. So, to point a finger at the essential meaning that emerges out of all of them: During the interval when a past thought has ceased and the next thought has not yet arisen, isn't there a fresh consciousness of the present—a clear, naked awareness that has never changed, even by a hair's breadth? Oh, just that is how pristine awareness is present! Then, insofar as you do not remain in just that state, doesn't a thought suddenly arise? That is a creative expression of pristine awareness itself. However, if you do not recognize it as soon as it arises, if a series of thoughts flows out, that is called the "chain of delusion," and it

is the root of samsara. Simply recognizing thoughts as soon as they appear releases them in their own nature, such that they do not continue to proliferate, and if you relax and rest right there, then whatever thoughts arise, they are all uniformly released in the expanse of pristine awareness, the dharmakāya. Just this is the main practice in which the view and meditation of cutting through are united.

When he says "people with lesser intelligence," he means those whose minds may feel overwhelmed, bewildered, and befuddled by all of the complexities and enumerations in the midst of the profound and vast aspects of the path, such as the detailed philosophical teachings of the Middle Way, the stages of the bodhisattva path, the stages of generation and completion, the peaceful and wrathful maṇḍalas, the myriad deities and demons and gods, and so forth.

Düdjom Rinpoché tells us that he will "point a finger at the essential meaning" of all the great teachings—both profound and vast—so that even for those of us with very poor intelligence, this should not be too difficult. These are pointing-out instructions to the nature of your own mind. So, you're at an interval when a past thought has ceased and the next thought has not yet arisen. Ask yourself, "Isn't there a fresh consciousness of the present—a clear, naked awareness that has never changed, even by a hair's breadth? Oh, just that is how pristine awareness is present!" It's right there in that interval between thoughts. That is where to look. Whether you ascertain it, well, that's an open question, but that is exactly where it is. That is how pristine awareness is present: clear, naked, never changing.

Nevertheless, as you are resting there, what happens? You don't stay right where you were, in the interval between thoughts. Rather, suddenly, doesn't a thought just show up out of nowhere? Now is the moment when you must recognize that this thought itself is a creative expression of pristine awareness. If, however, you do not recognize it in the very instant that it arises but rather allow a whole series of thoughts to flow out, then you have fallen into the "chain of delusion," and this itself is the root of samsara. That is the point when samsara begins again—and again and again. When you do not recognize a thought arising, it means you are unaware. Since it arises and you do not know it has arisen, you then fall into delusion, which is the root of samsara here and now. This is how samsara begins and continues cyclically.

Further, the very act of recognizing a thought as soon as it appears is what releases it in its own nature, which, ultimately, is that of empty pristine awareness. This recognition and release are what naturally stop the chain of thoughts from proliferating. Then you relax and rest. As you gain familiarity with the flow of recognizing and releasing, "then whatever thoughts arise, they are all uniformly released in the expanse of pristine awareness, the dharmakāya." This means you do not have to do anything apart from recognizing them in order to release them. Thus, you allow them to self-release in their own nature without your doing anything more than simply identifying them. Düdjom Rinpoché affirms that "just this is the main practice in which the view and meditation of cutting through are united."

Düdjom Rinpoché then concludes,

> Garab Dorjé declared,[4]
>
> > Mindfulness of the instant that pristine awareness suddenly arises
> > from the very nature of primordially pure, absolute space
> > is like finding a jewel from the depths of the ocean.
> > There is the dharmakāya, which has not been modified or
> > created by anyone.
>
> You must persevere relentlessly in this and meditate without distraction day and night. So do not let emptiness remain as an object of understanding—bring it into pristine awareness!

When he says, "do not let emptiness remain as an object of understanding," this means not to let it be confined to the space of mind as an object you only think about, reflect on, or meditate upon with the conditioned mind. Instead, "bring it into pristine awareness!" When it is with pristine awareness that you are aware of emptiness, there is no longer the cage created by mental processes. This is his quintessential and complete pith instruction.

A Brief Meditation: Resting in the Great Perfection

> Find a comfortable position in which your body, speech, and mind can be relaxed and at ease.
>
> The mind is easily aroused by such teachings, by reflecting upon

them, and by cutting through our false superimpositions about them. So, now take a moment to more fully settle the body, speech, and mind in their natural states.

For those of us with somewhat lesser intelligence, for whom "open presence" might be a bit too nebulous or may seem like an invitation to space out, for those of us who need a little bit of something to do that is in the spirit of cutting through to pristine awareness, first, rest your awareness right where it is, as you have done before.

Once again, all six doors of perception are open—we are not withdrawing but are vividly and discerningly aware of our closest neighbors, the activities of the mind, the thoughts that come and go.

Now, follow exactly those pith instructions that Düdjom Rinpoché gave to those of us with inferior faculties who perhaps get confused and maybe exhausted by the multiplicity, diversity, and complexity of so many teachings. While resting here, right in the very nature of awareness, vividly illuminate, with this inner glow of awareness, the phenomena that, in a manner of speaking, are the closest to the light—your innermost thoughts. Make sure that with the arising of each thought, it is brilliantly made manifest, illuminated immediately upon its arising, without letting even one go by unnoticed.

Exactly as he indicated, when a thought has subsided—like a wave on the surface of the ocean subsiding back into the sea—in that interval just after a thought has disappeared and just before the next wave of a thought arises, attend closely right there in that interval, to that vacuity. It is right there that pristine awareness reveals itself, uncloaked by thoughts, memories, the activities of the mind. It is right there in the intervals between the activities that the ever-present clear light of pristine awareness reveals itself unobstructedly. Practice now in silence, bearing in mind this guidance.

Are you aware of the space of awareness that encompasses your mind? While the activities of the mind come and go, this open, vast expanse of the space of awareness—illuminating the movements of the mind but never contracting into them, never expanding and never contracting, never coming and never going, always present, empty, and luminous, illuminating and knowing all that appears within it—is indivisible from the ground of being, the nature of existence. Resting there is the meditation of the Great Perfection.

Bring this meditation session to a close with these words of dedication:

By the merit of this practice, may we actualize the great transference rainbow body and bring all sentient beings, without exception, to that very state of realization.

6. The Main Practice: Conduct

The Utter Indivisibility of the View, Meditation, and Conduct

Düdjom Rinpoché has thus far addressed the view and the meditation and then turns to conduct. First, in order to see more clearly the utter indivisibility of the three, let's consider the integral role each one plays in supporting one another.

The view, of course, entails cutting through to pristine awareness and viewing reality from that perspective. However, for the view to be sustainable for even a few seconds, it must be sustained, or held, with a previously honed capacity for mindfulness. Otherwise, you might glimpse the view for a split second, but then, due to the ordinary distraction of an ordinary mind, you lose it again and perhaps cannot even quite remember what you experienced. So, in fact, for the view to occur, for it to be sustained at all, it has to have meditation, whereby you are resting in the view. Then, for whatever realization or experience you have of the view in meditation, it is certainly not sustainable unless there is a seamless segue from your formal meditation on the cushion into whatever you are doing off the cushion. Deeper realization or understanding of the view in meditation is sustainable only if it is supported with conduct. In this way, conduct is the safeguard for your practice to endure and prosper.

Thus, there is no Dzogchen conduct without it emerging from and seamlessly flowing forth from the meditation, and Dzogchen meditation is baseless unless it is thoroughly imbued with the Dzogchen view. Further, the notion that one can merely rest in choiceless awareness, calling it "be here now," "secular mindfulness," or "open monitoring" may have psychological benefits, but it is not Buddhist meditation, neither śamatha, vipaśyanā, nor Dzogchen, if it has no view of emptiness to support, sustain, and guide it and if it lacks any precise guidelines on the subtleties of ethical conduct to guard and uphold it.

Alongside the triad of view, meditation, and conduct within Buddhism is another crucial sequence with which you must become familiar. This sequence is fourfold, consisting of (1) understanding, (2) experience, (3) realization, and (4) acquiring confidence. First you gain understanding by hearing and reflecting on the Dharma. Then you enter into the practice of meditation and have firsthand experiences that are not just intellectual or conceptual—the experiential aspect is important to get a taste of how the teachings come alive through meditation, as well as to purify your mind when the psyche is being dredged. Finally, realization occurs, which is a transformative and liberative mode of knowing that is more than simply an experience. For that knowledge to be transformative, it must be sustainable, and when that occurs, one acquires confidence. Gaining an insightful meditative experience is like hammering a nail partway into a piece of wood. Although such an experience may penetrate the nature of reality to some extent, it easily fades away, like the nail being pulled out of the wood. Gaining genuine realization is like hammering the nail into the wood so that its head is flush with the surface. Such insight is enduring and transformative. Further still, acquiring confidence is like countersinking the nail so that its head is deeply buried inside the wood. Such confidence is irreversible, and it is this that forever liberates the mind from delusions. Post-meditative practice reinforces such realization so that the power of one's view, meditation, and conduct never diminishes.

HEART ADVICE ON GURU YOGA AND EMPTINESS

Guru Yoga as the Life Force of Dzogchen Conduct

Whether or not you are in strict retreat or simply planning to be, Düdjom Rinpoché's pith instructions on conduct are equally relevant. He writes,

> Now, as for the way to enhance the meditation with conduct and set out on the road of practice: Most importantly, as stated before, without being separated even for an instant from the recognition that regards your guru as an actual buddha, pray from the depths of your heart. This is called the "universal panacea

> of admiration and reverence." This is superior to any other method for dispelling obstacles and enhancing your practice, and you will proceed along all the paths with great momentum.

When he says "to enhance the meditation with conduct and set out on the road of practice," "the road" means we are going from here to there—here is samsara and "there" is buddhahood, and manifestly, in terms of our perspective, most of us have not yet reached "there." That is, we have not yet reached the place where we will continue traveling on the road and never fall off into the ditch, wander around in circles, or go backward. So, to "set out on the road of practice" is to reach the path and proceed along the path, which is the fourth ārya reality—namely, the reality of the path that leads to the cessation of suffering and its origins.

Further, "as for the way to enhance the meditation" implies that your conduct is not a dilution, distraction, or diminution of your meditation. The Bhutanese meditation master Drupön Lama Karma commented that as you proceed more and more deeply into śamatha practice, you might actually decrease your time on the cushion and increase your time off the cushion. In this case, that is not a weakening of your practice because you are empowering the many hours off the cushion with conduct and thereby enhancing your meditation. When you are going for walks with the four immeasurables, brewing your tea with pure vision, taking care of your home with mindfulness of the Dzogchen view, and so forth, you are completely following Dzogchen conduct, moment by moment—and your mind becomes Dharma. There is a classic Mahāyāna analogy of a man walking with a bowl filled to the brim with oil and an assassin is following closely behind him with a sword. If he spills even a drop of oil, the assassin would cut off his head. This is the kind of moment-by-moment vigilant attention that needs to be sustained between sessions. But unlike the person whose life is at stake, it is essential to maintain such an unbroken flow of discerning mindfulness while fully at ease.

This tells us the kind of fine-tuned continuity of conduct that is needed off the cushion, so that when you return to the cushion—having engaged between sessions in an ongoing flow of loving-kindness, compassion, guru yoga, and seeing the illusory nature of the phenomena arising to you—your practice is actually empowered by these between-session periods. In this way, there is no longer the frustrating process of alternating between distraction to a thousand objects while off the cushion and then trying to clean up the mess of your mind by restoring your mindfulness when you return to the cushion.

Deepening Guru Yoga with Admiration and Reverence

Düdjom Rinpoché then writes, "Most importantly, as stated before, without being separated even for an instant from the recognition that regards your guru as an actual buddha, pray from the depths of your heart. This is called the 'universal panacea of admiration and reverence.' This is superior to any other method for dispelling obstacles and enhancing your practice, and you will proceed along all the paths with great momentum." When he says "admiration and reverence," since this is guru yoga, then it is admiration and reverence for the guru, which, as mentioned earlier, is far, far beyond simply liking the guru because you think his or her good qualities are so appealing. It is very easy to like a pleasant person, but if you are practicing authentically, then you are experiencing vast, boundless reverence and admiration instead of a superficial attraction that ebbs and flows with the aversion and attachment of a mind immersed in samsara.

Regarding the phrase "the 'universal panacea of admiration and reverence,'" bear in mind that the object of this literally inconceivable admiration and reverence must be your actual guru, who is a buddha manifesting as your guru—be it Buddha Śākyamuni, Samantabhadra, Amitābha, Avalokiteśvara, Tārā, or Guru Rinpoché. You are not admiring and revering the human being whom you think of as your guru based on your own impure perceptions and concepts.

When you see and hear your guru in human form, what you are experiencing with your physical senses and mental faculties is a reflection of what you are capable of witnessing, given the limitations of your karma and the impurities of your own mind. If you are an *āryabodhisattva* or a vidyādhara, then what you experience will be radically different from what an ordinary person experiences. The degree of your mental purity, the strength of your karmic momentum from past lives, and the effect of your karma in this lifetime will all determine the degree to which you can see transcendent virtues in your human gurus.

Here is an analogy to reflect upon for a long time. Insofar as the teachings and conduct of your human guru are in harmony with the Dharma that he or she is imparting to you, your actual Dzogchen guru, Samantabhadra, may be likened to the sun, and your experience of your human guru may be likened to the flame of a candle held at arm's length in front of the sun. While the flame of the candle is incomparably fainter than the light of the sun, its energy originates from the energy of the sun and its flame does not obscure the brilliant light of the sun. Rather, the light of the sun shines through the candle flame.

Conversely, insofar as the guru's teachings and conduct do not accord with those of Samantabhadra—or Buddha Śākyamuni, Padmasambhava, Vimalamitra, and so forth—then your experience of the guru is like viewing a yellow, flame-shaped piece of cardboard placed at arm's length in front of the sun. It may resemble a flame, but the cardboard actually obstructs the light of the sun. Such a person should never be regarded as your guru, let alone as a buddha, and if one does engage in guru yoga with regard to that person, this will only lead one away from the path to enlightenment.

The five faculties that turn into the five powers when cultivated extensively along the Mahāyāna path are faith, intelligence, samādhi, enthusiasm, and mindfulness. When your faith, the first of these, overrides your intelligence, your powers of discernment are eclipsed by uncritical faith. In other words, by blindly accepting whatever the lama does as perfect and assuming the lama is infallible, omniscient, and so forth, you jettison your intelligence. That is neither Dzogchen nor guru yoga. His Holiness the Dalai Lama has clearly stated that you should never sacrifice intelligence on the altar of faith. Similarly, you should never sacrifice faith on the altar of your intelligence, thinking that you are smarter than your guru or that you know better. Instead, you must continue to apply your intelligence—humbly questioning your guru when something in his or her teachings or conduct seems amiss—balanced with faith, just as samādhi must be balanced with enthusiasm. Finally, the central of those five faculties, which enables you to balance the other four, is mindfulness of, or bearing in mind, the authentic teachings of the Buddha so that you never stray from the path.

Bearing in mind the balance that needs to be cultivated between faith and intelligence, one needs, in an ongoing way, to discern whether the teachings and conduct of one's guru are compatible with the authentic Dharma, be it of the Śrāvakayāna, Mahāyāna, or Vajrayāna, as revealed by Buddha Śākyamuni, Vajradhara, Samantabhadra, and Padmasambhava. If one practices guru yoga toward a lama whose teachings and conduct are incompatible with those of the Buddha, then the guru is for you like a yellow, flame-shaped piece of cardboard held in front of the sun, blocking the sun of authentic Dharma and conduct, while emitting no light of divine virtue of his or her own.

Moreover, all the planets formed together from the same source, the sun, and that is the origin of all the energy in the earth. Therefore, when you light a candle, the energy that is released originated from the sun. Likewise, all the virtues of your guru that you are able to perceive actually originate from your ultimate refuge and are not separate from it. The guru's virtues and those of Samantabhadra are indivisible. So, for swift blessings you need the blessings of the guru, the light from whom is closer to you and more easily accessible than that of Samantabhadra. You need a human guru who looks like a human being, probably appears to have some of your own limitations, has a personality, seems to forget things, and makes mistakes. In other words, the guru appears to be a lot like you, which makes it easier to relate to him or her and, therefore, to receive the guru's blessings. However, for deep blessings, those come from the bright sun of your *yidam*—the manifestation of the buddha with whom you feel the closest connection—whom you eventually come to realize as being identical to your own innermost nature.

Returning to the text, Düdjom Rinpoché says that "the 'universal panacea of admiration and reverence'" is "superior to any other method for dispelling obstacles and enhancing your practice." The word "panacea" means that it heals all the afflictions and obscurations of the mind. And "admiration and reverence" are the most powerful single method for "dispelling obstacles and enhancing your practice." When you completely embody and embrace the meaning of admiration and reverence toward your authentic guru in this way, "you will proceed along all the paths"—the paths of accumulation, preparation, seeing, meditation, and no more training—"with great momentum."

There is no mere sentient being who is worthy of the kind of admiration and reverence cited here. They may be worthy of respect, but that is not what Düdjom Rinpoché is referring to here. Further, anyone who yearns for admiration and reverence is not an authentic Dharma practitioner but is taking refuge in the eight mundane concerns. This type of person is not worthy of admiration or reverence.

When arousing faith, admiration, and reverence for Samantabhadra, such devotion is not directed to a blue icon, an abstraction, or a construct of your own cognition; rather, it is for the Buddha. You have the capacity to deepen your sense of admiration and reverence when you truly understand the qualities of the Buddha. If your devotion is focused on your guru as you perceive him or her, this is like focusing on the candle flame rather than on the sun. Your human guru may transmit the wisdom and compassion of the Buddha, but in authentic guru yoga, your conceptual construct of your guru dissolves into emptiness, and out of emptiness you view your guru as a pure embodiment of Samantabhadra, and you can thereby receive the teachings and blessings of this ultimate refuge.

When Düdjom Rinpoché says "without being separated even for an instant from the recognition that regards your guru as an actual buddha," this means to develop a baseline of admiration and reverence for the guru as a buddha. In order to develop that kind of reverence, it is crucial to have reverence for an actual buddha. If you do not have real reverence and admiration for Buddha Śākyamuni or Samantabhadra, then to say that you are viewing your guru as an actual buddha is feeble. So, cultivate an increasingly deep sense of admiration and reverence for the Buddha and then for "your guru as an actual buddha." The Buddha was not simply a man who lived two thousand six hundred years ago and then died. He was a nirmāṇakāya, a divine emanation of Samantabhadra. That same buddha is listening to you, witnessing you, and granting you blessings right now. The Buddha is no less real or present now than he was then—but this will become a tangible experience only for those with pure vision.

How to Arouse Admiration and Reverence

There are two ways to arouse such faith, admiration, reverence, devotion, and worship so that the depth of pure vision can arise. One is by learning about the lives and works of enlightened beings, such as Buddha Śākyamuni, Padmasambhava, Nāgārjuna, Atiśa, Jé Tsongkhapa, Sakya Paṇḍita, Milarepa, Shabkar Rinpoché, His Holiness the Dalai Lama, and so forth. You may, for example, read a book such as Bhikkhu Ñāṇamoli's *Life of the Buddha*, and as you immerse yourself in the Buddha's life story, immense reverence for this historical person and an eager desire to know more about his teachings may arise. You may then read the classic Sanskrit *Buddhacarita*, or *Life of the Buddha*, by Aśvaghoṣa, written in the second century of the Common Era. You may then feel inspired by the impact that the Buddha Śākyamuni had on India two thousand six hundred years ago through this present day, transforming the lives of millions of people with his virtue, compassion, and wisdom.

In this way, you learn of the Buddha by way of living tradition and not only from translations of ancient texts. From this, you may experience reverence, admiration, and faith in the Buddha and then take refuge in this being, his pure teachings, and the supreme community who authentically upholds his teachings. You may then continue by reading the life stories of later realized masters such as Nāgārjuna, Asaṅga, Padmasambhava, Atiśa, Milarepa, Sakya Paṇḍita, Longchen Rabjampa, and Jé Tsongkhapa. With the admiration and reverence that is aroused by appreciating their great realizations and enlightened deeds, you may then be inspired to learn more about their teachings and put them into practice. A deep, enduring sense of taking refuge in these buddhas, the forms of Dharma that each of them taught, and the lineages of their enlightened disciples may then arise, thus forming the basis for your ultimately taking refuge in your own buddha nature.

The second way to arouse such devotion is by first studying and practicing the sublime Dharma of the Buddha and other enlightened beings, and on that basis, faith will arise for those who embodied and revealed that Dharma. For example, if you truly fathom the meaning of the teachings on emptiness and dependent origination in the Prajñāpāramitā teachings of the second turning of the wheel of Dharma, you may realize that only a buddha could have revealed such a Dharma, regardless of whether you find any historical basis for that belief. You will see that those teachings are compatible with, yet surpass in depth and scope, the teachings on emptiness and dependent origination in the Pāli canon. Similarly, when you appreciate the Mahāyāna teachings on bodhicitta, the bodhisattva way of life, and buddha nature, you will see that they too subsume yet transcend the teachings on renunciation and the pursuit of one's own liberation as taught in the Pāli canon. Moreover, if you realize—first through conceptual understanding and then through your own direct experience—the profundity of Vajrayāna in general and Dzogchen in particular, which encompass yet surpass the teachings in the Sūtrayāna, then you will know that those teachings too could only have originated from perfectly enlightened beings.

Two Types of Teachings

There are two types of teachings that can further give rise to deeper admiration and reverence. First, there is the Dharma of scripture, which is imparted in the sūtras, tantras, and great commentaries. Scriptural teachings are those that are written down so you can read them, study them, reflect upon them, and practice them. Second, there is the Dharma of realization, which is not something you receive from the outside, but, rather, it arises from within through authentic practice. The Dharma of scripture is the launching pad for the Dharma of realization, and it is the Dharma of realization in which you will eventually take deeper refuge than you could possibly take in the content of books or the spoken word.

In order to see how these two types of teachings can arouse deeper admiration and reverence, consider the scriptural Dharma here in Düdjom Rinpoché's root text. If you truly fathom the meaning of this text and delve deeply into the practice, thereby penetrating into the Dharma of realization, then reverence will naturally flow forth for the person, Düdjom Rinpoché, based upon the scriptural teachings and your own realization, without needing to know anything about his life. You then recognize that the person who taught this text must be a buddha.

Further, once you have experienced such depth of admiration and reverence for the Buddha, you may then take refuge in the person whom you regard as your Dzogchen guru. As mentioned earlier, to do so requires a realization of the emptiness of inherent nature of all phenomena and an intuitive understanding of the all-pervasive nature of dharmakāya, or buddha nature, that permeates the mindstreams of all sentient beings. Then, when you have understood what it means to receive the four empowerments, you can realize the experiential referent of this statement: "Without being separated even for an instant from the recognition that regards your guru as an actual buddha, pray from the depths of your heart."

All the reverence that you feel for Buddha Śākyamuni—as well as for Samantabhadra, Padmasambhava, Tārā, Düdjom Rinpoché, and so on— is now personified as your guru, having all the qualities and virtues of a buddha. With that level of admiration, reverence, faith, and devotion, *now* you are able to comprehend the Dzogchen view, the indispensable basis for practicing authentic Dzogchen meditation. Then you are ready to blend your meditative experience with Dzogchen conduct.

Unveiling Your Actual Nature as a Buddha

One way you can approach, or get closer to, actualizing yourself as a buddha is by making offerings to and praising the guru, Buddha Śākyamuni, Samantabhadra, and so forth. In this way, offerings and praise are all expressions of your own pristine awareness. Further, when you offer with admiration and reverence all of your virtues of the three times—past, present, and future—and all that is good in your life to the cultivation and realization of pristine awareness, you are really praising and admiring your own buddha nature, which means that you yearn for the manifestation of that more than anything else.

In Christianity, there are many references to the centrality of the love of God, or *amor dei* in Latin. Yet, why does God need to be loved, and what is the love of God? According to St. Augustine, it is the passionate yearning to *know* God and then to achieve mystical union with him. A passionate, all-consuming flame of longing to know God by way of Jesus Christ is akin to the reverence, admiration, love, and adoration of the guru as a means to realizing the nature of Samantabhadra. Much as Jesus declared, "I am the way and the truth and the life. No one comes to the Father except through me,"[1] so is it true in Vajrayāna Buddhism that there is no way to achieve the perfect enlightenment of Samantabhadra except by way of the guru.

Everything from the past, present, and future that you have that is good and everything that you are is offered in praise, reverence, and admiration of Samantabhadra, the personification of your own pristine awareness, which is the source of all virtue and well-being. With intense admiration and reverence, you first *approach* the guru as the outer manifestation of your own pristine awareness and then *actualize* the indivisibility of the guru's vajra body, speech, and mind with your own body, speech, and mind. If you dissolve without trace the ordinary perception of your human guru into the primordial nonduality of the dharmakāya and the *dharmadhātu*, the absolute space of phenomena—that is, the emptiness that is indivisible from primordial consciousness and is replete with all the qualities of enlightenment—and then out of that emptiness, you now see an appearance that looks like a human being, you will recognize at the same time that this is merely an illusory apparition.

If you can view that being as an actual buddha and pray from the depths of your heart for guidance and blessings, then you are much closer to realizing yourself as a buddha. That is why you practice guru yoga.

How can you further shift from embodying the limitations of a sentient being to manifesting fully as a buddha? First, recognize that it is impossible to be both a sentient being *and* a buddha at the same time and from the same perspective, for a sentient being and a buddha each have very different and mutually incompatible sets of qualities. You are either a sentient being or a buddha, but you cannot be both. Viewed from your ordinary perspective, your guru may appear as human based upon the perceptions conditioned by your dualistic mind, karma, and mental afflictions. Yet, from the perspective of pristine awareness, both you and your guru appear as buddhas.

The only common thread that connects a sentient being and a buddha is the sheer luminosity and cognizance of awareness. A buddha's dharmakāya is luminous and cognizant. Its luminosity—as the primordial consciousness of the full range of phenomena—illuminates the three realms of existence, the six classes of sentient beings, and nirvana. The cognizance of the dharmakāya—as the primordial consciousness of the actual nature of reality—fathoms ultimate reality, the dharmadhātu. The consciousness of sentient beings is also luminous and cognizant, making manifest and knowing ourselves, others, and the world as we experience it. When the essential nature of our awareness is in no way obscured by the veils of our dualistic mind and mental afflictions, it is none other than the luminosity and cognizance of the dharmakāya.

In your practice, if you rest in that sheer luminosity and cognizance, then you are resting right on the borderland between you as a sentient being and you as you are viewed from pristine awareness, your own pristine awareness. From the perspective of your own pristine awareness, you are a buddha, you have always been a buddha. There was never any moment in time when you actually became a sentient being. When viewed from radically different perspectives, there is no incompatibility or contradiction, and that is due to the crucial point of emptiness.

There are many examples of such complementarity in quantum physics. Is light a wave or a particle? One thing cannot be a wave and a particle at the same time, for they have completely different, incompatible characteristics. However, from the perspective of one system of measurement, a photon, for example, is a particle, but according to another system of measurement, it is a wave. Prior to and independent of any system of measurement, a photon cannot even be said to exist. Prior to the act of measurement, its status is indeterminate. Similarly, what is your actual nature, independent of the perspective of a dualistic mind and independent of pristine awareness? From the perspective of a dualistic mind caught in samsara, you do exist conventionally, but from the perspective of your pristine awareness, you have never existed as a sentient being at all. Your existence as a sentient being is a reality that totally obscures a deeper reality—your buddha nature.

If you identify yourself simply on the basis of your body and mind as you experience them now—neither of which has ever actually been you or yours—then the self you so designate is indeed a sentient being. However, the body and mind have no real owner but are merely appropriated. It is like moving into and taking possession of an abandoned house. In Tibetan, the term translated as "sentient being" is *semchen*, which literally means "mind possessor." However, both mental appearances and the awareness of them are devoid of any agent who is the real observer of mental events. So they are devoid of what we might have thought was "the mind." Conversely, "the mind" is not found anywhere outside of mental appearances and awareness of them, so the existence of "a mind" is indeterminate.

In Tibetan, we are also called *lüchen*, meaning "corporeal beings," or more literally, "body possessors." While the body is composed of matter and energy, sensory appearances of the body are devoid of matter, and when we engage in ontological analysis of how the body actually exists, it is not found either within these immaterial appearances or anywhere apart from them. So its existence too is indeterminate.

As for the nature of energy, the Nobel Prize–winning physicist Richard Feynman comments in *The Feynman Lectures on Physics* that the conservation of energy is a mathematical principle, not a description of a mechanism or anything concrete. He states, "It is important to realize that in physics today, we have no knowledge of what energy *is*."[2] Therefore, mind, matter, and energy have only a nominal existence—they exist only in a manner of speaking—and the words "mind," "matter," and "energy" have no inherently existent referents outside of language itself.

On the other hand, you may believe that you exist as a person separately from your body and mind. Düdjom Lingpa writes in his great work *The Essence of Profound Mysteries: Guidance for Revealing One's Own Face as the Nature of Reality, the Great Perfection*,[3] "So-called personal identity is this very sense of 'I am' that appears to be real, which we experience on all occasions during the day and night, in dreams, during the intermediate period, and in future lives. Moreover, from the very beginning, there is an 'I'-grasping consciousness that exists in latent form, and then on occasion a subsequent consciousness and conceptualization bring this to mind, stabilize it and fortify it, and in this manner cling to it, and that is self-grasping." In a continuous stream, there is an appearance of a "me" that appears to be real, and there is a state of consciousness that grasps to it. Within samsara, this self-grasping consciousness is always present in a latent way within the mindstream, but at times it is brought to the fore through subtle and coarse conceptualization. This is the root of what makes us think we are sentient beings, over and over and over again.

In the practice of vipaśyanā, one actively investigates whether or not such an "I" actually exists. Explaining how to go about this type of systematic investigation, Düdjom Lingpa continues, "If that identity exists, from what outer or inner phenomena of the physical world or its sentient inhabitants does it emerge? Or in particular, from what part of your own body and mind does it emerge? Upon investigating what kind of an agent it is that emerges and so on, you will come to the conclusion that it has no origin." Turning then to the location of such a self, or personal identity, he writes, "Regarding the search for the essential nature of an identity that remains in the interim, if that identity were to exist, there should be something that can be determined as a real, substantial entity for which its location and that which is located there can be identified as distinctly different." Yet, no such location can be found either inside or outside the body. As for what happens to you when you cease to exist, he writes, "Likewise, upon investigating the essential nature of the place to which your so-called identity goes and the essential nature of the one who goes, you will come to the conclusion that there is no way there could be any place for it to go or anyone who goes."

Having found that there is no real origin, location, or destination to what you thought was you, he concludes, "Therefore, if you are wondering what it is that appears as your so-called identity, in fact it appears while being nonexistent, like a hallucination. Know as well that even though an *identity* may be described with words, the referent of that description is not determined to exist, even as one speaks about it. This is like speaking about the horns of a hare."

On the other hand, your existence as a sentient being is a reality of sorts, for you experience pleasure and pain, influence others and your environment, engage in actions, and experience their consequences. This is an obscurative reality, though, in that it totally obscures the deeper reality of your true nature as a buddha. However, if you identify yourself on the basis of your pristine awareness—which is replete with all the enlightened qualities of the dharmakāya, sambhogakāya, and nirmāṇakāya—then you may indeed regard yourself as a buddha, which is your ultimate nature. Even then, pristine awareness is also not inherently existent. Its essential nature is emptiness, which corresponds to the dharmakāya; its manifest nature is unborn, unconditioned luminosity, which corresponds to the sambhogakāya; and its all-pervasive compassion is the aspect of the nirmāṇakāya. These same qualities can be viewed in your guru, who also does not ultimately exist.

This is the gravitas, enormity, and majesty of Düdjom Rinpoché's paragraph on conduct, which is the key to enhancing your practice, reaching the path, and proceeding along the path to achieving rainbow body in this lifetime. However, even if you achieve śamatha and gain siddhis, extrasensory perception, and so forth, if you have no practice of guru yoga, then you have no chance of manifestly becoming a buddha in this lifetime. If you cannot view your guru as an actual buddha, then you will be unable to view yourself as an actual buddha without being delusional.

Conduct as an Antidote to the Addiction to Rumination

If you want to bring an end to your existence as a sentient being, then quit acting like one. Every time you slip into rumination, think a thought, get caught in the grip of an emotion or a desire, and tumble into dualistic grasping, you are acting like a sentient being. You will never bring an end to your existence as a sentient being if you keep acting like one, and this is what Dzogchen conduct is all about. Contrarily, if you want to be a buddha, then act like one. The conduct of the Great Perfection is no less than perfect.

We are literally addicted to rumination (Skt. *vikalpa*), which is obsessive, compulsive, delusional thinking. It is an addiction that we did not first acquire in childhood, adolescence, or early adulthood—this is an addiction that traces back to countless previous lifetimes.

The only way to begin to break this addiction is to be consistent in your commitment not to engage in rumination, both on and off the cushion. Otherwise, if your resolve is sporadic, occurring only when you are in formal meditation but then you return to your old habits when you are off the cushion, this would be like an alcoholic who abstains from alcohol in the morning but starts drinking again in the evening. In order to be truly free from the addiction, one must be sober one hundred percent of the time. Similarly, if you are to be free from your addiction to rumination, you must avoid it at all times, both on and off the cushion. If you do not break the habit in this lifetime, then you are going to remain addicted for innumerable future lifetimes.

If you are serious about engaging in the practice for which this text was intended, then here is the way to maintain continuity: When a thought arises, do not identify with it or appropriate it. Bear in mind that from the perspective of pure vision, as in the Vajrayāna stage of generation, all thoughts arise as manifestations of dharmakāya, so thoughts are not the problem. For even after you achieve śamatha, thoughts still crop up. It is not a matter of stopping thoughts or speech. However, discernment is necessary both on and off the cushion so that you can recognize when thoughts and speech are and are not appropriate.

Further, in Dzogchen conduct, you are not keeping the body frozen in one place, refusing to speak, and blocking thoughts, desires, or emotions—rather, you are allowing them to arise uninhibitedly, without encouragement or censorship, affirmation or repudiation, acceptance or denial. You are allowing all the movements of body, speech, and mind to take place as needed, and you are viewing them all from the primordial stillness of awareness. In this way, you are not acting like a sentient being, you are witnessing the activities of a sentient being with your closest approximation to pristine awareness, resting in the sheer luminosity and cognizance of your awareness. These teachings of Düdjom Rinpoché are intended for people who truly want to do everything they can to overcome the noxious addictions to rumination and dualistic grasping and thus to achieve rainbow body in this lifetime.

Deeper Relaxation

In order to begin to release the addictions that fuel and perpetuate your delusions, greater relaxation is needed. In regard to settling body, speech, and mind in their natural states, you can never relax too much—it will come in increasingly subtler ways. The only person who has perfected relaxation is a buddha. Only a buddha can accomplish everything without any effort whatsoever, which means only a buddha has achieved the perfection, or transcendence, of relaxation.

In this same vein, it takes no effort to be aware of being aware; it is not something you force or try to accomplish. If this feels inaccessible to you, then simply be aware that you are not unconscious right now, and notice how much effort it takes to do so. It requires some effort to attend to daily matters, but it takes no effort at all to be aware of being aware because you were already aware before you even thought about it. Settling body, speech, and mind in their natural states and then resting in that effortlessness is strongly emphasized in Dzogchen, and its significance is not to be overlooked. The great mahāsiddha and guru to the Thirteenth Dalai Lama,

Tertön Lerab Lingpa, wrote in his teachings on settling your respiration in its natural rhythm, "Train in calming the movements of your respiration just until you do not notice them, thereby settling your speech in its natural state."[4] If you are feeling tight, bored, distracted, irritable, and so on, you may think the practices are not working and that you are not progressing much. The solution to this is to relax more and more deeply.

Return to this repeatedly until you are breathing in a sustainable way and your respiration—and, therefore, your speech—has settled in its natural rhythm. Even before that, however, it is only when you have settled your body more deeply in relaxation, stillness, and vigilance—so that it comes to rest in its natural state—that the body's channels open and the prāṇas flow freely, thus enabling the breathing to settle in its natural state. Further, when your breathing is so shallow that it is almost imperceptible, now you are actually ready to settle your mind in its natural state. You cannot skip any of these three phases, thinking that instead you should just strive harder and push through challenges. Striving in that way is not sustainable and does not lead to the path. Moreover, you must move through these phases sequentially—settling and resting first the body, then the speech, then the mind—in order for them to be effectual. The answer lies in greater and greater relaxation, such that the body, speech, and mind can come to settle and rest. It is then that you become a suitable vessel for reaching the path—through generating uncontrived and stable bodhicitta with a mind that is truly serviceable.

Taking this a step further, you can then infuse the practice of settling body, speech, and mind first with a disappropriation of the body, whereby you are no longer identifying with tactile sensations or with this body as being your own. Beyond that, release even the conceptual designation "body." It is not a body but is simply a host of insubstantial, empty appearances arising. Then release the inner speech of the mind, or your respiration, as it was never yours. It is not *your* breathing—it consists of insubstantial, ownerless, and noninherently existent sensations related to the breath. Likewise, then, for the mind, release your appropriation and identification with memories, images, desires, and so forth, as they are all empty appearances. In this way, you stop reifying the body, speech, and mind. Appropriation and reification are analogous to a hermit crab who appropriates a shell that never belonged to it and that will be inhabited by that particular hermit crab for only a short time.

SPECIAL ADVICE ON OVERCOMING FAULTS IN PRACTICE

Conduct: Remedying Laxity and Excitation

Düdjom Rinpoché provides pith instructions on the conduct needed to remedy the extremes of laxity and excitation. He writes,

> Regarding defects in the meditation, if laxity and dullness set in, arouse your awareness. When there is scattering and excitation, relax your consciousness from within.

When he says, "Regarding defects in the meditation," this is in the context of conduct, which includes special pith instructions both for formal sessions and between sessions. At this point, you have identified the view and are sustaining it with meditation. Then in the post-meditative state, you are doing your best to sustain the pristine, unwavering flow of mindfulness throughout the course of the day. Nevertheless, problems may still arise.

The line, "Regarding defects in the meditation, if laxity and dullness set in, arouse your awareness," echoes the universal instruction for śamatha meditation in terms of how to respond to laxity and dullness—that is, you should refresh and "arouse your awareness."

Then, "When there is scattering and excitation, relax your consciousness from within." When scattering, excitation, agitation, and dispersal occur, a classic response might be to bear down and try harder to concentrate. There are many authentic śamatha instructions wherein one is told to apply specific antidotes, such as reflecting on death, impermanence, and the sufferings of samsara until the scattering and excitation subside. However, within the Mahāmudrā and Dzogchen traditions, one is commonly taught to relax more deeply, releasing the energy that arouses that agitation. Further, the real problem is not that the mind is scattered or excited but that your awareness has been caught in the vortex of scattering and excitation. In order to release this merging of awareness with the agitation of the mind, again, relax. If you are taking the mind as the path, then through familiarization, you gradually learn how to maintain that stillness, which is analogous to scientists observing a hurricane's great swirling mass of clouds from the vantage point of a space station. Whether the mind is agitated or calm, ruminating or silent, then up in the space station of your awareness, you are not affected one way or another because you are above even the highest level of atmosphere that is perturbed by weather.

On the other hand, you get caught in the weather of the mind when you grasp to it and identify with it. You did not see the thought, memory, or mental image when it first arose, so it caught you from behind and swept you away. One way to break the chain is simply to cut the flow of thoughts. The other way is to observe the thoughts passively without identifying with them. When your awareness is like Velcro, it sticks to everything that arises in the mind, but when it's like Teflon, you observe the vicissitudes of the mind from the outside and do not get stuck.

In this way, the problem is not the fact that your mind is agitated, the problem comes from not seeing discursive thoughts right when they first arise and therefore getting sucked into them. If you are caught up in them, it is actually the tentacles of your own grasping that ensnare you in these chains of thoughts. In this case, you can contract more tightly in an effort to overcome the thoughts, but this will usually cause you to become more immersed in the thoughts as being real, as something to be tangled with. Or you can simply relax the energy of grasping and allow the thoughts to release themselves naturally and effortlessly. Let go of the tiring effort that goes into grasping. If you are holding on to all of the angry, resentful, anxious thoughts that arise, then invariably this will exhaust you further. Instead, release the effort of grasping and reification, and relax in the ease and stillness of awareness.

Engaging with Reality from the Throne of Rigpa

Now, what type of awareness is this that we either arouse or relax? Düdjom Rinpoché writes,

> This should not be an enmeshed mindfulness in which you deliberately try to take the rapidly moving mindful awareness of the meditator and continuously thread it tight. Rather, with the mindfulness of simply not forgetting the consciousness of your own nature, continuously sustain this during all activities of eating, lying down, walking, and standing, both during meditative equipoise and the post-meditative state.

In other words, your mindfulness should not be enmeshed, entangled, caught up, or constricted by thoughts. In this Dzogchen approach, do not deliberately try to thread your mindfulness tightly to an object, as if you are bearing down to keep it from straying. Though there are approaches to śamatha where this type of tightly threaded "enmeshed mindfulness" is indeed appropriate and necessary, this is not the approach here within the actual context of Dzogchen view, meditation, and conduct.

The root text continues, "Rather, with the mindfulness of simply not forgetting the consciousness of your own nature, continuously sustain this during all activities of eating, lying down, walking, and standing, both during meditative equipoise and the post-meditative state." When he says not to forget "the consciousness of your own nature," ultimately, "your own nature" is pristine awareness. Thus, optimally, this instruction means you maintain your mindfulness of resting in pristine awareness throughout your daily conduct, both on and off the cushion. This can be done in multiple ways if you are accomplished in śamatha, have identified the view, and are sustaining it with mindfulness in meditation. Here in the context of conduct, then, in all your activities, never lose awareness of your essential, fundamental nature, which is rigpa. When you are cooking, washing clothes, going for a walk, and so on, although the mind and body are in motion, and thoughts and sensory appearances are arising, you remain steadfast in your conduct in between sessions, having turned off all the nine valves of your sentient being's body, speech, and mind. In this manner, you are not doing anything at all as a sentient being, as you are never losing the consciousness of your own pristine awareness, and are resting there in that primordially timeless space of dharmakāya. Whereas from the outside, people see you simply doing various activities as if you were a sentient being. As the accomplished yogi Drubwang Rinpoché said, "Although I do appear like a human person outwardly, my mental state is so different."

In sum, "continuously sustain this" mindfulness "during all activities of eating, lying down, walking, and standing, both during meditative equipoise and the post-meditative state." You are never wavering from knowing the consciousness of your own actual nature.

However, what does this mean for those of us who are still relative novices and especially those of us who are not in retreat and who have outer responsibilities calling on our attention? How can those of us who are not vidyādharas apply this to our current way of life when we have a lot of time for post-meditative conduct and probably somewhat less time for formal meditation sessions? To the best of our ability, we should maintain that ongoing awareness of awareness itself—which is a ray of pristine awareness—without being distracted.

Recall that in the method for achieving śamatha revealed to Düdjom Lingpa by the Lake-Born Vajra, the first of the four types of mindfulness is single-pointed mindfulness in which you are able to identify clearly the stillness of awareness in contrast to the movements of the mind and to recognize both simultaneously.[5] Off the cushion, while you are attending to the necessities of everyday life with its multitude of appearances coming and going, you can do what is needed while remaining aware of the stillness of your awareness. You can go for a walk and be aware of the stillness of your awareness, and, although it is not so easy, you can even be speaking and certainly listening while aware of the stillness of your awareness without distraction. From that stillness, you can examine whether the words that are arising might be flowing spontaneously out of a space that you cannot identify. Or, you might notice an inspiration, as if on a mental teleprompter, that catalyzes your next words for someone else's benefit. From where does your ability to draw an analogy, express an image, or share a memory actually arise?

To hone this practice of simply not forgetting, in some meditative sessions, after having settled body, speech, and mind and when your awareness has come to rest in a state that is relaxed, still, and clear, see if you can simply continue resting without letting your awareness be set in motion—without being distracted, without forgetfulness, without being drawn away. There may be noise outside, movement in the field of visual appearances, or else memories, thoughts, images, emotions, and desires may arise, but, without trying to make anything stop, your mind rests effortlessly in the stillness of awareness. In the midst of the movements of samsara—the samsara of your body, mind, the surrounding environment, and everyone who populates it—in the conditioned world of motion that is coming and going, rest in your facsimile of nirvana, in this stillness of awareness, without being distracted or drawn away. This is a pith instruction. It is not yet śamatha without a sign; it is not yet taking the mind as the path; it is not mindfulness of breathing. It is just "Sit there and don't be distracted."

In terms of view, meditation, and conduct, there *is* a difference between meditative equipoise and the post-meditative state, between the way you apply the instructions on conduct during meditation and the way you apply them between sessions of formal meditation. Yangthang Rinpoché wrote near the beginning of his pith instructions, *A Summary of the View, Meditation, and Conduct,* "If you wish to look into the mirror of the actual nature of your mind, do not look outward. Rather, look inward. Looking outward involves the delusion of reification. By looking inward, you observe your own mind."[6] This instruction is specifically a prelude to Yangthang Rinpoché's instruction on how to achieve śamatha, as a preliminary to realizing the empty, essential nature of the mind and then cutting through the conditioned mind to pristine awareness. Accordingly, when in meditation, you are *not* directing your attention to external things, such as cooking, eating, or walking, which all involve looking outward and which all occur between sessions. Rather, when you are in meditative equipoise, do not look outward. In śamatha, no attention is deliberately given to any of the five sensory fields. As mentioned earlier, by practicing śamatha in this way, sooner or later all of the five physical senses will dissolve into the substrate. Further, by not looking outward, nothing will upset you in the environment since you are explicitly not grasping at impure appearances and therefore reifying them. By looking inward, into the actual nature of the mind, it becomes vividly clear that everything you witness consists of your own appearances, none of which can harm you.

When Yangthang Rinpoché writes, "By looking inward, you observe your own mind," this points to ascertaining the actual nature of your mind, or the *cittatā,* which is nirvana. Having even glimpsed the nirvana that is the emptiness of your own mind, you then know beyond doubt that you can be utterly free of suffering because you have seen nirvana, and it is right there within you. If you know you can be free, then you know everyone can be free. From that place, great compassion and bodhicitta arise spontaneously.

Thus, prior to achieving śamatha, I encourage you to devote a major part of your practice while on the cushion to śamatha, wherein you direct the attention inward and do not let it flow outward. Between sessions, however, when you must be looking outward simply in order to engage in daily activities, it is not too soon to apply Düdjom Rinpoché's advice on the conduct of Dzogchen: "With the mindfulness of simply not forgetting the consciousness of your own nature, continuously sustain this during all activities." Then, the "simply not forgetting" can be sufficient to maintain the continuity of your mindfulness of the stillness of awareness until you return to your next formal session.

Düdjom Rinpoché continues,

Whatever joys, sorrows, afflictive thoughts, and so forth may arise, never react to them with either hope or fear, acceptance or rejection, and never counteract them with antidotes and so forth. Rather, whatever feelings of joy and sorrow are there, rest in their own essential nature: nakedly, vividly, and lucidly. For everything that occurs, there is nothing but this one crucial point, so don't confuse yourself with a lot of thinking!

This is straight Dzogchen lojong. There are many other ways to attend to appearances in the mind—such as cultivating the four immeasurables, doing practices for purifying and transforming the mind, as well as applying antidotes to mental afflictions. Yet, on that basis, you may then go for the pinnacle of lojong in which you are neither working to purify nor making efforts to transform your mind—because insofar as you are able to engage in this, the mind heals, purifies, and releases itself of its own accord, with no effort. It is important to know experientially that you can respond to all the fluctuations—the darkness, clouds, thunder, lightning, sun, and warmth—in your mind without "hope or fear, acceptance or rejection" and without trying to do anything about it or counteracting it "with antidotes and so forth." But you also must not fuse with anything that arises, or you will surely be carried away by it. This is Dzogchen conduct.

Rather than applying antidotes to problems that arise in the mind, "whatever feelings of joy and sorrow are there, rest in their own essential nature." This is crucial. Resting in their "essential nature" means to see a feeling as a feeling and a thought as a thought, without identifying with them or superimposing concepts on them. As the Buddha counseled in his pith instructions to Bāhiya, "In the seen, let there be only the seen; in the heard, let there be only the heard; in the tactilely sensed, let there be only the tactilely sensed; and in the mentally perceived, let there be only the mentally perceived."

Again, resting "in their own essential nature" means to see mental events as mental events, rather than viewing them as "I" or "mine," to be lucid with respect to waking experience, and thereby, to be free. This is different from trying to understand the mind by examining its manifest nature in terms of all the thoughts, desires, and emotions that arise in relation to their referents: "I'm happy about this, sad about that, upset about something else." The mind's manifest nature refers to the wide range of mental events that arise from moment to moment, consisting of the various types of thoughts, emotions, feelings, memories, and so forth. That is the focus when practicing the close application of mindfulness to the mind, but here you seek to separate your awareness from the mind. It was your past karma and kleśas that threw you into this relationship with your mind, and it is your dualistic grasping that has been tormenting you from beginningless lifetimes and perpetuating samsara. To escape this, dissolve that mind first into the substrate consciousness and then dissolve the substrate consciousness into pristine awareness. Then, "rest in their own essential nature: nakedly, vividly, and lucidly. For everything that occurs, there is nothing but this one crucial point, so don't confuse yourself with a lot of thinking!"

Practicing from the Heart

Düdjom Rinpoché continues, speaking to his students who have followed his experiential guidance every step of the way:

> There is no need to meditate separately on emptiness as an antidote for the thoughts and mental afflictions to be abandoned. As soon as you recognize with pristine awareness whatever is to be abandoned, it will release itself, like a snake unraveling its knots. It is common for people to know how to talk about this final, hidden meaning of the clear light vajra essence, but without knowing how to put it into practice, their words are like the squawking recitations of a parrot. We have such tremendous merit!

This is not the same as "be here now," choiceless awareness, or bare attention. Rather, on the basis of having completely turned your mind and whole life around through the four revolutions in outlook and utterly upgraded your coarse mind to the subtle mind, achieved śamatha, and apprehended the emptiness of inherent nature of all apprehended objects, you then know there is nothing out there from its own side nor is there any apprehending mind in here from its own side. Because it is empty, then any division between subject and object is also empty and is only nominally existent. As Düdjom Rinpoché states in his *Illumination of Primordial Wisdom*, "Apart from being the delusive appearances of one's own mind, in actuality, nothing whatsoever is determined to exist. Appearances do indeed appear, but real things are not real. Regard these simply as illusory apparitions, which, like the appearances of a dream, appear vividly and randomly, even though they do not exist."[7]

Once you have been introduced to the view and have learned both to sustain it by resting in meditation and to maintain it in the post-meditative state, if you see a tendency for reification arising, know that it is simply a delusive movement of the mind. So simply observe it, but do not identify with it, and by all means, do not reify such grasping! That which binds you is itself empty of inherent nature. So, at this point in your path, you would not need yet another meditation on emptiness to serve as an antidote to the mental afflictions, for your realization of pristine awareness is already enough. There are intimations and facsimiles of this approach in Padmasambhava's teachings on śamatha without a sign, where he teaches simply to invert awareness in upon that which is observing, upon that which is meditating, and then to release awareness into space. There is no conceptual analysis, investigation, or reasoning taking place, yet that may be enough to cut through to pristine awareness.

Düdjom Rinpoché continues in the root text, "As soon as you recognize with pristine awareness whatever is to be abandoned, it will release itself." You are recognizing what is to be abandoned not with your substrate consciousness or with your human mind but with pristine awareness itself. Then a thought or mental affliction "will release itself, like a snake unraveling its knots." This is very much like what takes place in the unraveling or releasing of the knots in the channels around your cakras, which are subtle physical correlates of the patterns formed within your configured mind.

Moreover, "It is common for people to know how to talk about this final, hidden meaning of the clear light vajra essence." That is, it is very easy to talk about Dzogchen, "but without knowing how to put it into practice, their words are like the squawking recitations of a parrot. We have such tremendous merit!" The inconceivable merit of being able to receive this guidance, practice it, and realize it is without comparison.

Like a Feather Consumed in Fire

Düdjom Rinpoché continues,

> Still, there is more to consider carefully and understand. Since beginningless lifetimes until now, the mortal enemy that has bound us in samsara is the duality of the apprehender and the

apprehended. Now, by the kindness of the guru, you have been introduced to the indwelling dharmakāya, so those two disappear without a trace, like a feather consumed in fire. Doesn't that satisfy your heart?

When he writes, "Since beginningless lifetimes until now, the mortal enemy," this means the mortal enemy that is out to crush us in every single lifetime and has succeeded thus far—until now. Will our mortal enemy conquer us again in this lifetime and will we die as ordinary beings yet again? This is our chance to break the cycle with these very pith instructions, so let's prioritize them. We should not take other things to be more important and thus be drawn away from this opportunity. Samsara will always be knocking on your door, by way of friends, loved ones, mental problems, health problems, and so on. It is called a "mortal enemy that has bound us in samsara" because the root of all the problems in samsara since beginningless time "is the duality of the apprehender and the apprehended," of subject and object, of us and them. Samsara begins in the very moment we slip into dualistic grasping, not billions of years ago but in every moment. That is the beginningless beginning of samsara.

However, he says, "Now, by the kindness of the guru, you have been introduced to the indwelling dharmakāya, so those two disappear without a trace, like a feather consumed in fire." When he says "those two," he is referring to the reifying division between the apprehending mind "over here" and the apprehended object "over there." It is the very appearance of a division that vanishes "without a trace, like a feather consumed in a fire," when you realize the indwelling mind of clear light, the dharmakāya, free of even the subtlest conceptual elaborations of dual appearance. This is an advanced stage, which takes place when you become a matured vidyādhara, but it comes about thanks to "the kindness of the guru," who is the one who reveals to you the nondual, "indwelling dharmakāya."

"Doesn't that satisfy your heart?" Is there something more? Were you looking for some Dharma better than this? Are you satisfied?

If you are having a hard time experiencing that kind of satisfaction just yet, begin with genuine well-being. You may not yet be experiencing the bliss of śamatha, much less the immutable, great bliss of the dharmakāya, but what you can expect sooner rather than later, something the likes of which you may never have experienced before, is peace of mind: mental peace, inner peace. It's not blissful. It's not exciting, but it's certainly better than having a mind that is just yammering and nagging and complaining and whining. It is certainly better than that. Moreover, it is sustainable. So, first, discover peace of mind. This is why it is so helpful to meditate on the benefits of a practice before fully committing to it. For example, we are taught to meditate first on the benefits of patience before really trying to overcome anger. Meditate first on the benefits of bodhicitta, then cultivate bodhicitta. Likewise, meditate on the benefits of śamatha, then practice wholeheartedly with confidence. As the Buddha declared of the śamatha practice of mindfulness of breathing, "Just as in the last month of the hot season, when a mass of dust and dirt has swirled up, a great rain cloud out of season disperses it and quells it on the spot, so too concentration by mindfulness of breathing, when developed and cultivated, is peaceful, sublime, an ambrosial dwelling, and it disperses and quells on the spot unwholesome states whenever they arise."[8]

In this way, even before you are experiencing the joy and bliss of bodhicitta, of śamatha, of vipaśyanā, and so forth, you are content because you know what you are doing is so immensely meaningful—in fact, there is nothing more meaningful you can possibly do. Can you be content in a sustainable way? Can you find satisfaction when simply being mindful of your breath or of thoughts coming and going while resting in the stillness of awareness? Can you find happiness, genuine well-being, in the sense of knowing from the depths of your heart, "This is exactly what I want to be doing; I'm so happy to be able to do just this. I'm resting in awareness of awareness, and this is the direct path." Then, won't your heart be satisfied?

Düdjom Rinpoché then continues,

Now that you have received profound practical instructions on a swift path such as this, if you don't put it into practice, this will be like putting a wish-fulfilling jewel in the mouth of a corpse—what a waste! Practice without letting your heart rot!

Now, if you are one of those navigators in ancient times who goes out into the great ocean looking for a wish-fulfilling jewel, you cast your net down over and over again, and perhaps finally, after years and years, you pull up your net, and lo and behold, there's a wish-fulfilling jewel there! You know what you are supposed to do with it, right? You polish it, put it on an altar, put offerings in front of it, and then you pray to it for whatever you may want. Then, according to Buddhist lore, it will give you anything you want—

hedonically, that is. But you have to treat it with a bit of respect first; clean it up and put some nice offerings out, and then make your prayers. What you certainly wouldn't do is to say, "At last, I've got a wish-fulfilling jewel. Oh, and I know there's a corpse over there. Why don't I put it in its mouth?" Well, that's just not the best thing to do with a wish-fulfilling jewel!

That is, you must treat the wish-fulfilling jewel of these "profound practical instructions" with the utmost respect, because you truly see what it is that is being given to you. If you hold the pursuit of hedonic pleasures as your primary aim, then your life will pass without putting these profound and liberating instructions into practice, which, in this context, would be like "putting a wish-fulfilling jewel in the mouth of a corpse—what a waste!" So, practice sincerely and earnestly, "without letting your heart rot!"

How to Respond to Involuntary Thoughts

Düdjom Rinpoché now addresses those who may be practicing authentically but who have not fully kept up with him in his experiential guidance—those who are still beginners. He writes,

> **Beginners will find that they get carried away from mindfulness by streams of negative thoughts, resulting in quite a few subtle thoughts suddenly slipping by unnoticed. After a while, when vivid mindfulness has returned, regret arises with the thought, "I was distracted." However, at that time, without doing anything such as cutting off the thoughts that have already entered or feeling regret about having been distracted, it is enough simply to sustain the stream of vivid mindfulness that has returned and settle naturally right there.**

When the guardrails of mindfulness crumble and forgetfulness ensues, negative thoughts may pull you away—desires, memories, emotions, and so on—"resulting in quite a few subtle thoughts suddenly slipping by unnoticed." You know it well: you are resting in awareness, and meanwhile, there's this sub-commentary going on that you are not even noticing: "Oh! That conversation that was going on!" You were multitasking. Then, "After a while, when vivid mindfulness has returned, regret arises with the thought, 'I was distracted.'" It's retrospective, since you are thinking a new thought about the past: "I was distracted." So, you just came back to the present moment, and what do you do? You start thinking. Instead of drowning in a swimming pool of thoughts, now you're drowning in a bathtub of self-reflection. If you are thinking, then once again, you are not doing the practice. You are distracted in the very moment when you are thinking, "I was distracted." Instead, when the thought arises, "I was distracted," simply observe it—don't think it! Then it does not harm you. Otherwise, you are once again caught in the spin cycle of rumination: "I'm not making any progress. Maybe I should do something else." There is no end to those thoughts if you identify with them.

Düdjom Rinpoché continues his kind counsel to beginners: "However, at that time, without doing anything such as cutting off the thoughts that have already entered. . . ." Don't cut them off. You keep on thinking, "Oh, I shouldn't be having so many thoughts. I'm going to start culling the herd. I'm going to start killing off some of the thoughts, particularly the bad ones." But he says not to do that. Don't stop thoughts; rather, stop identifying with them. Without "feeling regret about having been distracted, it is enough simply to sustain the stream of vivid mindfulness that has returned and settle naturally right there." So, keep it simple—do not compound conceptualization by whining about it. When the vividness of mindfulness returns, then just rejoice and "settle naturally right there"—right in the midst of whatever thoughts of regret, distraction, frustration, and so forth may still linger, like wisps of clouds dissolving after a storm. Settle there while resting in the stillness of your awareness without being moved by the thoughts.

Düdjom Rinpoché instructs us further,

> It is commonly said that you should not reject thoughts but regard them as the dharmakāya. However, until the power of vipaśyanā has fully manifested, if you rest in a vacuous śamatha while merely pretending that "it's the dharmakāya," there is the danger that you may slip into an ethically unspecified equanimity without being able to discern anything. So in the beginning stages, whatever thoughts arise, nakedly observe them without investigating, analyzing, or reflecting upon them at all. Like an old man watching children at play, simply remain as the one who recognizes the thoughts, without evaluating them or attributing any importance to them. If you rest in that way, the increasing stillness of your naturally settled nonconceptuality will suddenly and spontaneously disintegrate, and

in that very instant, naked, brilliant, primordial consciousness
that transcends the mind will arise.

Before manifestly realizing emptiness through vipaśyanā, regarding thoughts
"as the dharmakāya" may be a matter of mere imagination—just as you may
be imagining in the stage of generation practices that all appearances are
creative displays of nirmāṇakāya, all sounds are sambhogakāya, and all
thoughts are displays of the dharmakāya. However, by the time you progress
further along the path, there will come a point when thoughts and appearances are no longer arising as impure; instead, they are actually arising for
you as pure displays of the indwelling mind of clear light, the union of great
bliss and emptiness. This is beyond mere imagination, for it is what you are
truly seeing. This is especially the case when you have become a vidyādhara,
have achieved the first bodhisattva *bhūmi* on the Vajrayāna path, and are
dwelling in pristine awareness. Then from that perspective, all of the activities of the mind can validly be viewed as pure displays of the dharmakāya.

So, "until the power of vipaśyanā has fully manifested," whereby you are
seeing the emptiness of inherent nature of all phenomena, "if you rest in a
vacuous śamatha while merely pretending that 'it's the dharmakāya,' there
is the danger that you may slip into an ethically unspecified equanimity
without being able to discern anything." In other words, resting in the conditioned awareness of your coarse mental consciousness, you may simply
pretend that awareness, thoughts, and all other mental activities are the
dharmakāya, but this may lead into a stupor-like state of what is elsewhere
known as stagnant, or flawed, śamatha: "an ethically unspecified equanimity" in which you are not discerning anything.

Düdjom Rinpoché thus advises that "in the beginning stages, whatever
thoughts arise, nakedly observe them without investigating, analyzing, or
reflecting upon them at all." In this manner, "like an old man watching children at play, simply remain as the one who recognizes the thoughts, without
evaluating them or attributing any importance to them"—that is, observe
them without preference. It is important to note that this is like an old man
watching other people's children or grandchildren at play, such that he feels
no direct responsibility for them and knows he can relax without needing
to do anything. Their parents are nearby and will look after them.

If you continue in this practice—which is directly parallel to that of "taking the impure mind as the path," as taught by the Lake-Born Vajra—you
will eventually come to a naturally settled stillness, which is the ordinary

śamatha of the path. But this "increasing stillness" is nonetheless the stillness of the conditioned mind, even as it eventually comes to dissolve into the actual substrate, illuminated by the substrate consciousness. What Düdjom Rinpoché is saying next is that at a certain point, the bubble of this increasing, or growing, stillness of the conditioned mind will burst, thus revealing the uncontrived, primordial stillness of primordial consciousness: "If you rest in that way, the increasing stillness of your naturally settled nonconceptuality will suddenly and spontaneously disintegrate, and in that very instant, naked, brilliant, primordial consciousness that transcends the mind will arise."

This takes place within the context of meditative equipoise, where "naked" means unmediated or unveiled. Insofar as words can capture it, Düdjom Rinpoché is now pointing to what it is like to experience pristine awareness: "naked, brilliant, primordial consciousness that transcends the mind will arise." When he says "transcends the mind," this means the experience is entirely beyond that which makes you a sentient being—that is, it is not within the scope, dimension, potentials, or limitations of a sentient being's mind. However, this initial breakthrough to rigpa does not necessarily mean you have become a matured vidyādhara.

Preparing the Mind for Further Stages of the Path

Düdjom Rinpoché then continues,

> At the time of the path, even if such an experience does not come without being mingled with the meditative experiences of bliss, luminosity, or nonconceptuality, if you do not cling to them as supreme—and can settle without even a hair's breadth of craving, pride, hope, or fear toward them—that will prevent them from becoming grounds for leading you astray.

When he writes "At the time of the path," this refers to an experience of pristine awareness that is naked and, therefore, unmediated and nonconceptual. Pristine awareness is knowing pristine awareness directly and nondually; it is not as though the mind, as a separate subject, is identifying and recognizing pristine awareness as an object through the veils of a sentient being's mind.

Nevertheless, at this point, "even if such an experience does not come without being mingled with the meditative experiences of bliss, luminosity, or nonconceptuality, if you do not cling to them as supreme—and can settle without even a hair's breadth of craving, pride, hope, or fear toward them—that will prevent them from becoming grounds for leading you astray." Nakedly experiencing pristine awareness means that you have entered the Dzogchen path, for you have now identified within yourself the essential nature that is the ground dharmakāya, which means you now have an authentic, naked experience to take as the path of cutting through: you have identified *path pristine awareness*. So, at this point you would actually have entered the Dzogchen path, but you might still falter, which is why Düdjom Rinpoché immediately offers guidance for how not to go astray.

Early in your experience of pristine awareness, you may not yet have completely transcended the mind all the time. Since at some level you are still identifying yourself as a sentient being who has a mind, then your experience of rigpa will still "not come without being mingled with the meditative experiences of bliss, luminosity, and nonconceptuality." Having achieved śamatha, this triad now occurs simultaneously, whereas prior to achieving śamatha, these meditative experiences arose piecemeal. The experience of them all at once can create a strong temptation to simply linger in the substrate consciousness, but it is imperative not to cling to these meditative experiences, taking them to be supreme. The danger is that this very clinging will obscure your experience of pristine awareness, throwing you back into the essential nature of ignorance that is the substrate, and thus preventing you from fully realizing pristine awareness's own emptiness of inherent existence, which is its essential nature. That is, if you are too enthralled by the bliss, luminosity, and nonconceptuality that arise from your meditative forays into pristine awareness, you may not have the motivation to take the steps necessary to realize vipaśyanā in union with your śamatha in pristine awareness. Nevertheless, your newly found śamatha in pristine awareness must unite with vipaśyanā for any progress on the path to ensue.

When Düdjom Rinpoché writes, "If you do not cling to them as supreme—and can settle without even a hair's breadth of craving, pride, hope, or fear," he is referring to the craving or preference for the extraordinary bliss that arises from realizing rigpa. Settling "without even a hair's breadth" means you have not even a smidgen of preference for bliss over non-bliss or any attachment to luminosity and nonconceptuality. By so doing, "that will prevent [those meditative experiences] from becoming grounds for leading you astray," and you are then laying the foundation for your later experience of all of samsara and nirvāṇa being of one taste.

Otherwise, if you are still preferring nirvana to samsara, bliss to non-bliss, and so on, then you are throwing boulders on your own path: You are obstructing your own path to the deepening realization of rigpa and ultimately the realization of the "one taste." Likewise with pride, if you are thinking, "Oh, all those poor people who have not yet realized rigpa—thank goodness I'm not one of them. I'm better than them," then you have blocked your path. There is no difference between buddhas and sentient beings from the perspective of pristine awareness. Likewise with hope—are you hoping to achieve something? If so, you have blocked yourself from acquiring unwavering confidence. Are you grasping to fear? Then you have blocked yourself with that, too. These are just four ways you can put up a great, big titanium wall right in front of you, between you and where you want to go. If you cling to them, you have said, "I'm going to block myself. If nobody else will, I'll do it." So, that is why Düdjom Rinpoché warns us in advance.

Abandon Appropriation and Reification

What about where we are now? If you examine your own practice right now, it may be that you are still overtaken by upheavals and that you get caught in thoughts, merging with them as they arise. Even so, you may find that on occasion you are indeed able to observe a thought, image, or memory as it arises in the space of your awareness without merging with it. However, when it comes to emotions and desires, it is much more difficult to see sadness, fear, depression, low self-esteem, anxiety, and so on arise while maintaining a sense of spaciousness between the emotion and your naked awareness that is observing it without preference. The ability to "let there be just the mentally perceived" without focusing on the referents of mental events may be intermittent at best.

The nun Vajirā recognized that a chariot is not something really "out there" but is rather a mere construct that comes into existence nominally by the power of conceptual designation. In this way, she saw that the same is true of herself as a person. Yet, the same is not true for the perceptions of appearances, as they are experienced nonconceptually and without labels. The appearance of the color of a chariot, its texture when you touch it, the smell of its wood, and so forth, do not compose the chariot itself—that is, no chariot emerges simply from the appearances of what you see, hear, smell, taste, and touch. It is only the conceptual mind that imputes "the chariot" upon those appearances.

However, regarding the truth of suffering and its causes, or the first and second ārya realities, she saw these as real. When you are experiencing physical pain and mental suffering, you cannot simply choose to designate it conceptually as a pleasant feeling and then expect it to change. Just as if you got hit by a truck, you would not think it happened merely because you conceptually designated a truck. Likewise, if somebody hits you in the jaw, it is hard to make the pain disappear by thinking it is empty of inherent existence. In this way, Vajirā did not see suffering as something merely conceptually designated. The teachings on the second ārya reality identify karma and the mental afflictions—all rooted in attachment, hatred, and delusion—as the source of suffering. The real diseases of the mind are these afflictions—or more literally, afflicters—and not the mere symptoms of unhappiness and anxiety. People generally point to the sources of these states of mental distress as being outside of the mind, but in actuality it is the internal diseases of delusion, hatred, attachment, pride, envy, and so on that attack us from within. So, you may acknowledge that all external entities are just conceptual constructs, as the chariot is a construct, and, as Vajirā saw, your very identity as a sentient being is a construct too. But what about suffering itself, and what about the tormenting mental afflictions themselves? Are they merely conceptual constructs?

For Vajirā, the reality of suffering and its inner sources are real. However, the bodhisattva Śāntideva asserts that reifying not only objective physical phenomena but subjective mental states—viewing them as real or inherently existent—including feelings of joy and sorrow, is the true cause of suffering. Since the one who experiences feelings is not inherently real, the feelings that are experienced must also be illusory. By not appropriating them or identifying with them, and by not conceiving of them as existing from their own side, but rather by viewing them as empty appearances, their potential for harming or benefiting us is dispelled.

The way to become permanently free of the tyranny of these constructed illusions is first to achieve śamatha and then to follow this with intensive practice of vipaśyanā, after which one can unite śamatha and vipaśyanā in a powerful state of meditative equipoise. There are some very rare individuals who can achieve śamatha *by way of* vipaśyanā in the realization of emptiness. But it is extremely difficult to realize the noninherent, illusory, and, therefore, misleading nature of suffering and have this insight be truly transformative and liberating if that insight is not first rooted in śamatha, such that your mind has become serviceable and is capable of sustaining such realizations. Again, as Karma Chagmé wrote, the greater your śamatha, the greater your vipaśyanā—just as a small flame arises from a small piece of wood and a bonfire blazes up from a large pile of wood.

If you can view suffering from the perspective of a mind that is free from the five obscurations and richly imbued with the five dhyāna factors, then when mental or physical suffering arises, with the aid of vipaśyanā, you can penetrate through the veils of suffering to the ultimate reality, or actual nature, of the mind. Further, by contemplating the true nature of the mental afflicter and who it is that is experiencing the suffering, you can then get to the root: The one who is experiencing the suffering is not real, and, therefore, that which you are experiencing has to be equally unreal. This symmetry is such that, conversely, if you think you are real, then the suffering you are experiencing is going to be viewed and experienced as real.

By first coming to a strong conviction about the emptiness of inherent nature of all apprehended objects—nuclear weapons, war, a meteor striking Earth, the sun, the moon, and so on—based on profoundly stable samādhi and blazingly clear *prajñā* (or discerning intelligence), you are primed perfectly to realize this crucial truth. This is the avenue to break through to pristine awareness.

In Atiśa's *Seven-Point Mind Training*, he says to "regard phenomena as if they were dreams,"[9] which means to recognize that phenomena appear but are not really there—they are like a dream but are not actually a dream. In the same way, when you turn inward and examine the delusive appearances of your own mind, you will find them to be equally devoid of inherent existence. By so doing, it becomes apparent that all of these internal and external appearances can no longer hurt you.

Even quantum physicists say that phenomena do not exist in the manner in which they appear, just as elementary particles—the fundamental building blocks of the material world—do not exist prior to and independent of the act of measuring them. As Niels Bohr, one of the principal pioneers of quantum physics, wrote, "radiation in free space as well as isolated material particles are abstractions, their properties on the quantum theory being definable and observable only through their interaction with other systems."[10]

That is, as he is often quoted as having said, everything we call real is made of things that cannot be regarded as real. "Nevertheless," Bohr continued, "these abstractions are, as we shall see, indispensable for a description of experience in connection with our ordinary space-time view."[11] In his statement that "radiation in free space as well as isolated material particles are abstractions," he points out that the bases of designation of imputed objects do not exist from their own side, and in his comment that these abstractions are "indispensable for a description of experience in connection with our ordinary space-time view," he acknowledges their conventional existence in terms of dependent origination. To fully grasp the balance of these two statements brings one very close to the astonished awe one will experience when glimpsing the Middle Way itself. As Bohr remarked at a meeting of philosophers in Copenhagen, "those who are not shocked when they first come across quantum theory cannot possibly have understood it."[12]

Thus, let alone becoming attached to the marvelous experiences of bliss, luminosity, and nonconceptuality, how can you "settle without even a hair's breadth of craving, pride, hope, or fear" toward mental afflictions exactly at the moment that they arise—so that they too will not become grounds for leading you astray? It is a two-step method that you can practice right now, wherever you are on the path: Do not appropriate and do not reify. Rest unwaveringly in awareness, nonconceptually, without thinking about it, simply experiencing it. Then, when an emotion comes up, you see it coming up—just as when you see a thought come up and have learned to recognize it as soon as it arises. Likewise, an emotion comes up, a sense of unease, or else a sense of something like laxity—which is not an emotion but a subjective state—and as soon as it comes up, recognize it immediately. That's it.

There is a Tibetan aphorism according to which a pig shows up at the kitchen door in a Tibetan house. Imagine that the lady of the kitchen weighs a hundred pounds and the pig is three hundred pounds. If she smacks it on the snout right when it comes in, it will leave. But if she lets the pig get all the way into the kitchen, it will be impossible to get him out—and who is going to have more to eat, the hundred-pound cook or the three-hundred-pound pig? Following this analogy, pick up the scent of the emotion as soon as it comes in. See it. Don't feed it. Most importantly and explicitly—and following the classic teachings of the Buddhadharma—do not appropriate it. Do not be sad about being sad. Do not be sad that sadness has arisen; rather, view it as if it is somebody else's problem, like an old man watching someone else's children at play. Then, second, do not reify it. If you are not really here, then it is not really there. These are the pith instructions for how to abandon appropriation and reification and, thus, how not to get caught in the grip of mental afflictions.

Bringing Clear Discernment to Your Experiences

Düdjom Rinpoché continues his cautionary advice, which applies to Dzogchen practitioners at all levels:

> **It is important that you continuously abandon distraction and meditate with single-pointed mindfulness and determination. By straying into sporadic practice and intellectual understanding, you will feel special because of your smattering of śamatha; and, without bringing clear discernment to your experiences, your knowledge that consists of mere lip service will be of no benefit.**

It is crucial to "continuously abandon distraction and meditate with single-pointed mindfulness and determination." In the teachings common to the Mahāyāna, it is generally accepted that once you have achieved śamatha and are resting in the substrate consciousness, you then must achieve śamatha anew, as it were, but this time focused on emptiness, because you do not achieve the fusion of śamatha-vipaśyanā unless your śamatha is fully empowered with insight into emptiness. That is, when you are not satisfied with the bliss, luminosity, and nonconceptuality that arise from śamatha alone, because you know it can and will eventually be lost, you take the next step by piercing through the conditioned mind with the sharp, discerning sword of vipaśyanā, reinforced with a śamatha-trained mind that is stable, clear, and vivid. It is this union of śamatha-vipaśyanā that the Buddha uniquely and unprecedently revealed as the path to liberation.

It is at this point that you realize the actual nature of the substrate consciousness: that it is neither autonomous nor inherently existent. As Nāgārjuna wrote in his *Bodhicittavivāraṇa*, "When iron approaches a magnet, it quickly spins into place. Although it has no mind, it appears as though it did. In the same way, the substrate consciousness has no true existence, yet when it comes [from a previous life] and goes [to the next], it moves just as though it were real. And so it takes hold of another lifetime in existence."[13] In other words, as the substrate consciousness transmigrates from one place to another, from lifetime to lifetime, it seems as if it moves through space, but this is an illusion. It is simply a matter of shifting appearances, like watching a 3D movie, in which there is the appearance of movement, but it is unreal.

This insight into the emptiness of the substrate and substrate consciousness—which are the ground of your samsara—directly prepares you to realize pristine awareness, and from there you must then achieve śamatha in rigpa, as it were. That is, you must stabilize your practice of Dzogchen meditation until you are able to rest unwaveringly in rigpa, both during sessions of meditative equipoise and through the post-meditative periods. As mentioned earlier, a few very gifted individuals, with tremendous spiritual momentum from their past lives, may freshly achieve śamatha by following the instructions given here on how to rest in rigpa; but they must have actually identified rigpa first and not simply be resting in their coarse, human, mental consciousness.

Through vipaśyanā joined with identification of rigpa, you will realize not only that all phenomena are empty of inherent existence but also that all appearances of samsara and nirvana are equally pure displays of pristine awareness. So, in a sense, there are three progressive phases of attaining śamatha: first, the śamatha that enables you to rest nonconceptually in the substrate consciousness; then, the śamatha that is fused with realization of emptiness in vipaśyanā; and then, the śamatha that rests unwaveringly in pristine awareness. Therefore, the instructions to "continuously abandon distraction and meditate with single-pointed mindfulness and determination" should apply at any stage of the path at which you may be practicing now.

When Düdjom Rinpoché writes, "By straying into sporadic practice and intellectual understanding," "sporadic practice" means that even after you have identified rigpa, but before you become a fully matured vidyādhara, there might be the temptation to sink into a bit of complacency. When he says "straying into . . . intellectual understanding," this means that even after glimpsing totally nonconceptual primordial consciousness, once again you get caught up in conceptualization about it. Further, the phrase "you will feel special because of your smattering of śamatha" may refer to the smidgen of śamatha you have achieved in your realization of rigpa, or it may refer to your smattering of ordinary śamatha, without yet having fully identified rigpa, depending where you are on the path as you receive these teachings. As a parallel in the Mahāyāna teachings, however, even the āryabodhisattva on the first bodhisattva ground has to keep returning to the realization of emptiness with the fusion of śamatha-vipaśyanā. This enables the āryabodhisattva to experience increasingly deeper purification through repeated experiences of the meditative equipoise in which one directly perceives emptiness and then to engage in the illusion-like virtues of the six transcendences, or the six pāramitās, with ever-greater power and scope.

So, "without bringing clear discernment to your experiences, your knowledge that consists of mere lip service will be of no benefit." Even ordinary śamatha—with a sentient being's mind—is undoubtedly very important, but if you are just resting in stillness without venturing into vipaśyanā, seeking to fathom the actual nature of the mind and all phenomena, then that is a mistake. His Holiness the Dalai Lama has emphasized this for decades. In most lineages of Mahāmudrā and Dzogchen, even before you seek to achieve śamatha, it is essential to explore the origin, location, and destination of your mind. If you are struggling with upheavals—inner, outer, or secret—there are two things that can protect your mind and help you progress toward the path: these are the two forms of bodhicitta, at both the obscurative and ultimate dimensions of reality. Cultivating these two forms of bodhicitta directly encompasses the cultivation of great compassion as well as gaining genuine insight into emptiness. In this way, when the upheaval that arises is outer, or environmental, then you know that it is only a dreamlike experience of appearances and is not really "out there." The same is true for upheavals in your body and mind—the inner and secret upheavals, respectively—which also have no existence in and of themselves.

In this spirit, you could practice Asaṅga's method of mindfulness of breathing with the awareness that there is not actually any body here at all that is solid or inherently existent. Your body is entirely composed of appearances, and even those appearances exist only conventionally. This is analogous to the border between Canada and the United States. It is there, but only in a manner of speaking, and your body is no more substantial or inherently real than the border between these two countries. Yet, merely conceptually designated, conditioned phenomena do have causal efficacy, such that there are wars over borders in which people die due to hatred, greed, violence, and cruelty. It is appearances of getting a bullet in your head, burning, drowning, and so on that kill you. Appearances are not inherently real, but of course they have causal efficacy. So, do not doubt for a second that the merely conceptually designated phenomena of your own body, for example, have causal efficacy.

Especially when your body is in pain, then, it can be deeply transformative to meditate with mindfulness of breathing, recalling the Cittamātra view as you are meditating on the sensations. Bear in mind the sensations of the breath, but there is no breath. There is no air. There is no gas. There are no molecules. There are no lungs; there's no heart; there's no liver; there's no navel cakra. There are appearances, yes, but they are not really there at all in the way they appear. Suddenly, the mind becomes so much more spacious, and that is just from a Cittamātra viewpoint. But then why not infuse the sweetness of Dzogchen into it, where of course your mind itself is no more inherently existent than your body? It is just an appearance—appearances all the way up and all the way down. Everything that appears consists only of appearances to your mind, including—because this does not contradict Prāsaṅgika Madhyamaka—the appearances of a chariot. Think of the chariot. It is only an appearance to your mind that you have conceptually designated. That is why what you have conceptually designated also appears to your mind—and not only appearances of colors and smells and tastes, and so forth.

Therefore, in order to bring "clear discernment to your experiences" you must continue to study the depth and breadth of the Dharma so that you understand where particular teachings fit within the scope of authentic Dharma teachings. Go back to the Buddha's own teachings and those who you know are authoritative. For the Theravāda, after the Buddha, there is no one more authoritative than Buddhaghosa, just as for the Gelukpa tradition, there is no one more authoritative than Tsongkhapa and in terms of the systematization of Dzogchen, there is no one more authoritative than Longchenpa. Go back to the gold standard, to the authentic treatises and the authentic teachers, and rely on them. Then, when you measure your experiences against the gold standard, you will know with raw honesty where you are on the path, and your knowledge will transcend mere lip service. Then, when you speak the Dharma to others, it will truly be of benefit.

SUSTAINING PRACTICE WITH CONTINUOUS MEDITATION

Düdjom Rinpoché then reminds his listeners of ancient sayings from the Dzogchen tradition, each of which have been quoted for centuries:

> The Great Perfection teachings state, "Understanding is like a patch, for it comes off" and "Meditative experiences are

> like mist, for they vanish." This is how many meditators are deceived by even minor good or bad circumstances and get lost in them. Even though meditation has been planted in your mindstream, if you do not meditate continuously, the profound practical instructions will remain in your books; and with your stubborn, untamed mind that has become insensitive to the Dharma, your practice will become jaded, so that no authentic meditation will ever arise. Old meditators who are still novices at practice are in danger of dying with their heads encrusted in salt, so they should watch out!

The line "Understanding is like a patch, for it comes off" drives home the point that in the sequence of (1) understanding, (2) experience, (3) realization, and (4) acquiring confidence, it is critical not to confuse mere conceptual understanding of the teachings for any of the higher levels gained from diligent practice. All the things we learn with our minds in this life, we will forget, so the analogy is quite literal: Mere conceptual understanding will surely peel away at death, if not long before. Likewise, "Meditative experiences are like mist, for they vanish." That is, meditative experiences come and go—unlike genuine realization, they are not sustainable. As extraordinary as some meditative experiences can be at the time, they quickly fade into memories. Yet, if you cling to them and overevaluate such experiences, you may think you have accomplished something enduring, when in fact you have not. The greatest danger here is that, thinking you have attained a degree of realization that you have not, you might give up on doing the very practices needed to attain that realization. So, then, not only are you left with a mere memory rather than transformative realization, but you believe you are beyond the very practices that would lead you to the actual realization, had you not deceived yourself. Therefore, understanding should never be conflated with meditative experience, meditative experiences should never be conflated with realization, and realization should never be conflated with achieving confidence.

Düdjom Rinpoché continues, "This is how many meditators are deceived by even minor good or bad circumstances and get lost in them. Even though meditation has been planted in your mindstream, if you do not meditate continuously, the profound practical instructions will remain in your books; and with your stubborn, untamed mind that has become insensitive to the Dharma, your practice will become jaded, so that no authentic meditation will ever arise. Old meditators who are still novices at practice are in danger of dying with their heads encrusted in salt, so they should watch out!" That is, as a seasoned practitioner, you may pride yourself on the number of years spent in practice and retreat, but this in itself does not count for much, apart from gaining genuine realization and acquiring confidence. So, "watch out!" Do not die with your head "encrusted in salt"—that is, do not die jaded or disappointed with yourself.

Düdjom Rinpoché continues,

> By acquainting yourself with practice continuously in this way for a long time, eventually, due to any one of the contributing conditions of admiration, reverence, and so forth, experiences will be elevated to realizations, and you will nakedly and vividly perceive pristine awareness.

He is speaking again to people who have not yet stabilized their realization of rigpa but do have the sincere aspiration, are keeping their samayas, and so forth. In order to do so, acquaint "yourself with practice continuously in this way for a long time" and eventually, because of the depth of your admiration, reverence, and so forth, what began as fleeting meditative experiences will rise to the level of realization, and "you will nakedly and vividly perceive pristine awareness." Since he refers to "admiration, reverence, and so forth," as the crucial contributing conditions that will catalyze this shift, it is important to turn again to ever subtler guidance in guru yoga.

What Kind of Guru Yoga Is Needed?

You can admire people for all kinds of things: for their intellect, athletic abilities, talents and skills, beauty, sense of humor, and so on. When you have extraordinarily gifted and accomplished teachers, it is easy to admire them for their astounding erudition, kindness, humility, intelligence, and other virtues. Yet, you are seeing only what you can see as a sentient being, which consists of their human qualities, and you are admiring them, perhaps even revering them, only for those. However, this misses the point of authentic guru yoga entirely, as you are basically on the fast track to idolatry and, sooner or later, disappointment.

When Düdjom Rinpoché writes, "By acquainting yourself with practice continuously in this way for a long time, eventually, due to any one of the contributing conditions of admiration, reverence, and so forth, experiences will be elevated to realizations," he is pointing to the fact that it is authentic reverence and devotion that will catalyze a quantum leap in your practice, taking you from the level of unstable experiences to sustainable and transformative realization. Nevertheless, there is only one kind of being who is worthy of this level of boundless, inconceivable admiration, reverence, faith, devotion, prayer, worship, and so forth—only one. Not even a tenth-stage āryabodhisattva is worthy, for that is still a sentient being. For the depth of admiration and reverence, worship, faith, and devotion referred to here, who is worthy? Only Samantabhadra, the primordial Buddha, Vajradhara. Or if you want a historical figure, Buddha Śākyamuni. Buddha Śākyamuni is an embodiment of Samantabhadra. Samantabhadra is the dharmakāya. Buddha Śākyamuni was an embodiment of the dharmakāya so that beings like ourselves who are not āryabodhisattvas could actually listen to him, see him, touch him, and so on.

That is the one who is worthy of infinite, boundless, inconceivable faith, devotion, reverence, worship, and prayer: the one to whom you call for blessings. Blessings come from Samantabhadra, Vajradhara, or Buddha Śākyamuni, no less. Buddha Śākyamuni's mind was the mind of Samantabhadra, so he is no less worthy of devotion, faith, and reverence than Samantabhadra. This is a samyaksambuddha, endowed with the thirty-two signs, eighty symbols, and all the qualities of the Buddha's speech; all the qualities of the Buddha-mind. This is why, when His Holiness the Dalai Lama speaks of Buddha Śākyamuni, you can see him deeply moved with emotion. He understands. That is the being who is deserving of and appropriate to the kind of faith and reverence called for here, which is necessary for the practice and realization of Dzogchen.

Devotion is not a matter of thinking, "This one has incredible erudition and all these wonderful qualities." That's all very fine, but these qualities are like the light from a candle flame, while the qualities of a buddha are like sunrays. The person you can see is like the candle flame, and the sun is behind it. The sublime qualities of the Buddha don't obscure the human qualities. Isn't it wonderful that Tsongkhapa could memorize thirty pages a day? Isn't it extraordinary that Sakya Paṇḍita managed to master all five fields of knowledge, including Sanskrit? But those are still just a sentient being's qualities, not worthy of this kind of worship.

So, as a test of your guru yoga, let's say somebody woke you up in the middle of the night and asked, "Who's your object of refuge?" You should answer without hesitation, "Vajradhara." Go right to the real one: Vajra-dhara, Samantabhadra. And then suppose he asks, "Can you elaborate?" You would reply, "Oh, Buddha Śākyamuni." That's perfectly fine. And then he'd say, "Do you have anything to add?" And you would respond, "Well, yes, it's dharmakāya manifesting as my yidam; as Tārā, Padmasambhava, Mañjuśrī, Cakrasaṃvara, Avalokiteśvara, Vajrayoginī." Tārā has all the wisdom, the power, the compassion, of Samantabhadra, no less. She's not only a very compassionate female archetype; she is a complete buddha. She has all the wisdom of Mañjuśrī and all the power of Vajrapāṇi. Each yidam embodies specific aspects of the dharmakāya, but each one of them also encompasses the entirety of the body, speech, mind, sublime qualities, and enlightened activities of all the buddhas. When you envision Vajradhara or Samantabhadra, you are focusing on the aspect of the limitless dharmakāya. Fundamentally, you need to know that this dharmakāya is your ultimate guru, whether upon waking up from sleep with a start or when breathing your last in this life.

Ask yourself, then, who is the one, specifically, whom you may wish to escort you through the portals of death into the bardo? It may be Samanta-bhadra manifesting as Tārā, or Padmasambhava, but nothing less. Then you have that personal relationship with the *iṣṭadevatā*, or personal deity. Among the myriad manifestations of Samantabhadra, know that "this is the one I choose. This is my iṣṭadevatā." Nevertheless, whether it be she or he, peaceful, enriching, powerful, or ferocious—whichever of the four manifestations—whether he or she appears as white, yellow, red, or deep blue, know that it is all of them showing this particular face. But your faith is faith in Vajradhara, Buddha Śākyamuni. At this point, it becomes per-sonal. For some of you, it's White Tārā, for others, it's Padmasambhava, for another, it's Mañjuśrī, for yet others, Samantabhadra. But it's not just Mañjuśrī: it is Samantabhadra as him. That is a crucial point.

I have personally seen in many Tibetans the kind of heartfelt faith and devotion that comes when one is raised with these kinds of ideas, culturally. Likewise, many Christians raised with faith in Jesus Christ, God the Father, and the Trinity, have that same kind of faith in an ultimate source of ref-uge. It is said that faith is the mother of all virtues; it changes a whole life. Sometimes we need a historical person, not just something that may seem abstract, like the ground of being or primordial consciousness, to embody this ultimate source of refuge. You can look to Jesus of Nazareth or you can look to Buddha Śākyamuni in northern India. Look at his life story. Look at his teachings. Look at the impact he had during his time and even now, two thousand six hundred years later. Then you have a glimpse of what it means to be a buddha in this world.

From that place of refuge in a historical person as the bedrock example of what it means to manifest enlightenment, then if you are practicing Mahāyāna or Vajrayāna, you start to see that majesty, depth, and glory of a fully enlightened being manifesting as Tārā or whoever your yidam may be. If your mind is steeped in Dharma in this way, and you have conviction in the three principles taught by Maitreya in the *Uttaratantra*, as mentioned earlier, and you have found a guru who is truly qualified—then you may dissolve the human appearances by which the guru presents himself or herself to you and look straight through to the presence of the dharmakāya, Samantabhadra, who is actually there.

If you give infinite admiration and reverence to a person with finite virtues, it's a mismatch. Infinite meets infinite; finite meets finite. No matter how wonderful the human virtues of a guru may be, to think, on the basis of those human qualities, "That person is a buddha" is a complete mistake. Recognize those qualities as wonderful virtues, worthy of respect, but not as the full personification of the infinite ground of being.

If you are practicing Theravāda Buddhism, then it is fine simply to pay your respect to the human guru. In that context, your guru is seen as an emissary of the Buddha, and that is appropriate. But in Dzogchen, however magnificent the accomplishments of the lama may be that you can witness, that you can understand and wrap your mind around, you must dissolve it all into emptiness. If you see any ordinary flaws and human foibles, you dissolve those into emptiness as well because we are assuming at this point that the person is a qualified guru and not someone who is leading others astray with either conduct or teaching. Nevertheless, even if he or she seems to you to be a perfect lama, you are still viewing at the level of a sentient being and not a buddha.

I often think of Atiśa as the perfect guru and Padmasambhava as the perfect mahāsiddha. No one else performed those extraordinary siddhis in Tibet; the work had Padmasambhava's name on it. But when I ask, in the whole history of India, who is the perfect guru, I think of Atiśa: he was a perfect bodhisattva, a perfect paṇḍita, a perfect mahāsiddha, a perfect example, a perfect monk, with perfect generosity, and so on. When practicing guru yoga, however, you take your view even of that marvelous human being and dissolve the person it looks upon into emptiness. Then, *from your yidam,* manifest Atiśa, manifest His Holiness the Dalai Lama, manifest Garchen Rinpoché, or any other authentic lama. But there has to be a dissolution into emptiness first, just as you dissolve yourself in emptiness.

If you don't do that, then you are just pretending all over again. As His Holiness the Dalai Lama says, if you've not realized emptiness, and you're going through all the motions of Vajrayāna, thinking, "I'm the deity, reciting this mantra, and doing this visualization," and you have not yet realized emptiness, then it is just all playtime. It is pretending, and no one has ever achieved enlightenment by pretending. But if you can see that where the guru is, there is the dharmakāya, and the guru is the conduit for all the blessings of the dharmakāya, then you can fall on your knees and press your face to the ground in worship without fear of idolatry.

If there is to be a catalyst from our side powerful enough to catapult us to realization beyond our current capacity, then it has to be a practice of guru yoga on that order, and no less. Then, "experiences will be elevated to realizations, and you will nakedly and vividly perceive pristine awareness."

When Thoughts Arise as Meditation

Düdjom Rinpoché then elaborates on how thoughts can release themselves:

> As if removing a veil from your head, you will feel wide open and perfectly balanced. This is called "the supreme seeing that does not see." From that time onward, thoughts will arise as meditation, and stillness and movement equally release themselves. At first, releasing thoughts by recognizing them is like meeting someone you already know. After a while, thoughts release themselves, just as a snake unravels its own knots. Finally, thoughts are released without causing benefit or harm, like a thief in an empty house. These three phases occur progressively, and a strong conviction arises from within that all phenomena are apparitions of your own pristine awareness alone.

This is still in the context of conduct, and, as you can see, the triad of view, meditation, and conduct are inextricably integrated. That is, if you remove the view, there is no Dzogchen meditation or conduct. If you remove meditation, then there is no sustainability of the view and, therefore, no conduct. If you remove conduct, then there is no stability of meditation. If you remove any one part, the whole crumbles.

When he says, "As if removing a veil from your head, you will feel wide open and perfectly balanced," he is suggesting that in retrospect, you will feel that your experience prior to this was claustrophobic, as if there were a veil on your head, or even worse, that you may have felt stuck inside your head. But then, like removing a veil, you will suddenly feel a vast openness and sublime sense of balance that is free from the activities of the dualistic mind—it is a homogeneity and symmetry that is without the bifurcation of subject and object, my side and your side, this and that.

Düdjom Rinpoché continues, "This is called 'the supreme seeing that does not see.' From that time onward, thoughts will arise as meditation, and stillness and movement equally release themselves." This "supreme seeing that does not see" is a reference to a realization of emptiness that echoes the language of the Prajñāpāramitā sūtras. Up until that point, you might still be perturbed by the nagging, obsessive, compulsive occurrences of thoughts, seeing them as distractions, a dilution of your awareness, and maybe even as obstacles. However, now that you have broken through to this dimension of realizing emptiness and pristine awareness nondually, thoughts arise *as* meditation, because you see their emptiness even as they arise. This is similar to the way that the emanations of the four kinds of nirmāṇakāyas that spontaneously and effortlessly flow out in all directions to serve the needs of sentient beings are not obstructions of dharmakāya—they are expressions of dharmakāya. So, "thoughts will arise as meditation" because you see them clearly as expressions of pristine awareness, not as something to suppress or terminate. Prior to this point, you may have preferred stillness over movement, just as you may prefer nirvana over samsara. This is common, as movement seems unsettling and stillness seems peaceful. At this point, though, you are diving deeply into that one taste where stillness releases itself and movements need no external antidote or anything to remedy them. Instead, they all "equally release themselves."

He then explains three ways that thoughts can release themselves. First, the sheer recognition of thoughts causes them to release, "like meeting someone you already know." This is called "naked release." Second is "release upon arising," which comes by the power of deeper familiarization. This is not the same as recognition, which involves a subtle form of "doing" in order for them to release. Rather, they simply arise, and without your even recognizing them, they simply have no hold, no traction. They have no ability to lead to a chain of thoughts. They just arise and then vanish, like sparks disappearing into the sky. This is compared to a snake that unravels its own knots. In the third phase, whether they linger or pass quickly, thoughts have no power to influence you, either to improve your awareness, or to distract, dilute, or dull your awareness. This is called "self-release" and is compared to a thief in an empty house, who will depart without having caused either benefit or harm. Düdjom Rinpoché concludes that "these three phases occur progressively, and a strong conviction arises from within that all phenomena are apparitions of your own pristine awareness alone."

Yangthang Rinpoché said that it is particularly in the third phase that thoughts actually empower your realization of pristine awareness. They are arising *as* meditation because rather than distracting you from pristine awareness, they are empowering your realization of pristine awareness, and in that way, they serve as aids to your practice.

Additionally, there is a fourth type of release called "primordial release." Pristine awareness constitutes this primordial release because pristine awareness has never been bound by thoughts, unlike your dualistic mind. From the perspective of pristine awareness, there has always been primordial release, or liberation, but from the perspective of a practitioner in the process of being liberated from a conditioned mind, there are those three ways in which thoughts release themselves progressively over the course of the actual evolution of practice.

Generally, in the Sūtrayāna, it is stated that in order to realize how utterly delusive and misleading appearances are, you must use your intelligence to investigate the actual nature of phenomena in contrast to the way they appear. That is, simply applying bare attention to appearances is not enough to break through the obscurative manner in which they are experienced. If all you are doing is observing appearances that are undoubtedly misleading you about the actual nature of reality, this would be like carefully listening to someone who is lying to you without ever questioning the validity of what they are saying. The essential point here is that phenomena appear as if they exist from their own side, by their own intrinsic nature, but in reality, neither subjective nor objective phenomena exist in that way. In order to transcend the deceptive, misleading nature of all appearances, sensory and mental, it is necessary to use reasoning of the kind that Nāgārjuna uses in his ontological analyses of phenomena.

By contrast, in Dzogchen, one can gain realization of the same emptiness—there is only one emptiness—without analysis, in a purely nonconceptual way. This is specifically true in the case of individuals with superior faculties who are swiftly able to cut through the dualistic mind to unconditioned, pristine awareness. Then, by viewing reality from that perspective, they effortlessly realize that all phenomena are empty of their own inherent nature and are pure expressions of pristine awareness. The path of Dzogchen is presented as being effortless. It is effortless to rest in awareness and simply let thoughts come and go without exerting effort to appropriate them. Conversely, it actually requires effort to appropriate thoughts and be obsessed, compelled, and deluded by them. As you master taking the mind as the path—and even more so, śamatha without a sign—then you know that you were effortlessly aware of being aware even before you learned how to meditate. With practice, the *awareness* of the awareness that was already there occurs constantly and effortlessly.

A clear indication of this is that when you recall being aware of an event, you can remember both the event and your being aware of it at the time. You wouldn't be able to remember being aware of that event if you weren't aware of being aware of it at the time. That awareness of being aware is constant and effortless in every conscious moment. Likewise, when you are engaging in the śamatha practice of being aware of being aware, or awareness of awareness, that is effortless. The only effort needed is not to let your attention be distracted elsewhere, but that is a gentle effort, like holding a little bird in a closed hand—neither too tight, nor too loose.

Sooner or later, your śamatha practice is going to culminate in awareness of awareness. On that basis, without engaging in detailed logical analyses, you may swiftly realize the empty, essential nature of your own mind by recognizing its emptiness of origin, location, and destination. Then you are poised to realize the manifest nature of the unborn luminosity of awareness, resulting in your realization of trekchö—and on that basis, tögal—which will take you all the way to perfect enlightenment.

These three phases of releasing thoughts correspond to ever-deepening stages of relaxation and, therefore, the release of the effort of appropriating thoughts. When you relinquish the effort of appropriating thoughts, then they respond, in turn, by subtly and steadily releasing themselves. Then "a strong conviction arises from within that all phenomena are apparitions of your own pristine awareness alone." This includes all phenomena, whether pleasant or unpleasant, virtuous or nonvirtuous. As "apparitions of your own pristine awareness," they are equally of one taste. Rather than a dog paddling forever in the ocean of samsara, washed to and fro by your likes and dislikes, you will then be dwelling in a vast sky of blessings.

THE CULMINATION OF THE VIEW, MEDITATION, AND CONDUCT

Düdjom Rinpoché continues,

> Emptiness is stirred by a whirlpool of compassion, any preference for nirvana or samsara is extinguished, and you will realize that there are no distinctions of good and bad regarding buddhas and sentient beings. Whatever you do, your joyous mind never wavers from the actual nature of reality, so you continuously rest day and night in an open expanse. As the Great Perfection teachings state, "Realization is like space— without change."

When he writes, "Emptiness is stirred by a whirlpool of compassion," this occurs in the ocean of blessings where everything is arising as blessings of dharmakāya, sambhogakāya, and nirmāṇakāya. Regarding the idea "any preference for nirvana or samsara is extinguished," the great meditation master and scholar Dilgo Khyentsé Rinpoché said that when you are coming to the end of the bodhisattva path and are on the cusp of achieving perfect awakening, you will view the whole of samsara and nirvana with complete equanimity—without any preference for nirvana over samsara.

Further, Düdjom Rinpoché assures us that "whatever you do, your joyous mind never wavers from the actual nature of reality," which is the immutable, unborn, unceasing bliss of *dharmatā*. In this way, "you continuously rest day and night in an open expanse. As the Great Perfection teachings state, 'Realization is like space—without change.'"

Here Düdjom Rinpoché is approaching the conclusion of his presentation on the road of practice. Thus, he gives a preview of the culmination of this Dzogchen path, writing,

> Accordingly, such yogins appear in ordinary human form, but their minds dwell in the effortless enlightened view of the dharmakāya, enabling them to progress without activity along the bodhisattva grounds and paths. Finally, both their cognition

> and phenomena are extinguished: like the space inside a broken
> pot, their bodies dissolve into minute particles, and their minds
> dissolve into the actual nature of reality. This is called "dwelling
> as the youthful vase kāya, the inner luminosity of the primor-
> dial ground, absolute space." This is what will come to pass.

When he says that "such yogins appear in ordinary human form," this means
that they look just the same as before. If they were walking down the street,
no one might notice anything different about them. Yet inwardly, "their
minds dwell in the effortless enlightened view of the dharmakāya, enabling
them to progress without activity along the bodhisattva grounds and paths."
They have completely deactivated their body, speech, and mind as sentient
beings. So, while they still look like normal people, since their minds view
all phenomena effortlessly from the perspective of the dharmakāya, they
are able to progress swiftly along the ten bodhisattva grounds without exer-
tion in the myriad outer activities of a bodhisattva. Thus they complete the
fourth of the five paths, the path of meditation, and proceed to the fifth,
"the path of no more training."

Further, "both their cognition and phenomena"—that is, all of the impure
appearances within the whole field of samsara, including both the subjective
mindsets and the phenomena of which one is aware—"are extinguished."

When he writes that "their bodies dissolve into minute particles," this
means that their bodies eventually dissolve into the energy of primordial
consciousness. That is, "like the space inside a broken pot"—which is exactly
the same before the pot existed, as it breaks, and after it is gone altogether—
the material body returns to the ultimate ground of being. Moreover, "their
minds dissolve into the actual nature of reality," which means that the configured mind of a sentient being dissolves irreversibly into the primordial
dharmatā. Düdjom Rinpoché then uses deeply symbolic and technical terminology, unique to the Dzogchen tradition, to describe the enlightenment
that is achieved in this way. It is called "dwelling as the youthful vase kāya,
the inner luminosity of the primordial ground, absolute space."

The "youthful vase kāya" is said to abide in such a way that the primordial
consciousness that is present as the ground is not made manifest in its coarse
aspect of outer luminosity, but rather it abides in the manner of a subtle,
inner luminosity—without transference, change, aging, or degeneration. It
is often explained in terms of analogies. As the *Tantra of the Reverberation
of Sound* states, "In the jeweled palace of the *citta* [mind], its essential nature

is the aspect of original purity; the radiance of the kāya is the synthesis of emptiness and luminosity; it is perfectly complete with face and arms, in the manner of a kāya within a vase; and it abides spontaneously as a sphere of light. Compassion appears distinctly as each color of light."

Khatog Getsé Paṇchen Gyurmé Tsewang Chogdrub (1761–1829) explains that the youthful vase kāya has the essential nature of the dharmakāya, in which the knowing aspect of the outer luminosity is "dissolved yet not dull," just as the light of a crystal is analogously thought to disappear inside the crystal when it is not shining. When a crystal is covered with a cloth or held in a dark room, the light that would be refracted outwards when the same crystal is held up in the sunlight does not in fact shine outward, but according to this analogy, the potential for that brilliance is still there. Similarly, the inner luminosity of the dharmakāya abides without change, but in its dharmakāya aspect is invisible to others. Its manifest nature, on the other hand, is luminosity that remains nonconceptual, and is the basis for the two kinds of *rūpakāya* (that is, the sambhogakāya and nirmāṇakāya) to arise. The compassion of the youthful vase kāya engages in such a way that the actual nature of the inexhaustible ornamental wheels of the body, speech, and mind of all *tathāgata*s are able to appear as objects of perception for disciples, just as the image of the moon is able to appear in a water vessel as long as there is water in it. The way that the youthful vase kāya abides in the absolute space of phenomena is stated in the *Tantra of the Luminous Expanse*: "Its essential nature is emptiness; luminosity—the kāya of primordial consciousness—is its manifest nature; it is impartial compassion. The great indivisibility of these is the primordial buddha."[14]

Düdjom Rinpoché then ties everything together, concluding,

> That is the culmination of the view, meditation, and conduct, so it is called "the actualization of the fruition where there is nothing to achieve." Moreover, these demarcations of meditative experiences and realizations may occur in a normative sequence, without prescribed order, or all at once, according to the specific capacities of different individuals. But at the time of the fruition, there are no differences.

When he writes that "it is called 'the actualization of the fruition where there is nothing to achieve,'" there is nothing to achieve because, from this perspective, you now recognize that you have always been a buddha. Likewise, there was never any point in time when you actually came into existence as a sentient being. Having already been a buddha from timeless beginning, there is nothing to achieve, and you now know that with certainty—it is not simply an article of faith or belief.

In addition, "these demarcations of meditative experiences and realizations may occur in a normative sequence," which means that they may occur sequentially in a very orderly fashion, as in a person of low faculties. Or they may occur "without prescribed order," as in a person of medium faculties who is able to bypass the gradual cultivation of śamatha and vipaśyanā by swiftly recognizing pristine awareness and then proceeding directly to the practice of trekchö—continuing to rest effortlessly in pristine awareness. Or realizations may occur "all at once," as in the case of those with superior faculties, who simply hear the teachings and simultaneously gain realization. These distinctions in meditative experiences and realizations occur "according to the specific capacities of different individuals"—that is, it is based on the magnitude of karmic momentum each individual brings into this lifetime, which is something you cannot control or force. Yet, "at the time of the fruition," or when you achieve the perfect enlightenment of a buddha, "there are no differences." In other words, at the culmination of the path, when buddhahood is actualized, the qualities of a perfectly enlightened buddha—a samyaksambuddha—are always the same. In another tantra revealed to Düdjom Lingpa, *The Enlightened View of Samantabhadra*, the Lake-Born Vajra says the following:[15]

> Finally, the bonds of subtle cognitive obscurations are severed from your heart, and your limpid body, like space dissolving into space, extends limitlessly into the absolute space of phenomena, free of conceptual elaboration, as the primordially pure youthful vase kāya. This is the originally pure dharmakāya made manifest, so it is authentic perfect enlightenment.... Thus there is (1) natural liberation, the dharmakāya of entering the womb; (2) union, the dharmakāya of nonduality; and (3) transference, the dharmakāya of primordial consciousness. However you are liberated among these three ways, the unwavering dharmakāya manifests limitlessly as displays of the kāyas and facets of primordial consciousness. By means of rūpakāyas manifesting in various ways to train every individual, you serve the needs of sentient beings until the ocean of sentient existence is empty, like a moon and its reflections in water.

Distinguishing between Meditative Experiences and Authentic Realization

It is crucial to be able to distinguish between the unimaginable variety of nyam, or meditative experiences, and *tokpa*, or authentic realization. In short, meditative experiences—as meaningful as they may seem at the time—come and go. But authentic realizations, especially when fortified with deep and prolonged familiarization, result in the purification of mental afflictions and obscurations, the arousal of great compassion, profound insight into emptiness, and other virtues, as well as a more robust and sustainable sense of genuine well-being that carries one through good times and bad, thus transforming one's very being and entire way of viewing reality. By recognizing this clear and vitally important distinction, you prevent the risk of mistaking mere meditative experiences for genuine realization, thinking that you are further along than you actually are.

To elaborate, a danger in not being able to distinguish between meditative experiences and actual realization is that there are many accounts of people claiming realizations in ways that are not in accordance with the Buddha's teachings. Many people desperately want to think they have achieved some degree of enlightenment, and they come to this conclusion without checking with qualified lamas to determine whether their assessment of their own experiences and insights are actually valid and correspond to stages of the path as taught according to the various yānas of Buddhism. In his commentary to *The Sharp Vajra of Conscious Awareness Tantra*, titled *The Essence of Clear Meaning*, Düdjom Lingpa writes, "So cut through your false assumptions by devoting yourself to a sublime spiritual mentor who knows how to draw forth the crucial points of this path correctly, without ever being separated from him. Even if you lack such good fortune [of meeting a qualified spiritual mentor], it is indispensable that you, without falling into indolence, properly read, realize, and familiarize yourself with the pith instructions of the vidyādharas of the past who have achieved siddhis by way of this path."[16] The problem here is that if people have overestimated their own experiences and realizations, then they will no longer apply themselves to achieving what they erroneously think they have already attained. Having deluded themselves, they are then bound to delude others who don't know any better.

As a word of caution, as you continue in your own practice, you may have some extraordinary breakthroughs, but be humble and be cautious in evaluating your experiences. Many people think they have achieved śamatha and one or more of the dhyānas, but they are mistaken, for their experiences don't correspond to the most authoritative sources—such as the writings of Asaṅga and Buddhaghosa—on these stages of samādhi. The same is true of the achievement of vipaśyanā and higher realizations. If you think you have achieved great realization when, in fact, you have not (and if you take your own perspective as ultimate regardless of whether your guru tells you otherwise), then you are stuck and no further progress is to be made until you let go of your exaggerated evaluation of your experiences.

Accordingly, rely closely on the authentic teachings of vidyādharas for guidance on how to assess practice accurately. In *The Vajra Essence*, following his precise teaching on "taking the impure mind as the path as the entryway to cutting through," the Lake-Born Vajra said, "This is called *ordinary śamatha of the path*, and if you achieve stability in it for a long time, you will have achieved the critical feature of stability in your mindstream. However, know that among unrefined people in this degenerate era, very few appear to achieve more than fleeting stability."[17] Even though that was written with regard to Tibet about 150 years ago, it is ever more relevant in this modern, degenerate era.

The Lake-Born Vajra continues, saying, "At this time, for some people their supreme chosen deity will appear, and they will still their minds there." That is, some people may have a vision of Mañjuśrī or Tārā, for example, and they will settle their minds there. Then, "Visions of buddhafields appear to some, and they stabilize and settle their minds on these. Some particularly experience bliss, luminosity, or nonconceptuality, and they settle there. To others, images of their guru, rainbows, lights, and bindus appear, so they remain there, and so forth. Understand that due to the functioning of the channels and elements of each individual, experiences are not the same for everyone."[18] It is extremely common for people to have what are, in fact, nyam, or meditative experiences, and for them to mistake these nyam for tokpa, or authentic realization. While the experiences themselves can be beneficial and inspiring, to mistake them for something higher is dangerous and can hinder one from actually achieving genuine realization, thereby stunting any growth toward reaching the path, much less actualizing buddhahood.

7. POST-MEDITATIVE PRACTICE

Düdjom Rinpoché has now finished the core pith instruction for the whole text, upon which the foundation of view, meditation, and conduct is laid. The third and final topic in his root text is that of post-meditative experience. One might think that the post-meditative state is the whole of conduct, yet it is a separate section. As we saw, many of the instructions on conduct do pertain directly to how to fine-tune one's practice during formal sessions of meditation, in addition to how to maintain the continuity of practice between sessions. Here, the instructions on post-meditation will focus more explicitly on how to behave when engaged in activities undertaken in relationship with other sentient beings, while still indicating the integration and utter indivisibility of the Dzogchen view, meditation, and conduct.

First, Düdjom Rinpoché emphasizes the importance of maintaining vigilance in the post-meditative state—by stationing the sentry of your mindfulness and introspection on continuous watch—in order to be able to maintain your ethical commitments at all levels of practice: Śrāvakayāna, Bodhisattvayāna, and Vajrayāna. He writes,

> Regarding the post-meditative practice of keeping your samayas and vows and integrating all your activities of this life with Dharma, if you strive in the cultivation of the view, meditation, and conduct yet are not skilled in the methods of practice between sessions, your vows and samayas will degenerate. If that happens, in the short term there will be interferences and obstacles to progressing along the bodhisattva grounds and paths, and finally you will definitely fall into Avīci Hell. So it is of the utmost importance that, without ever being separated from the sentry of mindfulness and introspection, you are unmistaken in determining what is to be adopted and

what is to be rejected. As the great Ācārya [Padmasambhava] declared,

> While my view is higher than the sky,
> my conduct regarding cause and effect is finer than barley flour.

Even when you have actually achieved high degrees of realization and your samādhi is honed, it may be tempting to think that you can then relax regarding your ethics, believing that with your newfound realization, you can behave spontaneously in any way you like. This is a profound error. Whether you have gained high realization or not, if you allow your samayas and vows to degenerate, perhaps adopting a casual attitude, then "in the short term there will be interferences and obstacles to progressing along the bodhisattva grounds and paths, and finally you will definitely fall into Avīci Hell." Such a rebirth in hell is not punishment meted out by a supreme being but rather is the natural consequence of such misconduct in accordance with the laws of karma. Simply put, Düdjom Rinpoché's statement points to the fact that if you disregard your samayas and vows, then you are going to encounter a horde of problems, possibly even in this life but certainly in the hereafter. In order to prevent these completely avoidable challenges, "it is of the utmost importance that, without ever being separated from the sentry of mindfulness and introspection"—that is, to monitor your behavior—"you are unmistaken in determining what is to be adopted and what is to be rejected."

We then come to a very famous quotation by the great Ācārya, or Master, Padmasambhava: "While my view is higher than the sky, my conduct regarding cause and effect is finer than barley flour." Simply put, the higher you progress in your practice, the finer your ethical intelligence must become, for your deeds actually gain power—for good or for ill—the more deeply you understand the actual nature of reality and the laws of cause and effect. All of your actions of body, speech, and mind have consequences. Every deliberate action has consequences, so be careful of the seeds you sow because you will be reaping the harvest.

SAMAYAS AND THE GURU-DISCIPLE RELATIONSHIP

Düdjom Rinpoché continues by saying that if one can maintain the key samayas of body, speech, and mind with respect to your guru, this will encapsulate all the many types of samayas and vows that need to be maintained:

Therefore, reject a casual, crude attitude, and behave with care in terms of cause and effect. Keep your samayas and precisely maintain your vows at subtler and subtler levels, and you will not be contaminated by the stains of faults and downfalls. Although there are many kinds of Secret Mantra samayas, in brief, they are synthesized as the samayas of your root guru's enlightened body, speech, and mind. It is said that if you regard your guru as an ordinary person even for an instant, this will delay your accomplishment of siddhis by months and years. Why? This is because of the crucial point that the guru is a sacred field, as it is said,

> **Because Vajradhara said that siddhis follow after the master.**

Here, Düdjom Rinpoché is providing guidance for how to keep your samayas pertaining to the view of your guru. These samayas are traditionally elaborated in terms of how to honor the root guru's enlightened body, speech, and mind and are included in appendix 4 of this volume, according to Düdjom Rinpoché's own explanation of them. Optimally, when he speaks here of the view you should hold toward your guru, he is referring to people who have mastered dwelling in rigpa, where they are seeing their own face as Samantabhadra and viewing all phenomena with pure vision. However, if, somehow, they should fall back into ordinary vision for even an instant—the ordinary conception of themselves or their guru—then they will delay their "accomplishment of siddhis by months and years." This is because the guru is known as "a sacred field."

You may have encountered this idea of a sacred field before. For instance, your parents are a sacred field, even if you did not have great parents—they still gave birth to you, took care of you as well as they could, and enabled you to survive in whatever ways they were able, otherwise you wouldn't be here right now. Any of your actions pertaining to your parents—be they virtuous or nonvirtuous—are going to be accentuated by the power of their being a sacred field, wherein there is an acceleration, or an enhancement, of the power of the karma that you accrue, for better or worse. In other words, because of the immensely close connection you have to your parents—they provided the grounds for your conception and survival, after all—then all karma associated with them, positive or negative, will be enhanced and accentuated. That is true not only of your parents but of beings who are extraordinary fields of merit in themselves, such as bodhisattvas who have entered the path and especially āryabodhisattvas. Any harm you do in relationship to such holy beings will be accentuated. Then, all the more so is this true of your guru as a sacred, momentous field. That is, any virtuous or nonvirtuous activity toward the guru will be accentuated due to this exceptionally powerful karmic connection, and especially due to the gravitas of the guru's ability to protect you from the lower realms and to lead you to perfect enlightenment. Thus, it is extremely important for you to come to understand the samayas of your root guru's enlightened body, speech, and mind, and how these can encompass appropriate ethical guidelines for your interactions with all other sentient beings as well.

Düdjom Rinpoché continues, highlighting the pivotal importance of your decision to take someone as your guru,

> Therefore, whoever you are, until you first accept someone as your guru, you are on your own. But from the moment that you devote yourself to a guru and become linked with him through empowerments and practical instructions, then you have no choice but to keep your samayas. At the conclusion of the four empowerments, you bowed in front of the guru as the principal deity of the maṇḍala and vowed to him,

> From now on, I offer myself
> to you as your servant.
> Please accept me as your disciple
> and make use of even the smallest part of me.

When he says, "whoever you are, until you first accept someone as your guru, you are on your own," this highlights the fact that the choice is in our hands. No one will force you to take on the responsibilities of a relationship with a Mahāyāna or Vajrayāna guru. You need to see for yourself why you need to establish a relationship with an authentic guru if you wish to reach and proceed along the path swiftly. You have been on your own for countless past lifetimes, and if you would like to continue in this way, then you have that freedom. But when you see that that route is only perpetuating your samsara and not leading you away from suffering and its inner causes, then it is time to seek out an authentic guru who will guide you clearly toward and along the authentic path. Understanding the nature of an authentic relationship with a Vajrayāna guru, as explained earlier, you then need to ask yourself all the questions regarding whether this is an authentic guru and whether this is the right guru for you: (1) Are their teachings authentic? (2) Does their behavior accord with their teachings? (3) When you carefully put what they teach into practice, does it benefit you personally? When you decide to ask someone to be your guru, you are asking that person to take on the tremendous responsibility, not only in this lifetime, but in all your future lifetimes, of guiding you to your own perfect enlightenment. Pause and think what a grave responsibility you are placing on the guru by making that request. It's "heavy," which is the meaning of the Sanskrit word *guru*. I don't think you've ever asked anybody in this lifetime—not your wife or husband, parents, relatives, boss, benefactor, or employees—for such a huge grant, commitment, or gift. But if you do decide to make this solemn request, then, "from the moment that you devote yourself to a guru and become linked with him [or her] through empowerments and practical instructions, then you have no choice but to keep your samayas."

It is important to understand that apart from the exceptional cases of tulkus identified as children (or very devout Tibetan families where children may be steeped in Vajrayāna empowerments from an early age), establishing this guru-disciple relationship with a Vajrayāna guru is only to be done by adults, just as you cannot become a fully ordained monk or nun unless you are sufficiently mature. You then check carefully, as an adult, whether or not the guru and the teachings of the guru are authentic and whether or not the behavior of the guru is in accordance with the teachings. It is the disciples' responsibility to check these things with certainty and not devote themselves to the guru out of blind faith. Then, if you receive samayas, empowerment, pith instructions, and thus establish a guru-disciple relationship, it is your moral obligation "to keep your samayas," which requires you to learn what these are.[1]

To elaborate, Düdjom Rinpoché reminds Vajrayāna disciples, "At the conclusion of the four empowerments, you bowed in front of the guru as the principal deity of the maṇḍala and vowed to him [or her], 'From now on, I offer myself to you as your servant. Please accept me as your disciple and make use of even the smallest part of me.'" Be careful here, because if you think you are doing your guru a favor by offering yourself as his or her servant, then you are mistaken. Your guru doesn't need a servant. It sounds as though you are making an offering—which at one level you are—but at the same time what you are asking for is a gift that you will never be able to repay until you have achieved perfect enlightenment. Remember that what you are surrendering yourself to is pristine awareness—not to another sentient being. There are no masters and slaves here when speaking of gurus and disciples. But since your guru is qualified to guide you correctly, you can be confident that the things the guru may ask of you will only be to your own benefit along the path. Knowing this clearly, you can entrust yourself to the providence of the omniscient and all-compassionate buddha who will guide and care for you in the person of this authentic guru, even and precisely when the guru must correct your behavior or your way of thinking, or teach you crucial lessons about your mental afflictions that are at first not easy to bear.

Düdjom Rinpoché continues,

> With that oath, however great and noble you may be, haven't you sworn your allegiance to the guru? Likewise, regarding the vow, "Whatever the principal deity commands, I shall do all that you say," from that time forward, do you have the right not to do whatever he says? If you do not fulfill your oath, you cannot be called anything but a "samaya-breaker," as disagreeable as that label may be.

"Samaya-breaker" means simply, yet importantly, that you took samayas and then broke them. In a culture steeped in Vajrayāna Buddhism, such as that of Tibet, this is a deeply shameful epithet, so Düdjom Rinpoché's words would have landed searingly on his listeners. The humility that this oath of allegiance calls forth is, again, the humility of surrendering everything we were grasping to as being "me"—as a sentient being—so that our guru may lead us by the hand to discover our infinitely greater, identityless identity of buddhahood.

He continues,

> Furthermore, nowhere is it said that you must keep your samayas perfectly with great gurus who have many attendants and much wealth, power, and authority but not with minor gurus who accept a low status and live as beggars. Regardless of who it is, you should understand the crucial points of the advantages and risks of such a relationship, for it won't do to be

like a dull-witted old nag. Therefore, as if you were preparing medicinal substances, settle your mind in its natural state and carefully consider whether the need to keep the samayas is for the guru's sake or for your own sake. If it is for the guru's sake, you may as well set them aside this very day. But if not, there is no point in throwing ashes on your own head!

When Düdjom Rinpoché says, "nowhere is it said that you must keep your samayas perfectly with great gurus who have many attendants and much wealth, power, and authority but not with minor gurus who accept a low status and live as beggars," this means that you should not discriminate and place your devotion more strongly upon a guru with a higher social status than one with a lower status, if they are both genuine, authentic gurus. If you have that kind of attitude, breaking your samayas or behaving casually with gurus who are less well known, then you have completely missed the whole point. Devotion to an authentic guru must not be corrupted by worldly concepts of who deserves profound reverence versus casual familiarity, for such concepts all boil down to the eight mundane concerns.

Regardless of whether the guru you are approaching is world-renowned or relatively hidden, "you should understand the crucial points of the advantages and risks of such a relationship, for it won't do to be like a dull-witted old nag." So, don't think you have entered Vajrayāna blindfolded, but rather make every effort to "understand the crucial points of the advantages and risks" of the guru-disciple relationship in advance. Then your practice will be supported by such genuine understanding.

Regarding the analogy, "Therefore, as if you were preparing medicinal substances," when I was living with the great Tibetan Dr. Yeshi Dhonden during my early twenties, I saw this done many times. When Tibetan doctors are preparing a single herbal pill that has thirty-five ingredients, you can imagine how meticulous, how careful they have to be, because if you get the proportions wrong, it could turn into something that can make you ill. So, with that kind of conscientious care, "settle your mind in its natural state and carefully consider whether the need to keep the samayas is for the guru's sake or for your own sake." Are you keeping your samayas merely to please the guru, to try to make him or her happy, or is it for your own sake because you understand that it will bring you inconceivable benefit in the near and long term? Düdjom Rinpoché challenges us, "If it is for the guru's sake, you may as well set them aside this very day." However, if you recognize that the whole point of the guru-disciple relationship—including taking vows and samayas and receiving empowerments and pith instructions—is all for your benefit, and that none of it was for the guru, then "there is no point in throwing ashes on your own head!" In other words, don't be your own worst enemy, and as the idiom might be understood more readily in English, "don't dig your own grave."

SAMAYAS AND SPIRITUAL FRIENDS

After addressing the samayas with respect to the guru, Düdjom Rinpoché then turns to the second classic topic within Vajrayāna samayas—namely, how to relate to your spiritual community:

> In general, the samayas regarding your spiritual relatives and friends consist of looking charitably upon everyone who has entered the door of the Buddha's teachings and of cultivating pure perception of them. Avoid all bias and disparagement regarding philosophical schools. In particular, all those who have the same guru and are included within the same maṇḍala are vajra siblings and friends, so renounce such attitudes as contempt, competitiveness, envy, and deceitfulness, and hold them dear to your heart in mutual harmony.

When he says, "your spiritual relatives," this refers to viewing those in your sangha, or spiritual community, as being your spiritual mother and father, brothers and sisters, children, and so on. At the broadest level, these samayas include "everyone who has entered the door of the Buddha's teachings" so that you train in regarding all such individuals, wherever they may be, with warmth and affection, and even beyond that, you cultivate pure perception by looking beyond ordinary appearances to envision how you would relate directly to the purity of their buddha nature. How would you relate to every Buddhist you ever meet or hear about if you perceived that he or she was already a bodhisattva highly advanced on the path?

Further, he says to "avoid all bias and disparagement regarding philosophical schools"—be it Śrāvakayāna, Madhyamaka, Yogācāra, or Zen, and beyond that, Christianity, Islam, Judaism, Hinduism, and so forth. Simply avoid the root mental affliction of thinking one's own views and practices are supreme while disparaging those of others. Recognize instead how the diversity of Dharma teachings can be of enormous benefit to sentient beings with very different inclinations and propensities, whether they fall within the explicit range of the Buddha Śākyamuni's teachings or outside it.

Then, focusing on a specific category of our spiritual family, Düdjom Rinpoché explains the meaning of our "vajra siblings and friends"—namely, "all those who have the same guru and are included within the same maṇḍala." Those who are "within the same maṇḍala" refers to those who have received empowerment from the same guru at the same time, or at least have received empowerment within the same maṇḍala—such as that of the Lake-Born Vajra, Guhyasamāja, Cakrasaṃvara, and so on—and with whom you thereafter have a strong karmic connection. They are all your "vajra siblings and friends, so renounce such attitudes as contempt, competitiveness, envy, and deceitfulness, and hold them dear to your heart in mutual harmony."

We are taught to cultivate a pure perception of spiritual family at the broadest level and view them charitably, never with contempt. This, of course, echoes what the Buddha taught with respect to all sentient beings in his discourse on loving-kindness, the *Karaṇīya Mettā Sutta*: "Let no one deceive another nor despise any person anywhere. In anger or ill will let no one wish any harm to another. Just as a mother would protect her only child even at the risk of her own life, even so let one cultivate a boundless heart toward all beings."[2] Hold no one in contempt or in disdain, ever, no matter what they've done, no matter how vile their behavior, no matter how toxic their mental afflictions. In this way, never look down on anyone, but instead maintain the awareness that in previous lifetimes (and possibly in this current lifetime), you have certainly engaged in similar nonvirtuous actions. If you try to fathom countless previous lifetimes, you realize that there is probably no evil that you have never committed. Although right now, perhaps you cannot even imagine engaging in such horrendous behavior, recognize that this is due to the blessings of your gurus, the Dharma, and your spiritual friends. See that you are subject to all of the same mental afflictions as those who engage in harmful actions of body, speech, and mind—these mental afflictions are simply waiting to be catalyzed so that deceit, contempt, hatred, violence, and so on can be aroused.

Yet, how do you actually maintain pure perception of someone when their behavior is clearly not pure? This needs a lot of wisdom. What do you do when you observe someone who is a spiritual friend, maybe a vajra sibling, and you see that on occasion, their behavior is really incompatible with Dharma? Clearly, we can avoid contempt and instead feel compassion, empathy, caring, generosity, warmth, kindness. It doesn't have to be competitive or envious or deceitful, certainly not disdainful or contemptuous, but how do we maintain pure perception in that situation? This is certainly *not* an invitation to neglect, discount, or minimize despicable behavior, whether on the part of the guru, your vajra siblings, or anybody else. Compassion should never be enabling of nonvirtuous behaviors. You have intelligence, and you are never asked to sacrifice it on the altar of "pure perception" whether in guru yoga or in Vajrayāna practice in general. To do so would be a violation of Dharma.

There is a balance between cultivating pure perception of your vajra siblings and being a true spiritual friend to them. Friends correct each other's behavior, or at least bring it to their attention, when they see it to be erroneous, misguided, or harmful. On some occasions, however, we may discover there was a justifiable reason for what had looked like misbehavior from the outside. So, listen with an open mind, but know that it is never permissible for anyone—neither the guru nor vajra siblings nor anyone else—to engage in unethical conduct.

One of the tutors of the Tenth Dalai Lama, a Gelukpa geshé known as Tsenshab Tsewang Samdrup (late eighteenth to early nineteenth century), wrote an explanation of the bodhisattva vow called *A Shining Garland of Jewels: Training in the Three Sets of Vows*,[3] including the eighteen root downfalls and forty-six misdeeds with respect to the bodhisattva vow in the lineage of Jowo Atiśa, following Nāgārjuna, Asaṅga, and Śāntideva. Training in the subtleties of avoiding the root downfalls and misdeeds against the bodhisattva vow provides clear guidelines for practice in relation to oneself and to all others, once one has committed oneself to the path for becoming a bodhisattva. Among the forty-six misdeeds within the bodhisattva vows, the sixteenth reads as follows: "In response to someone's physical or verbal misconduct, if one sees that one is able to forcefully correct them, but one fails to do so in order to maintain their good opinion of oneself, that is the misdeed of not correcting others despite their mental afflictions."[4] In other words, if you see that someone is acting improperly, it is a misdeed if you do not confront them about it for fear of how they might react.

Similarly, the thirty-eighth of those forty-six misdeeds says, "If there is someone who is engaging in conduct that would be detrimental to them in this and future lives, but out of anger or laziness one does not rationally show them how they can abstain from such vices, that is the misdeed of not rationally showing such conduct to be unconscientious."[5] That is, if someone is engaging in misconduct but you do not want to show them how they can abstain from such vices simply because, out of hatred or aversion, you do not want to deal with them, or, out of laziness, do not feel like concerning yourself with them, then this, too, is a misdeed.

By failing to correct someone's conduct for fear of hurting the other person's feelings, not wanting them to think badly of you, wanting to remain friends with them, not liking them, being lazy, and so on, you have then committed at least one of these forty-six misdeeds. You have a moral obligation to uphold the bodhisattva vows, and it is these vows that will support you in following the path to its culmination.

Use your intelligence wisely to discern ethical conduct from misconduct when you observe that a spiritual friend or vajra sibling is behaving in a way that seems incompatible with Dharma. Instead of feeling contempt, you can nurture compassion, empathy, care, generosity, warmth, loving-kindness, and an abundance of other ways to "hold them dear to your heart in mutual harmony," as Düdjom Rinpoché says.

This one paragraph contains his pith instructions that summarize samayas toward your spiritual friends and family, your sangha.

SAMAYAS AND SENTIENT BEINGS

Düdjom Rinpoché first gave guidance on how to keep and maintain samayas with respect to the guru, then to Dharma friends, and now he completes this triad by providing guidance on how to uphold samayas regarding all sentient beings in general. He says,

> Consider, "All sentient beings, without exception, have been our kind parents. How sad that they are tormented by the terrible miseries of endless samsara! If I do not protect them, who will?" Unable to bear this thought, train your mind in the cultivation of compassion. By means of your body, speech, and mind, make whatever efforts you can to do only that which is beneficial, and dedicate all your virtue for the benefit of others.

Here, Düdjom Rinpoché exhorts us to consider the fact that all sentient beings have been our kind parents in previous lifetimes. Feeling the sadness that "they are tormented by the terrible miseries of endless samsara" and being "unable to bear this thought, train your mind in the cultivation of compassion" so that you can rise up to protect them from further suffering. This guides us into a particular form of compassion, known as "unbearable compassion," which is the visceral experience of not being able to bear the thought of others' suffering. This unbearable compassion arises especially for those who have never heard a word of authentic Dharma and instead are bound by the eight worldly dharmas, or the eight mundane concerns, which simply perpetuate their cycles of birth, aging, sickness, and death.

The eight mundane concerns are the only ones most people will ever know in this lifetime. Once again, these eight consist of attachment to gain and aversion to loss, attachment to hedonic pleasure and aversion to samsaric discomfort, attachment to praise and aversion to being rebuked, and attachment to having a good reputation and aversion to having a bad reputation. These are all rooted firmly in the three poisons of attachment, hatred, and delusion. Insofar as these eight are your primary concerns and therefore form the lens through which all of your actions and concerns are filtered, there will never be a way out of samsara. Seeing how blinding, smothering, and wrought with suffering your obsession with these concerns becomes for you personally, can you bear the thought of others being tormented endlessly by these poisons and the mundane concerns they perpetuate?

Consider how different your life would be if you had never heard even a word of authentic Dharma. From this place of immense compassion, commit yourself to protecting others from the seeds of suffering—if you don't, then who will? Regarding anyone with whom you come into contact, know that you have some kind of karmic relationship with them—the cashier in the grocery store, the plumber who fixes your toilet, the person with whom you exchange smiles on the street, and so on. Cultivate unbearable compassion for them—a compassion that finds others' suffering at least as unbearable as you find your own. Moreover, recognize that their suffering is far greater than yours, since they have no genuine Dharma in which to take refuge from the perils of samsara. So, "By means of your body, speech, and mind, make whatever efforts you can to do only that which is beneficial, and dedicate all your virtue for the benefit of others."

REFINING YOUR CONDUCT FOR ADVANCED PRACTICE

Düdjom Rinpoché then encapsulates the pith instructions for a life devoted to Dharma:

At all times there are only three things to think about: the Dharma, the guru, and sentient beings. So do not let your intentions and actions deviate from those. Do not compete with those who bear the trappings and titles of realized adepts and monks. Rather, keep your mouth shut and control your own mind. This is of utmost importance, so don't be a fool.

If you fundamentally think of your own welfare solely in terms of future lifetimes, then you have good reason for the imperative to practice what we call "Dharma." But if you place your hopes in the roots of virtue that others may perform on your behalf after you are dead, it will be difficult to derive any benefit from them.

That is, do not let your intentions and actions deviate from serving the Dharma, the guru, and sentient beings. There is a lot of good advice and bad advice out there—from friends, relatives, therapists, and so on. However, almost all of it expires at the end of this lifetime. By contrast, the holy Dharma offers advice, counsel, and guidance that is truly of benefit in this and all future lifetimes and that actually leads to the path to be released from samsara and to achieve perfect awakening. All other advice pales in comparison.

"But if you place your hopes in the roots of virtue that others may perform on your behalf after you are dead, it will be difficult to derive any benefit from them." If, for your own welfare, you are depending not on your own practice but on the prayers and virtues performed by your lamas and Dharma friends after you die, then even their prayers will be of little use, because your own karma and habitual propensities are the primary factors that drive you through the experience of the intermediate period into your next lifetime.

Düdjom Rinpoché continues,

So turn your mind within, keep it there, and with a heartfelt spirit of emergence, hold your ground by applying mindfulness, determination, and strong enthusiasm to saturate your entire life with spiritual practice. Strike the crucial points of the main practice of the profound view and meditation; between formal meditation sessions, keep your [Vajrayāna] samayas, [bodhisattva] training, and [Śrāvakayāna] vows; and don't behave in any way that is contrary to what should and should not be done according to your vows. As a result, virtuous qualities will inevitably arise from within, for the Great Perfection is a path that will forcefully bring to enlightenment even those who have committed very evil deeds.

When he says "with a heartfelt spirit of emergence," this is the aspiration to emerge from samsara and toward nirvana with a definite conviction to do so. With this heartfelt spirit, "hold your ground by applying mindfulness, determination, and strong enthusiasm to saturate your entire life with spiritual practice." In other words, give up all attachment to this life and let your mind become Dharma. This means that there is no separation between the everyday occurrences of your life and the Dharma—your mind transforms everything it encounters into Dharma, without discrimination. In this way, everything you encounter in life serves you on the path to your own perfect awakening for the benefit of all.

With regard to Düdjom Rinpoché's next counsel, on how to strike the crucial points of view and meditation during the main practice and how to keep one's ethical training continuously between sessions, bear in mind that all these vows—Vajrayāna samayas, bodhisattva training, and Śrāvakayāna vows—serve to protect you. Just as when you go to a doctor and receive medical treatment and advice regarding your nutrition and lifestyle, this is all intended to help you heal. Samayas and vows are the same—they are there to protect you.

As a result of acting in accordance with your vows, "virtuous qualities will inevitably arise from within, for the Great Perfection is a path that will forcefully bring to enlightenment even those who have committed very evil deeds." You should not think that the terrible misdeeds from your past will deem you unworthy of practicing Dzogchen. Rather, especially for those who recognize they have done regrettable things in this life and in countless past lifetimes, "the Great Perfection is a path that will forcefully bring [you] to enlightenment." Holding this closely in your heart, it is crucial not to let your present be captive to the past.

How to Practice with Upheavals

Düdjom Rinpoché continues,

By the power of the extraordinary profundity of the Great Perfection, there will also be obstacles, just as great profit often

comes with great risk. This is because all the negative karma you
have accumulated in the past is catalyzed due to the potency
of these practical instructions, and this manifests externally as
the upheavals of demonic interferences and apparitions.

This is another crucial point. "Upheavals" are a very significant issue in
this profound path of Dzogchen, and for those who have already devoted
months or years to the intensive practice of śamatha, you already know
firsthand that Düdjom Rinpoché is speaking the truth here. You know
that unexpected and sometimes strange events arise environmentally, phys-
ically, and psychologically. Karma is stirred up. Outer, inner, and secret
upheavals—those pertaining to the environment, your physical body, and
your mind, respectively—are aroused because you are practicing authentically. Get used to that; it is a reality of this path. It doesn't necessarily
mean you are doing anything wrong or that your practice is misguided.
It may be that you are practicing incorrectly, in which case you check for
yourself, possibly ask your guru, and then if it becomes clear that there are
problems in your practice, correct them. But the point is that when you set
out on this path of the Great Perfection, it is so powerful that to progress
along this path, you will need to purify negative karma from past lives, let
alone from this lifetime. And this can catalyze a lot of difficulties, to put
it mildly.

The way to respond is to follow the teachings from Dodrupchen Rinpoché Jigmé Tenpé Nyima (1865–1926), Düdjom Lingpa's eldest son, in his
mind training titled *Transforming Felicity and Adversity into the Spiritual
Path*:

> In order not only to prevent all unfavorable circumstances and
> adversity from afflicting your mind but to cause them to elicit
> a sense of mental well-being—with respect to illness inside
> and with respect to enemies, demons, vicious gossip, and so on
> outside—you should put a stop to the appearance of their being
> something unwanted. Rather, train so that everything arises
> solely as something appealing to the mind. For that to happen,
> you should stop seeing those harmful situations as something
> wrong but give all your effort to the practice of seeing them as
> valuable. For, whether a situation is agreeable or not comes down
> to the way it is apprehended by the mind.[6]

Dodrupchen Rinpoché also advises us to anticipate whatever may arise with the forceful decision, "'From now on, whatever kind of adversity arises, I shall not quail.' In this way practice cultivating great courage."

So, do not lose heart, but recognize you are taking on a challenge that is truly awesome, that hardly anyone on the planet even has the opportunity to undertake. The opportunity to receive teachings like this from an authentic lineage and to have the leisure, confidence, and aspiration to put the teachings into practice is extremely rare. With this kind of commitment to such a superbly profound path, purification will take place in the form of upheavals being catalyzed. Be prepared that not all upheavals will be pleasant, for you do not purify past negative deeds just by having a really lovely time in retreat and a whole lot of wonderful meditative experiences. Negative karma is purified only by the arising of adversities—environmental, physical, and psychological—and you must recognize that that is the way it is. No one is punishing you—the buddhas never punish. But this purification of negative karma from within is necessary in order for you to progress along this path.

Some of these upheavals may be chronic, lasting for years; this simply means that there is a lot of karmic cleanup that needs to be done. The way to clean up the messes of your past—in this lifetime and past lifetimes—is by applying all the Dharma you have ever learned. Above all, do not appropriate or identify with the mental afflictions that arise around it. Do not cringe before adversities, but be of good cheer, be courageous, and apply all the Dharma you know. Whether it is awful things happening to you from outside, whether it is physical illness, or whether it manifests as inexplicable psychological upheavals, you have only one task: to continue practicing Dharma. And by so doing, whether these upheavals last for a day or a year or twenty, thirty, forty, fifty years, it is the purification of karma. It has to be purified, and the best way to purify it is to continue practicing and transforming it.

Of course, if you need to seek medical help for physical ailments or psychological guidance for mental traumas or challenges, then do not neglect this need: you can still practice Dharma while receiving all forms of care. Nevertheless, for everything else that arises as an upheaval, by practicing in the aforementioned ways, you come to recognize that no matter how long upheavals last, this purification of negative karma is a necessity in order to proceed toward and on the path.

In reliance upon refuge, bodhicitta, and guru yoga, the best way to purify your obscurations is to continue practicing and transforming everything that arises—both adversities and felicities—into the path to awakening. This is why lojong, or mind training, is the foundation of Vajrayāna and specifically Dzogchen practice. It is where real transformation occurs. Then, on the basis of that lojong, there is the perfection of lojong in Dzogchen, which you may recall is the transcendence of lojong. This means that you are no longer striving to train, purify, or transform your mind. This transcendence of mind training occurs because you have become so familiar with resting in pristine awareness that you simply observe all upheavals arise and release of their own accord, without any modification or interference from your mind. You do not need to wait to achieve such a state of perfection in order to begin to practice in this way.

Düdjom Rinpoché continues,

> **In the place where you practice, gods and demons may show their forms, call you by name, and take on the guise of your guru and make prophecies. Various terrifying apparitions may appear as meditative experiences or in your dreams, and it is possible that you may in fact be subject to beatings at the hands of others, theft, illness, and so on. All of these can arise in indeterminate ways.**

You may actually see these appearances as gods and demons or they may appear in a more familiar form, such as the form of your guru or someone else making prophecies. There may also be physical, outer upheavals such as being beaten, robbed, becoming ill, and so on. In such intensive, powerful practices as Düdjom Rinpoché has taught in this text, bear in mind that if the strength of your mind wanes because you are feeling overwhelmed by upheavals arising, and you thus fall into the habit of appropriating or identifying with the upheavals—thereby reifying them as being inherently real and succumbing to them with craving and aversion, hope and fear—then you are perpetuating your own samsara. So, it would be a tragedy if you enter into Dzogchen and then, as a result of the way you are responding to upheavals, instead of approaching the Great Perfection, you are simply continuing the ongoing cycle that you have experienced in countless previous lifetimes. Conversely, if you can maintain the continuity of your practice in the perfection of lojong and eventually the transcendence of lojong, then exactly these various experiences that you could ever so easily have seen as obstacles can actually empower you on the path and lead to the realization of siddhis.

Elaborating on a similar point, in *The Vajra Essence*, the Lake-Born Vajra proclaims, "Some teachers gain confidence in a relaxed, soothing state of bliss, telling others that this is the culmination of the view and meditation— and they get stuck there." That is, some have been practicing because they want to find bliss, and once they do so, they then regard it as the pinnacle of Dzogchen, the Great Perfection that is the unborn, unconditioned bliss of pristine awareness. But because they become attached to such bliss, still veiled by ignorance, they grasp to it and become stuck in a meditation whose result will never transcend samsara.

The Lake-Born Vajra continues, "Other teachers have an experience of luminosity in which visions of gods and demons arise, they gain confidence in a steady vividness of mindsets and appearances, and they teach this to others." For some, as they go deeper into such practice, they start experiencing a variety of visions that they regard as sacred. Encountering beings they regard as ultimate refuges and receiving guidance they regard as coming from ultimate authorities, they then reify these as being supreme. As they teach these things to others in this obscured way, unfortunately all they are teaching others is how to perpetuate their own samsara.

Moreover, "Some gain confidence in a clear, nonconceptual sense of vacuity, devoid of mindfulness of any movement, in which appearances are impeded, and they teach this to others." In these three steps, we see reification of the three qualities—bliss, luminosity, and nonconceptuality—that manifest incrementally, and then quite wondrously when you fully achieve śamatha, so that it becomes ever so easy to think "This is it." You may think the bliss, the luminosity, and the nonconceptuality are so extraordinary that they must be attributes of nirvana or rigpa—"This must be the Great Perfection!" However, if you cling to any of these three qualities, then you are turning your back on nirvana and simply perpetuating samsara.

The Lake-Born Vajra continues, warning that "others gain confidence in an unimpeded, unstructured state of consciousness and present this to others as the culmination of the view and meditation." This may occur, for example, in the practice of open presence. Perhaps due to ignorance or insufficient knowledge about the significance and role of śamatha and how the substrate consciousness manifests, some people may be introduced to the Dzogchen view, and, striving to sustain that view, they may encounter what they feel to be an unstructured state of consciousness. But most likely, it is the substrate consciousness—unstructured as a human mind, quasi-melted, but not the full melt of pristine awareness. Not knowing better, they may latch onto that, mistaking the substrate consciousness for pristine awareness. Over the centuries, lamas from multiple traditions of Tibetan Buddhism have all affirmed that it is very common for people to mistake this subtle continuum of consciousness—the subtle mind, or the substrate consciousness—for a realization of emptiness or of rigpa itself. But the Lake-Born Vajra states, "Those who identify the view and meditation in such ways do not rise above the three realms, for they have not realized the view of emptiness." In other words, they are stuck in a state where they still need to probe directly into *that which is experiencing* the bliss, luminosity, and nonconceptuality, into *that which is experiencing* the unimpeded, unstructured consciousness, and thus realize its emptiness of inherent nature, cutting through the very parameters and conceptual extremes of existence and nonexistence. Without doing so, they are merely perpetuating samsara: "They are imprisoned by that failing, and consequently they do not see the path to liberation and omniscience."[7]

His Holiness the Dalai Lama said that the role of the guru is to save you a lot of time, and recognizing the point explained here could certainly save you countless lifetimes. That is, if in this lifetime you latch on to any of these qualities of the substrate and regard them as ultimate, you will die an ordinary death. The clear light of death will actually manifest, yet you won't be able to recognize it—because during your lifetime, you thought you had already recognized the clear light. But it was only the substrate, and you had reinforced your habitual grasping to it by meditating there, with grasping, for a long time in this life. In that case, you would still be cast unknowingly into the bardo—transitioning from the unknowing state of the substrate to the brief but unrecognized appearance of the clear light and then into the bewilderment of the ensuing transitional phases.

You may not yet fully believe this now, but when your time comes, the truth of the continuity of consciousness after death will become all too apparent, and then you won't *believe* in the hereafter, you will *know* it. But if you only realize this at that point, it will be too late to do you much good.

According to advanced contemplatives who have passed lucidly through the dying process, the intermediate period and then their next rebirth, there is indeed a "lights out" phase at the culmination of the dying process. It occurs when, from the dying person's perspective, all appearances and mental processes have ceased, and one rests in the oblivion of the substrate, a blank vacuity. For a little while, you do unconsciously "rest in peace." But the trouble with being "dead" is that it doesn't last more than three days.[8] Then the clear light of death breaks through that darkness. If you have already identified the "path pristine awareness" while you were living, then when the "ground pristine awareness" manifests at the end of the dying process, you may dwell in this sublime samādhi, known in Tibetan as *tukdam*, for days or even weeks on end, during which your body is clinically dead but does not begin to decompose. This has been witnessed many times in the recent past, in the East and West, including occasions when realized lamas demonstrate tukdam when they die in hospitals, leaving their physicians utterly mystified at this phenomenon, which is completely inexplicable in terms of the current biomedical view of death.

If you have not identified pristine awareness, however, then this spontaneous manifestation of the ground clear light will last no longer than it takes to eat a bowl of food.[9] So this once-each-lifetime opportunity will have been missed yet again. Then you will be thrown into the wild ride of a series of disturbing, bizarre, and sometimes terrifying appearances as you transition from this life to the next. From there, who knows when you will ever encounter authentic transmissions, teachings, and guidance on Dzogchen again? So, to say that a qualified guru can save you a lot of time is something of an understatement.

If, on the other hand, you have achieved śamatha and *know* that this is all you have achieved, while you have not yet identified pristine awareness or been able to rest there, the achievement of śamatha alone can indeed be extremely beneficial at the time of death. Since you have not grasped to the experience of the substrate and substrate consciousness in the wrong way—as being something that it is not—then your familiarity with the substrate can enable you to remain lucid as you pass into the dying process, thus extending the time you remain in the "dark near-attainment" phase of resting in the substrate alone. Then, whether or not you actually recognize the clear light, you still have much better chances of remaining lucid through the ensuing phases of the transitional phase of the actual nature of reality and the transitional phase of becoming, and thus having the ability to put into practice pith instructions that you had received on the transitional phases while you were still alive.

Continuing with Düdjom Rinpoché's text, he warns,

> Psychologically, you may inexplicably experience intense misery and sadness that will make you want to weep. You may experience strong mental afflictions, and your sense of admiration and reverence, bodhicitta, and compassion may decline. Thoughts may arise as your enemies, nearly driving you mad. You may misinterpret words intended to help you, and losing the desire to remain in retreat, you may consider abandoning your solemn commitment. You may experience false views regarding your guru, doubts about the Dharma, and so on. In addition, you may suffer false accusations and a bad reputation, your friends may arise as enemies, and so forth. Various outer and inner undesirable circumstances may well emerge.

Amid your authentic practice, the welling up of secret upheavals such as grief, misery, and sadness may arise. When you are not only practicing śamatha but actually cut through to pristine awareness, this is going to dredge not only your psyche but the whole of your samsara from its depths. Therefore, whatever mental afflictions have not yet shown their face in this lifetime will inevitably be excavated from the deepest trenches of your mind. Further, the intensity of these mental afflictions may cause "your sense of admiration and reverence, bodhicitta, and compassion" to degrade and feel undermined or even worthless. At this point, you may really feel that all is lost, as though you are an utter failure. Then in the thick of that despair, "thoughts may arise as your enemies, nearly driving you mad. You may misinterpret words intended to help you." This may occur as words from your guru that were not really what you wanted to hear, and you think you know better. You may doubt whether your guru's words are emerging from that very deep wellspring of wisdom and compassion. As you follow your ruminations rather than your guru's guidance, you may lose "the desire to remain in retreat" and "consider abandoning your solemn commitment" to full-time practice. This has happened in the past, and it happens nowadays. There is a reason Düdjom Rinpoché is telling us this in advance, so we will recognize them simply as upheavals when such thoughts seem so convincing during our darkest times in retreat.

Further, "You may experience false views regarding your guru, doubts about the Dharma, and so on. In addition, you may suffer false accusations and a bad reputation, your friends may arise as enemies, and so forth. Various outer and inner undesirable circumstances may well emerge." This is where the object of your refuge is vital. If you are still taking refuge in your guru as a human being, that is pretty fragile because sometimes that human being will not live up to your expectations or will give guidance you do not want to hear. If you are looking upon a human being as a buddha, this is delusional. Your time of deepest crisis is precisely when you need to recognize the true nature of your ultimate refuge. As you drop the anchor of taking refuge all the way down to the ground of Samantabhadra—manifesting as Amitābha, Avalokiteśvara, Tārā, Guru Padmasambhava, Düdjom Lingpa, Düdjom Rinpoché, your own guru or gurus, and countless other beings—then that refuge will carry you through the most formidable of circumstances. You will hold fast, even when the howling winds of samsara seem to imperil you and threaten to drown you in its ocean.

Düdjom Rinpoché offers our lifeline at such times:

> Oh, these are all indications of upheavals, so recognize them! Here is the demarcation between profit and loss: If you embrace those obstacles by means of the crucial points of practice, they will turn into siddhis. If you fall under their influence, they will become hindrances. With pure samayas, admiration, reverence, and unfaltering courage, entrust your heart and mind to your guru, and earnestly pray to him with confidence in whatever he may do. By taking unfavorable circumstances as something desirable, and by striving diligently in your practice, eventually the substantiality of those circumstances will naturally dissolve, and they will instead empower your practice.

When he writes, "If you embrace those obstacles by means of the crucial points of practice, they will turn into siddhis," this again points to the enormous capacity of Dzogchen practice alone to be the ultimate lojong, or the transcendence of mind training. But without having a deep foundation in classical lojong—such as Atiśa's *Seven-Point Mind Training* and Dodrupchen's *Transforming Felicity and Adversity into the Spiritual Path*—whereby you are learning from moment to moment how to transform everything that happens to you into the path, and instead you try to skip over this and go directly to the transcendence of lojong in Dzogchen, you may find it very difficult. That is, if you are not actually able to view circumstances from the perspective of pristine awareness realizing emptiness, you may get knocked off your horse over and over again, as it were. So the proactively transformative practices of lojong may be in order—to correct mentally afflicted states of mind. But even resting in the stillness of conditioned awareness, while not reifying conditions as really having the positive or negative qualities they appear to have, may be enough to release many upheavals, especially the secret, or psychological, ones.

If you can remain unwavering in your dedication to practice, these upheavals may turn into siddhis, but "if you fall under their influence, they will become hindrances. With pure samayas, admiration, reverence, and unfaltering courage, entrust your heart and mind to your guru, and earnestly pray to him [or her] with confidence in whatever he [or she] may do." Authentic guru yoga is so difficult and yet so crucial, any cheaper imitation may be counterproductive altogether. But with authentic guru yoga, you can trust that you will emerge all the stronger from even the most formidable of upheavals.

To the transformative point of lojong, Düdjom Rinpoché writes, "By taking unfavorable circumstances as something desirable, and by striving diligently in your practice, eventually the substantiality of those circumstances will naturally dissolve, and they will instead empower your practice." You are becoming lucid with respect to unfavorable circumstances, and if you are not seeing them as objectively or inherently real but are instead viewing them as being like an illusion or a dream, then the situation itself will empower your practice.

MAKE YOUR MIND STRONG

Düdjom Rinpoché continues,

> Appearances will fade like mist, you will have even greater confidence in your guru and his practical instructions than you did before, and from now on you will find the fortitude to accept such upheavals with equanimity. Oh, this indicates that they are coming to an end, for by transforming such circumstances into the path, conditions for their termination are brought about. *A la la*, that is what we old fathers want! Don't behave like a fox sneaking up to a human corpse, with its haunches trembling in fear even as it longs to devour it. Make your mind strong.

In *The Seven-Point Mind Training*, one of the criteria to determine whether the practice is really working is that you are able to maintain an ongoing sense of well-being. You are not upset or fragile amid the myriad faces of felicity and adversity but are instead strong and steady like a great river. When you can maintain such equanimity, equipoise, and imperturbability through all the vicissitudes that your karma is dredging up for you, this is a sign of being a true, experienced practitioner. Again, remember that no one is doing this to you: all these appearances are your own appearances, being catalyzed from within. When you come to that kind of sustainable equanimity in the face of every kind of upheaval, "Oh, this indicates that they are coming to an end." The trials and tribulations are coming to an end because you have succeeded in practicing purely through them, "for by transforming such circumstances into the path, conditions for their termination are brought about." There is no end to samsara as long as you are perpetuating it, but there is an end to these outer, inner, and secret upheavals if and only if you become skillful in transmuting them into the path through the Sūtrayāna practices of lojong and then, ultimately, through Dzogchen by allowing them to arise and release themselves. Because you have not responded with the habitual influences of ignorance and the mental afflictions, conditions for the termination of the cycle of samsara itself are brought about. So, "Don't behave like a fox sneaking up to a human corpse, with its haunches trembling in fear even as it longs to devour it. Make your mind strong."

Conversely,

> Those with little merit, lax samayas and vows, flagrant false views, and a host of doubts, who make big commitments but whose practice is weak—such people, whose hearts stink like farts—request their guru's practical instructions only to leave them on their bookshelves. By fixating with a death grip on unfavorable conditions and then ruminating on them, they are easily snared by māras who lead them on the path to miserable states of existence. How very sad! Pray to your guru that this doesn't happen.

It may be easy to point your finger outward to all the other people you know who might fall victim to these flaws even while you fail to recognize these shortcomings in yourself. So examine yourself honestly and recognize such flaws within yourself again and again, with the resolve and determination to overcome them.

He continues, "By fixating with a death grip on unfavorable conditions and then ruminating on them, they are easily snared by māras who lead them on the path to miserable states of existence. How very sad! Pray to your guru that this doesn't happen." This is where blessings can arise vividly and indisputably for us. Sheer effort, aspiration, diligence, and discipline can only take us so far, and there is a point where we simply need to be uplifted on waves of blessings, especially to protect us from the assaults of māras that appear to us in disguise as "perfectly reasonable" doubts and spiritual laziness.

> Moreover, although it may be relatively easy for unfavorable circumstances to arise as the path, it is very difficult for favorable conditions to do so. Therefore, if those who pride themselves on their supposedly high level of realization devote themselves solely to achieving high status in this life, they are in danger of becoming servants of the māra of distraction, Devaputra. So you must be very careful. Understand that this is the test that determines the demarcation between meditators who go up or go down. Until the power of the qualities from your inner realizations is perfected, it is inappropriate to tell just anyone indiscriminately about your meditative experiences, so keep quiet. Furthermore, without boasting about how many months or years you have spent in retreat, devote yourself to practice for your whole life. Do not deceive yourself with your talk about emptiness, such that you dismiss the importance of virtuous deeds within the obscurative reality of cause and effect.

When Düdjom Rinpoché writes, "Moreover, although it may be relatively easy for unfavorable circumstances to arise as the path, it is very difficult for favorable conditions to do so," this means that when everything is agreeable, it is easy to be complacent and lose the determination to transform such felicity into the path. But, failing to transform favorable circumstances into the path, "if those who pride themselves on their supposedly high level of realization devote themselves solely to achieving high status in this life, they are in danger of becoming servants of the māra of distraction, Devaputra." This is one of the many ways to go astray, and thus lose one's way on the path.

This is especially so if you are starting to flourish in the practice and are reaping the benefits of authentic practice. Amid the experience of virtues, insights, or perhaps even realizations arising, the mind leaps into self-aggrandizement—for example, "*I* will be admired by many people, *I* will become renowned, people will respect me, worship me, and revere me." Practice then becomes shackled by pride and you thus become a servant of Devaputra, who is one of the four classic māras.[10] Devaputra specifically personifies the forces of lust and envy that become direct obstacles to virtue by distracting one to the objects of the desire realm.

Düdjom Rinpoché counsels that "you must be very careful. Understand that this is the test that determines the demarcation between meditators who go up or go down." It is a great fork in the road where you choose between the māra of pride and competitiveness, which will plummet you deeper into samsara, or the abolition of such delusion, which will manifest as utter humility dawning from realization. It is the latter that leads you toward the true pinnacle of the Great Perfection. Often you will see in some of the most accomplished contemplatives of modern times, both Buddhists and non-Buddhists, that the greater the realization and majesty of their accomplishments, the humbler they are. In sum, "Until the power of the qualities from your inner realizations is perfected, it is inappropriate to tell just anyone indiscriminately about your meditative experiences, so keep quiet."

Düdjom Rinpoché continues, "Furthermore, without boasting about how many months or years you have spent in retreat, devote yourself to practice for your whole life." It is crucially important not to measure your achievement or spiritual maturity simply by how long you have been in retreat, for not only can the quality of practice in retreat vary greatly, but there is no certainty as to how quickly one or another practitioner will progress in purifying his or her mind, much less gaining stability and realization. So do not fall prey to thinking either, "I've been in retreat for so long, why haven't I achieved more by now?" or "I've been in retreat for so long, I must really be special by now!"

Then, Düdjom Rinpoché repeats one of the direst warnings given by Dzogchen masters in particular: "Do not deceive yourself with your talk about emptiness, such that you dismiss the importance of virtuous deeds within the obscurative reality of cause and effect." Given the themes of transcending duality through the realization of rigpa, it is perhaps easy to get a taste of this nondual state and then mistakenly think that your own realization is so high that you now do not need to worry about the details of karmic cause and effect, or the distinctions of good and evil, because you may wrongly think your behaviors are arising purely from pristine awareness and are therefore all spontaneous, enlightened activities. But in this way, you just dig yourself deeper into the pit of samsara. As cannot be repeated too often, although phenomena are conceptually designated and are empty of inherent existence, this does *not* mean they do not have causal efficacy. Therefore, it is essential to engage in "virtuous deeds within the obscurative reality of cause and effect."

He continues,

> Do not linger in populated places for the sake of getting supplies by means of performing village rituals for subduing demons and so on. Keep pointless activities, unnecessary talking, and worthless thoughts to a minimum. Do not deceive others with what is incompatible with Dharma, such as pretense and guile. Do not engage in wrong livelihood by making indirect requests, flattery, and so on out of craving for desirable things. Do not associate with those whose views and conduct are incompatible with your own or with evil friends. Disclose your own faults, and do not speak of the hidden faults of others. All kinds of smoking are said to be tricks of demons that cause you to break your samayas, so earnestly avoid them. Although alcohol is to be relied upon as a samaya substance, do not carelessly drink it to the point of intoxication. Without discriminating, bring everyone along the path—including those with whom you have good and bad relations, those who faithfully serve you as well as those who distrust you, revile you, and treat you badly—and look after them with pure prayers.

Regarding the point, "Do not linger in populated places for the sake of getting supplies by means of performing village rituals for subduing demons and so on," it is quite common in Tibet for individuals to go into a village and market themselves for the sake of acquiring food or supplies, saying, for example, that they can perform exorcisms, subdue demons, and so forth.

Düdjom Rinpoché warns his disciples not to get involved in such things. But what would that look like in today's society? Are there ways one could become immersed in "marketing Dharma" and thus lose interest in a life of solitude and single-pointed practice?

Moreover, "Keep pointless activities, unnecessary talking, and worthless thoughts to a minimum." This describes a whole way of life. Regardless of how many hours per day you are actually in formal meditation, is your formal practice couched in a way of life that is saturated in the discipline and discretion of Dharma? In other words, is your conduct between sessions rising to meet the authentic Dzogchen view and meditation? In this section, Düdjom Rinpoché offers classic guidelines to ensure that your way of life does not undermine the hours you spend in formal practice.

He counsels, "Do not deceive others with what is incompatible with Dharma, such as pretense and guile. Do not engage in wrong livelihood by making indirect requests, flattery, and so on out of craving for desirable things. Do not associate with those whose views and conduct are incompatible with your own or with evil friends." When he says, "do not associate," this means not to fall under the influence of others' views and conduct if they are incompatible with or contrary to the Dharma that you are seeking to practice. Bear in mind how few people nowadays have any knowledge, appreciation, or faith in the view and conduct of Dzogchen. This refers to most people around you, including, in many cases, family members and friends. Take care not to fall under their influence, even as you continue to treat them with love and affection.

He next states, "Disclose your own faults, and do not speak of the hidden faults of others." It is often easy to see the faults of others, to fixate on them, and then want to talk about them, but if you consider that all appearances are your own appearances, then at the deepest level, you are criticizing yourself. So, without concerning yourself with what others will think of you, "disclose your own faults," and, taking care not to harm others, "do not speak of the hidden faults of others."

Regarding intoxicants, he begins, "All kinds of smoking are said to be tricks of demons that cause you to break your samayas, so earnestly avoid them." This prohibition against intoxicants includes not only tobacco but also psychedelics and other substances that can alter your state of mind. In addition, "Although alcohol is to be relied upon as a samaya substance, do not carelessly drink it to the point of intoxication." The term "samaya substance" refers specifically to food and drink that are meditatively dissolved into emptiness and then transformed—by the power of samādhi—into sacred substances to be offered and partaken of specifically in the context of a Vajrayāna ritual known as the *gaṇacakra*, or in Tibetan, *tsok*. So Düdjom Rinpoché's point is that one should not think that just because it was permitted to partake of a small amount of blessed alcohol in the context of a sacred ritual that it is then okay to indulge in excessive drinking at another time. This would be relying upon alcohol as an intoxicant, which is against all principles of Buddhist ethics.

Moreover, "Without discriminating, bring everyone along the path—including those with whom you have good and bad relations, those who faithfully serve you as well as those who distrust you, revile you, and treat you badly—and look after them with pure prayers." Within this instruction is found a manifestation of immeasurable impartiality. When it comes time to practice *tonglen* (a practice of giving joy and taking away suffering, conjoined with the breath) and the four immeasurables, focus especially on those with whom you have difficult relationships—"those who distrust you, revile you, and treat you badly," and maybe even those who abuse you or have abused you. If you can wholly and genuinely arouse the heartfelt aspiration for them to be free of suffering and the causes of suffering, and the aspiration that when the time is ripe, you may lead them to such freedom, then call for blessings that you may have the capacity to do so. If you can highlight those people whom you find very difficult, then the rest of the practice will go smoothly.

REMAIN STEADFAST TO THE END

Düdjom Rinpoché continues,

> At all times, inwardly keep your spirits high, without losing heart, and outwardly keep your deeds discreet. Wear worn-out clothes. Uplift everyone: the good, bad, and middling. Live frugally and keep to mountain hermitages. Hold as your ideal the life of a beggar. Emulate the life stories of the siddhas of the past. Not blaming your past karma, practice Dharma as purely as you can. Not blaming transient circumstances, remain steadfast, no matter what happens. In short, with your own mind as your witness, unite your entire life with Dharma so that when you die, you have left nothing undone and you

are not ashamed of yourself. The crucial point of all practices consists of this.

When Düdjom Rinpoché writes, "At all times, inwardly keep your spirits high, without losing heart, and outwardly keep your deeds discreet," this means to proceed with confidence and enthusiastic perseverance, keeping your virtues concealed as much as possible so that you do not fall prey to the māras of pride.

At the same time, "Uplift everyone: the good, bad, and middling"—that is, without exception, inspire others with virtue. And when he instructs us to "keep to mountain hermitages," this refers to practicing in conducive environments, even if in our present times that means an apartment in a bustling city where you can still seclude yourself and meditate without disturbances.

Further, "Not blaming your past karma, practice Dharma as purely as you can. Not blaming transient circumstances, remain steadfast, no matter what happens." When your practice falters and you lose the continuity of formal practice, especially by reducing the time you spend in meditation each day, it is easy to have excuses and reasons for doing so that may seem very compelling—such as dealing with a difficult relationship, addressing health problems, tending to parents, children, the weather, and so on. Düdjom Rinpoché says that regardless of what occurs, steadfastly maintain continuity in practice.

It is crucial that wherever you are devoting yourself to practice, you must already be cultivating a sense of the one taste—so that even when you must engage in outer activities, you never lose the continuity of mindfulness, introspection, and the vivid awareness that you are actually practicing some form of Dharma in each moment. In this way, "with your own mind as your witness, unite your entire life with Dharma so that when you die, you have left nothing undone and you are not ashamed of yourself. The crucial point of all practices consists of this." So, live each day with the awareness that it could very well be your last. Then, when your final day in this life does come, you will be able to look back on how you have spent your days, your weeks, your years, and you will not be ashamed. You will know with confidence that you have done your very best to take full advantage of the indescribably rare and precious opportunities granted to you by encountering the path of the Great Perfection.

He continues,

> When it comes time for you to die, renounce all your worldly possessions without being attached even to a needle. In the face of death, the best practitioners feel elated, the middling have no apprehension about death, and the least experience no regret when they will die. If you experience the clear light of realization continuously, day and night, there will be no intermediate period, and only the encasing of the body will be destroyed. Otherwise, if you have confidence that you will be liberated in the intermediate period, whatever you do is fine. If you do not have such confidence, having already gained some experience in training in the transference of consciousness, perform the deed when the time comes, and transfer your consciousness to the buddhafield of your choice. There you will progress along the remaining bodhisattva grounds and paths and achieve enlightenment.

When Düdjom Rinpoché writes, "When it comes time for you to die, renounce all your worldly possessions without being attached even to a needle," this is an urging to give everything away without attachment while you are still alive and able to do so consciously. Embrace this opportunity as a last act of generosity before you die and give away everything, even down to a needle. Moreover, "In the face of death, the best practitioners feel elated, the middling have no apprehension about death, and the least experience no regret." That is a classic teaching of the *lamrim*, or the stages of the path to enlightenment, where in the face of terrible injury, illness, or death, those of great capacity who are following the bodhisattva way of life feel happy. With regard to the body of this life, they can think, "Oh, good, that one is of no use anymore, and I'm going to get a new one." Those of middling, or medium, capacity who are devoted to the achievement of their own liberation and who know they have lived immensely meaningful lives, the fruits of which will be something that is in no way dangerous or fearful, "have no apprehension about death," or more importantly, what comes after death. For those of small capacity who are at least prioritizing their well-being in future lifetimes over their well-being in this lifetime, they "experience no regret."

"If you experience the clear light of realization continuously, day and night" means that if you have reached this point in your practice—having achieved śamatha, vipaśyanā, and cut through to pristine awareness—and you are able to rest continuously in the sublime joy that is devoid of dissatisfaction or suffering, then "there will be no intermediate period, and only the encasing of the body will be destroyed." This joy is what we aspire for, both for ourselves and everyone else, in the cultivation of immeasurable empathetic joy, *muditā*. At this point, we are extremely well prepared to recognize the mother clear light during the dying process and achieve enlightenment immediately.

When he writes, "Otherwise, if you have confidence that you will be liberated in the intermediate period," the "intermediate period" refers here to the bardo of dharmatā (or the "transitional phase of the actual nature of reality"), during which liberation can take place by way of recognizing the manifestations of your own pristine awareness as the peaceful and wrathful deities. If you have that confidence, then "whatever you do is fine." However, "If you do not have such confidence," but you have already gained experience by training in the transference of consciousness, or *powa*, then you will know how to actually "perform the deed when the time comes, and transfer your consciousness to the buddhafield of your choice." That is, through the power of your prayers, aspirations, and merit—along with tremendous blessings—you are able to take birth in a pure land, such as Sukhāvatī or Guru Rinpoché's Copper-Colored Mountain. Then, once you have been born in a pure land, you will be able to "progress along the remaining bodhisattva grounds and paths" and thus achieve the complete and authentic enlightenment of a buddha.

NOT JUST ANCIENT HISTORY

> Therefore, this precious lineage of ours is not just ancient history, for even these days there are individuals who come to the highest state of realization by following the paths of cutting through and the direct crossing over, and their material bodies dissolve into a mass of rainbow light.

Thus, Düdjom Rinpoché assures us that the accounts of mahāsiddhas achieving the rainbow body are not just old stories from the past, maintained in a reverent and nostalgic lineage, but they are living accounts that have been actualized again and again, even in the present day. Achieving enlightenment by way of Dzogchen is possible here and now. There is strong evidence to support this statement, clearly indicating that individuals are still achieving rainbow body in today's world. His Holiness Penor Rinpoché (1932–2009) stated in the year 2000 that he knew with certainty that there had been at least six people who had achieved rainbow body during his lifetime.[11]

While it is also obviously true that we are living in degenerate times, we should reflect carefully on His Holiness the Dalai Lama's comment, made in the early 1970s, that if we practice as Milarepa did, we will achieve realizations like those of Milarepa. It is widely known that Dzogchen is especially powerful during the most degenerate of times. So, now is the time to put Düdjom Rinpoché's assertion to the test of experience. By putting into practice the pith instructions of this sacred text, we may ascend along the path of Dzogchen to the pinnacle of achieving rainbow body in this very lifetime. It is up to us whether we take full advantage of the opportunities before us to reach the path to enlightenment and proceed to its culmination.

> **This being the case, do not throw away this jewel and then seek some trinket. You are extremely fortunate to have encountered such profound practical instructions, which are like the heart blood of the ḍākinīs. Keep your spirits high and meditate with joy! Disciples, cherish this text as the jewel of your heart, and it is possible that great benefits will arise.**

In other words, this text is not something merely to store on your bookshelf or something you will get around to later when you are not so busy. He says, "Do not throw away this jewel and then seek some trinket." Do not discount this for gimmicks that are presented as shortcuts to "enlightenment." Fascination with novelty is all too common. We seek the excitement of new teachers, new teachings, new practices. Instead, if you steadily practice and repeatedly return to the text, then these teachings will come alive and speak to you with flawless guidance. You will hear and understand things that you never understood before because the mind you are bringing to the text is different each time—transformed by your own practice.

Düdjom Rinpoché reminds us, "You are extremely fortunate to have encountered such profound practical instructions, which are like the heart blood of the ḍākinīs." When you receive teachings of this caliber, majesty, and proven efficacy, then know that what you have received is indescribably rare and precious. It is already extremely rare to be born as a human rather than as an animal, preta, hell being, and so on, let alone to be born as a human with the full leisure and opportunity to practice Dharma. That said, along with a precious human rebirth, it is even more rare and precious to encounter the profundity of these very teachings.

With enthusiasm, Düdjom Rinpoché concludes, "Keep your spirits high and meditate with joy! Disciples, cherish this text as the jewel of your heart, and it is possible that great benefits will arise."

The colophon of the text concludes with Düdjom Rinpoché's dedication prayer and blessing upon our practice:

> With the primary cause being the mountain retreat practice of the meditators of Ogmin Pema Öling, and the contributing condition being the request of the diligent practitioner Rigzang Dorjé, who possesses the jewel of indivisible faith and reverence, this was spoken by Jigdral Yeshé Dorjé, as heartfelt and concise advice for practice. May this be a cause for the forceful emergence of the primordial consciousness of realization in the mindstreams of fortunate beings.

8. COMMENTATOR'S CONCLUSION

Tragically, we see in the news every single day how we human beings are ravaging the environment and wiping out other species as well as tremendous numbers of our own human population. There are unquestionably people who are trying to find solutions to these problems, but there is also a great momentum behind the way we are undermining our very home here on Earth. For all that is being done and considering how worthwhile and meaningful all of these activities are—utilizing sustainable energy, preserving nature and natural habitats, and so forth—it is painfully obvious that it is not enough.

As hopeless as it all may seem, we can still take great confidence in the possibility of this trajectory changing course if we look at the impact of enlightened beings in the past: Buddha Śākyamuni, Nāgārjuna, Asaṅga, Padmasambhava, Jé Tsongkhapa, His Holiness the Dalai Lama, and the Paṇchen Lamas, to name a few—not to mention the other great beings, sages, and saints who have graced the world with their wisdom and compassion.

It was prophesied to Düdjom Lingpa in a pure vision that in this lineage "one hundred male and female disciples will surely attain the rainbow body of supreme transference."[1] This has not yet happened but can occur through the practice of these very teachings. If one individual, such as Buddha Śākyamuni or Jesus Christ, could bring about such monumental transformations during their time and through ensuing millennia, when the entirety of human civilization was not imperiled, as it is now, then imagine what one hundred beings, manifesting as buddhas, could do during these most catastrophic and degenerative times. What if one hundred beings should appear and manifest the wisdom, compassion, and powers of a fully enlightened being in this century?

Together with all the other efforts, which include promoting clean energy, preserving habitats, eliminating the burning of fossil fuels, and so forth, the emergence of even one hundred fully enlightened beings could be enough to turn the tide so that we may not only survive as a species but drastically diminish the amount of suffering that takes place. Then we, as a human species, might flourish spiritually and in every way—more than ever before—if a hundred beings should achieve enlightenment and manifest the qualities of enlightenment.

We have this wish-fulfilling jewel in the palm of our hands, along with the prophecies of this lineage. If not us, then who? In the instructions contained within this profound text, coupled with our immensely precious human rebirth, we have the complete causes and conditions to actualize buddhahood in this very lifetime. Let us all practice as sincerely and enthusiastically as we can. If we do, then that will be enough.

Let us all fathom the mind, the inner resources of our own minds. In so doing, may we first heal ourselves from the very root, and then turn outward and heal the world.

Appendix 1: The Science of Dharma: Meteorology, Astronomy, and Cosmology

His Holiness the Dalai Lama has commented on many occasions that there are scientific, philosophical, and religious aspects of Buddhism, and he correlates its scientific aspects especially with the first turning of the wheel of Dharma, which is rooted in the Buddha's teachings on the four ārya realities. Likewise, ethics, samādhi, and wisdom—the core elements of the path to liberation—are scientific, as are the four close applications of mindfulness and the four immeasurables. They are deemed scientific in that the theories and practices taught in each of those contexts are rational and lend themselves to experiential confirmation. They are not based simply on logic, as is most philosophy, or on the authority of others, as "religion" is commonly understood.

The second turning of the wheel of Dharma, with its emphasis on emptiness and dependent origination—which pertain to ontology and epistemology—in turn represents the most distinctively philosophical dimension of Buddhism. However, these teachings also lend themselves to confirmation both by logic and contemplative, experimental inquiry into "the objective clear light," which is equivalent to the absolute space of phenomena, or dharmadhātu.

Finally, the third turning of the wheel of Dharma, which focuses on buddha nature, the dharmakāya, or *tathāgatagarbha*, may be deemed religious in that it appeals to our innermost intuition pertaining to the "subjective clear light," or the ultimate, actual nature of the mind. Yet these teachings too are not based on blind faith but can be tested experientially by way of the deepest forms of meditation, in which one explores the nature and potentials of consciousness. All three of these approaches are integrated directly into the practice of Dzogchen.

Even as Buddhism has become a worldwide phenomenon, often known as a "wisdom tradition," there is, of course, another tradition rooted in rational and empirical knowledge that is also global, and that is science. Therefore, His Holiness the Dalai Lama said that the encounter and engagement between Buddhism and science is extremely important because in spirit, they bear much in common. They both adhere to the premise that one should not accept something merely on blind faith, just because it is believed by many people, just because it is a long-standing tradition, or just because it is in ancient books. Rather, you must investigate and come to know things firsthand. This goes back to the Pāli canon, in which the theme, "come and see for yourself"—in Pāli, *ehi passiko*—is prevalent. Moreover, as Āryadeva points out in his *Four Hundred Stanzas*, three qualities are necessary for a person to be a "suitable vessel" for studying and practicing Buddhism: one must be unbiased, discerningly intelligent, and have the aspiration to test the teachings by putting them into practice.[1] Those same qualities are equally essential for anyone who wishes to become a scientist.

Buddhism includes within its vast scope a kind of contemplative science, in that its methods entail primarily subjective inquiry rather than the objective forms of inquiry that prevail in all branches of Western science. His Holiness the Dalai Lama has often commented that when it comes to the physical sciences, there has been tremendous progress in advancing objective knowledge about the physical universe and thus the development of technology. However, when His Holiness was recently asked what he has learned about the mind from Western science, he replied, "Nothing! For that, I rely on the Nālandā tradition." Further, on multiple occasions he has commented, "When it comes to understanding the mind, Western science is still in kindergarten."

While the physical sciences have provided an enormous amount of knowledge about the external world of space, time, matter, and energy, when it comes to the mind sciences, modern scientists have not yet made any consensual discoveries about the nature of the mind-body relationship but have attempted to obscure the fact of this ignorance by assuming, for the most part, that the mind is what the brain does. Nor have they discovered the true causes of genuine well-being or of mental suffering. They also do not know with any scientific certainty the nature of consciousness, how it originates, what are its necessary and sufficient conditions, and what happens at death, nor have they even begun to fathom the role of consciousness in the natural world. A major blockage to progress in the mind sciences has been its domination by the metaphysical beliefs and limited methodologies of scientific materialism.

METEOROLOGY: OBSERVING THE WEATHER FORMATIONS OF YOUR MIND

Here is an extended analogy that may be of benefit in your practice. We all know that meteorology is the branch of science concerned with the processes and phenomena in the atmosphere, especially as a means of forecasting the weather. A meteorological observatory is a scientific establishment devoted to making particularly precise and detailed measurements of meteorological, geophysical, and related astronomical phenomena that impinge upon or influence the weather. There are many sites around the planet for measuring shifts in the weather—and one of them is your own physical experience of the world around you. Just hold up your index finger: "Ah, the wind is blowing from the west." You have just made a meteorological investigation! We can call that "folk meteorology." Then, over the last several decades, there are satellites in space that focus their cameras on the earth in order to record weather phenomena as they move across the planet. So meteorologists are able to look at weather both from within weather formations (that is, from instruments based on the ground and in the atmosphere) as well as from outside of the weather, since the satellites are completely untouched by the weather formations they are observing or photographing down in Earth's atmosphere.

Similarly, when you are practicing śamatha of any kind—mindfulness of breathing, focusing on a Buddha image, taking the mind as the path, and so on—you are observing the "weather formations," or patterns, of your mind, noticing whether or not they are peaceful, turbulent, calm, overcast, or clear. During these observations of causes and effects, there is the recognition that influences from the outside are causing your mind to be emotionally turbulent, caught up in rumination, and so forth. You are seeing that memories from the past are triggering emotions and desires, while fantasies about the future are triggering hopes and fears. By and large, unless you have mastered taking the mind as the path, you are observing the movements of the mind from within the mind.

Here, then, there is "folk meteorology of the mind," in which we can say, "Oh, I'm really upset today. I'm really, really disturbed. This happened this morning. I'm really quite afraid and anxious. Oh, I'm feeling so agitated right now. I'm feeling very calm right now. I'm feeling very loving. I'm feeling very irritable right now." At that point you are observing the mind from within the mind. You are observing the hurricane from within the hurricane, the tornado from within the tornado, the balmy breeze and the sunny warmth of Hawai'i while on the beaches of Waikiki. We all do that and everybody knows whether they're happy, sad, peaceful, or agitated. So in a sense, everyone is a folk psychologist, and to some extent we have some idea, primarily external, of what causes us to be friendly and unfriendly, happy and sad, peaceful and agitated, and so forth.

Yet, many of our conclusions are false or misleading, as we point to people and things outside of ourselves as the primary causes of our mental distress. Desperately scrounging for an answer to our dismay, we may point to the brain, our genes, our parents, other people, to losing a job, having a bad boss, a quarrel with a spouse, the weather, and so forth. Similarly, when we experience craving or desire, we point our finger in all the directions that are not actually the true source of our genuine well-being or even of our hedonic happiness. Once we turn "inside"—which is the meaning of the Tibetan word for a Buddhist, *nangpa*—we awaken to the fact that none of the primary causes of our joys or sorrows is to be found in the brain, the body, in other people, or the external environment. All of these can be and often are contributing conditions that may or may not catalyze mental states, just as water can be poured on the ground and it may or may not cause a seed to germinate. But if there are no seeds, then there is only wet dirt. If there are already seeds, then the water may cause them to germinate. Since the seeds were already there, the water simply catalyzed their germination and growth. In a corresponding way, the actual sources and primary causes of our happiness and sorrow are always to be found within.

So, we are all folk meteorologists of the mind, but then we can be professionally trained. We can develop a telescope of samādhi, whereby we can sustain focus on a point but also sustain focus on a field, such as the space of the mind. When we direct well-refined attention, samādhi, mindfulness, and introspection that are cultivated by way of mindfulness of breathing, for example, then we can turn that finely-honed telescope to the space of the mind, and with discerning intelligence and sustained samādhi, maintained by the power of mindfulness, we can observe the origins of mental afflictions, the origins of virtuous states and ethically unspecified states. We can observe internally how they arise and where they arise from. Once they are manifesting, they are in the present, and we can examine them closely with samādhi, backed by the discerning intelligence and wisdom of vipaśyanā, to see whether they are impermanent or permanent, changing or unchanging; whether they are veritable sources of well-being and happiness or they are not; and whether they are actually, really, "I" or "mine" or whether we are simply witnessing them and have some ability to influence them, but they are not us and they are not ours. We can investigate that.

Then over the course of many years of rigorous training, we can become professionals—professional meteorologists of the atmosphere of the mind, observing the current, the flows, the contaminations, and the purities, and we can observe it from the ground of our own minds within our own minds. But then as you also know, it is possible, once you have achieved śamatha, to be resting in awareness whose location is the form realm, which is not located in the human mind. The human mind is in the desire realm. Once you have achieved śamatha, since you've achieved at least access to the first dhyāna, then you can continue developing the telescope with vipaśyanā, and then, like those satellites outside of the atmosphere, from that vantage point, you can turn your attention to the human mind from outside of all of that—the calm, the dark, the smog, the clarity, the peacefulness, the hurricanes—and then you can investigate.

Then, by watching the weather patterns of your mind and observing cause and effect, from that distanced perspective, you can develop the ability to forecast the future weather of your mind. When you see that a mental affliction has arisen, you recognize it as such and then examine the detrimental influences it has on your mind and possibly on your behavior—if you haven't yet mastered the art of remaining "still like a piece of wood"[2] when your mind is upset. In this way, you learn to observe and investigate the mind from within, rather than just trying to make inferences about the mind based on other people's brain states, verbal reports, and behaviors. Further, the primary motivation for making such internal observations is to identify the true causes of mental distress and of genuine well-being. To do so, you are not looking at outer influences, such as the brain, genetics, other people, the environment, your spouse, childhood traumas, and so forth. All of those may be significant and may have watered the seeds in your mind, yet none of those is a primary cause. By identifying the true causes of suffering itself, which can only come from within the mind, you have the opportunity to awaken from the old, misleading self-hypnosis that "other people and outside circumstances" are the real causes of your happiness and suffering.

ASTRONOMY: USING THE TELESCOPE OF SAMĀDHI TO OBSERVE THE SPACE OF THE MIND

Now we turn to the science of astronomy to continue the extended analogy. Although it is very different from meteorology, we see that events observed by astronomy do impinge upon weather patterns. Astronomy is the branch of science that deals with celestial objects, space, and the physical universe as a whole. Within astronomy, there have been great discoveries through the evolution of increasingly sophisticated methods for observing astronomical phenomena. The Danish astronomer Tycho Brahe, for example, made precise, naked-eye measurements of the relative movements and distances of the planets. It was on the basis of those measurements that his student Johannes Kepler was able to formulate the three laws of planetary motion. Then there is Galileo, father of modern science, who refined the telescope first invented by the Dutch, and used it for the first time to observe the sun, moon, planets, and stars. With his increasingly powerful telescopes, he made unprecedented discoveries about a wide range of celestial phenomena, revolutionizing our understanding of the physical universe as a whole. In 1676, the Royal Observatory Greenwich, Britain's oldest scientific institution, was established by King Charles II for the specific and practical purpose of observing the motions of the planets and the locations of the fixed stars. Then, in 1904, Mount Wilson Observatory was established in the mountains above Pasadena, California, and soon afterward became famous for the installation of the one-hundred-inch Hooker Telescope, a reflecting telescope that was the world's largest telescope from 1917 to 1949. It was with this telescope that the renowned astronomer Edwin Hubble made his great discoveries, such as the fact that the Milky Way is just one of many galaxies in an ever-expanding universe. This telescope was used by Hubble and other astronomers to lead directly to our current understanding of the origins of the universe, the big bang model, the expanding universe, and so on. Most recently, in 2021, the James Webb Space Telescope was launched and, like the Hubble Telescope, orbits our planet outside of Earth's atmosphere and is directed into deep space. In a short period of time, they have used it to discover the most distant galaxy ever observed, which formed about 235 million years after the big bang.

Relating this back to contemplative inquiry, śamatha may be viewed as contemplative technology and vipaśyanā as contemplative science. When you use śamatha to turn your attention in upon the mind and investigate it by way of the vipaśyanā methods of inquiry known as *citta-satipaṭṭhāna*, or the "close application of mindfulness to the mind," you can then make many replicable, important discoveries about the mind and its relation to the rest of reality. Yet, as you penetrate through the atmosphere of the coarse mind, or psyche, by way of the practice of śamatha, the mind under observation actually dissolves, with all sensory and mental appearances fading away one by one into the empty, deep space of the substrate. From there, you invert your awareness in upon the source from which your mind emerged when you were conceived, from which it emerges every time you awake from deep sleep, and the source from which all thoughts, emotions, and desires emerge from moment to moment. This is the substrate consciousness, into which your mind and all mental processes dissolve every time you fall into deep sleep, when you faint, become comatose, have general anesthesia, and when you die.

Having achieved śamatha, you penetrate through the atmosphere and all the fluctuations of your human, coarse mind into the deep space of the substrate consciousness beyond the human mind. From that vantage point, you can explore another dimension of reality as a whole, known as the form realm. If you want to continue on this straight track of śamatha into the first, second, third, and fourth dhyānas in the form realm, and into the samāpattis, or the absorptions, of the formless realm, then you can explore firsthand with this powerful telescope of samādhi the four dimensions of the form realm, from which the desire realm (the known "universe" of modern science) emerges, and, beyond that, the four dimensions of the formless realm, from which the form realm emerges.

Great contemplatives throughout history have observed that the whole of the desire realm—the universe we perceive with our senses and physical instruments such as the James Webb Space Telescope—emerges from the form realm. Mathematicians infer mathematical laws that must fundamentally stem from this realm of pure forms, but it is only yogis who directly perceive this realm and the beings who inhabit it, in addition to the deeper formless realm from which the form realm emerges and into which it dissolves over the course of billions of years.

When you engage in the śamatha practice of "taking the mind as the path," for example, you are resting in your closest facsimile of the substrate consciousness, which is always luminous and cognizant, is unmoving, illuminates all appearances (without ever merging with them), and is aware of thoughts without ever thinking them. Resting in and sustaining that stillness in an unfluctuating way, you observe the movements, fluctuations, hurricanes, storms, and calm of the mind without sinking back into it—like a satellite that drops back to Earth, plunging into the ocean. Rather, like a satellite that remains in orbit, you are able to observe the mind but also to turn your attention outward to the deep space of the substrate, which is neither encapsulated inside your head nor inside anything at all. The substrate consciousness itself has no boundary, no limits, no shape, no form, no size: it is boundless. Once you have achieved śamatha, you have created something like a space station from which you can either look back on Earth or look into deep space and make discoveries about that vast domain of reality.

Just as astronomers have followed a technological evolution from Galileo right on through to the Hubble and then the James Webb Space Telescope, so, as professional astronomers of the mind, we can learn to replicate the discoveries of the preceding generations upon generations of yogis who have developed samādhi, going back to the Buddha and to the great *rishis* (Skt. *ṛṣi*) of pre-Buddhist India who had already explored and mapped out the multiple dimensions of the desire, form, and formless realms.

Thus, śamatha has the great boon of being above all the fluctuations of the suffering of suffering, but it is not above the suffering of change. When you are experiencing objects that are subsumed by the suffering of change, it can feel very nice in the present, as in the experiences of the bliss, luminosity, and nonconceptuality of samādhi. The bliss of samādhi due to achieving śamatha is a conditioned bliss that feels really good. But as we have seen, if you latch onto it and reify it, then it is only a matter of time before the power of your samādhi fades and your space station crashes to Earth once again, reverting you back to being an ordinary person with no samādhi. Or perhaps you will fall to one of the miserable states of existence, such as an animal, who cannot remember ever having experienced samādhi. Further, rebirth in all of the three realms of existence arises from the substrate consciousness. If one clings to the bliss of the substrate consciousness, this catalyzes rebirth in the desire realm; clinging to its luminosity gives rise to rebirth in the form realm; and clinging to its stillness and nonconceptuality leads to rebirth in the formless realm.

Cosmology: Investigating the Emptiness of Inherent Existence of All Phenomena

For the last dimension of this analogy, we turn to cosmology, the science of the origin, development, and evolution of the universe. Cosmology asks the final, ultimate, deepest questions about the physical universe as a whole: Whence does it arise, what is its nature, and what happens at the end? Of course, the James Webb Space Telescope may provide information and observations that alter and shift our notion of the nature of the cosmos as a whole, as the Hooker Telescope on Mount Wilson led us to understand the expanding universe and the fact that there are other galaxies in addition to our own, the estimate number of which has now reached two trillion galaxies—in our currently observable universe. So cosmology relies on the evolving technology at its disposal, just as astronomy does, but cosmology asks questions that are more fundamentally abstract, theoretical, even philosophical.

Thus, cosmology's investigation into the origin, location, and destination of the universe is akin to vipaśyanā, which includes the investigation into the origin, nature, and destination of the mind. With vipaśyanā, we examine the origins of the conditioned mind, the nature of the mind and its role in nature, and the destination of the mind, or what is going to happen to the mind at death and beyond. The Dzogchen practice of trekchö then goes far beyond that, cutting through both the coarse, human mind and the substrate consciousness to the unconditioned mind, which is unborn, unceasing, primordial consciousness that transcends all conceptual categories.

Galileo, following the lead of the Greek materialist philosopher Democritus, asserted that all qualia—or appearances to the senses, including colors, tastes, smells, and so on—"are no more than mere names" and that they reside only in consciousness, having no existence that is really out there in the world. More recently, a growing number of quantum physicists have drawn the same conclusion about matter, energy, space, and time: They have only a nominal existence but do not inherently exist "out there" in the imagined real, physical world. The investigations of vipaśyanā first show the fundamental role of the mind in terms of the three realms, and then, with its insight into emptiness, reveals not only that the three realms arise from the substrate consciousness but that the phenomena that we identify in the world of objects and subjects exist only in relation to our conceptual designations, having no existence outside of the substrate of each sentient being. This implies that there is, in a manner of speaking, one universe for each sentient being. All subjects and objects come into existence and depart from existence by the power of conceptual designation. None of these objects— not stars, planets, nebulae, the big bang, or elementary particles—bear any intrinsic, objective qualities of their own. Each entity that nominally bears its own characteristics is conceptually imputed on those characteristics, but it cannot ultimately be found either among or apart from those parts and qualities. The *Ratnamegha Sūtra* states, "All phenomena are preceded by mentation. When mentation is comprehended, all phenomena are comprehended. By bringing mentation under control, all things are brought under control."

By means of śamatha and vipaśyanā, we cut through the reification of the subjective and objective phenomena that we conceptually designate to realize their emptiness of inherent existence. By so doing, we realize the actual nature of the substrate as the dharmadhātu, the absolute space of phenomena in which relative space-time is expanding and contracting. The Buddha himself observed and reported on the cyclic expansion and contraction of the universe, which takes place over billions of years. The absolute space of the dharmadhātu, in which this oscillation occurs, is indivisible from primordial consciousness and from the energy of primordial consciousness, from which all matter and energy fundamentally emerge.

In modern cosmology the mind is assumed to be derivative of matter and energy, so it is not believed to play any fundamental role in the universe at large. However, this is simply an assumption based on an unquestioned metaphysical belief in the ontological primacy of matter. The eminent physicist Nima Arkani-Hamed, of the Institute for Advanced Study in Princeton, New Jersey, declared, "Many, many separate arguments, all very strong individually, suggest that the very notion of space-time is not a fundamental one. Space-time is doomed. There is no such thing as space-time, fundamentally in the actual, underlying description of the laws of physics. That's very startling, because what physics is supposed to be about is describing things as they happen in space and time. So if there is no space-time, it's not clear what physics is about. That's why this is a hard problem."[3] In other words, if space and time are not really "out there" and have only a nominal existence, then there is really nothing "in" space-time that is really out there. Therefore, all of the distant galaxies observed by the James Webb Space Telescope are not really "out there"—they arise for us relative to our systems of measurement, but are not inherently real since space is not inherently real. That is the cutting-edge conclusion of some of the premier quantum physicists of the current day. Among scientists, it is the quantum physicists who have the deepest insights into the nature of matter and energy, and it is they who provide the most compelling evidence and reasoning in the refutation of scientific materialism.

A Contemplative Observatory

Each of us is endowed with our own observatory for exploring the whole of reality from the inside out. While scientists have sought to explore reality from the outside in, and made extraordinary discoveries in the process, these methods have still left them in the dark about the fundamental role of the mind in the formation, evolution, and dissolution of the universe. It is with the power of samādhi, imbued with the insights of vipaśyanā, that we can probe into the nature of the whole of reality—in which consciousness is found to be fundamental—and thus make discoveries that lie beyond the scope of objective science alone.

Appendix 2: The Nuclear Fusion of Śamatha

Nuclear fusion is a reaction in which two or more atomic nuclei are combined, or united, to form one or more different atomic nuclei and subatomic particles. With the infusion of a small amount of energy into the system, this fusion can be catalyzed, with a much, much greater amount of energy being released from the atomic nuclei when they are fused. That is, the energy was already there in the atomic nucleus, and by infusing a small amount of energy into it, then an enormous amount of energy that was trapped or enclosed within each individual atomic nucleus is released—this type of nuclear reaction is what is empowering the sun and has been for 4.6 billion years.

This analogy is also very relevant to śamatha practice. To understand how, we turn to one of the most definitive and authoritative accounts of what it is like to actually achieve śamatha from a first-person perspective, found in Asaṅga's *Śrāvakabhūmi*, which is cited by Jé Tsongkhapa and other great scholars in various lamrim texts. Asaṅga writes, "The portent of the proximate occurrence of gross, easily discernible single-pointedness of mind and of mental and physical pliancy is a sensation of heaviness on the top of the head." That is, when you are about to achieve śamatha, an extraordinary energy from a deeper source is close to being released, which creates a sense of heaviness on top of the head. Asaṅga continues, "But this is not a harmful symptom. As soon as this happens, mental dysfunction, which is included among the mental afflictions that obstruct delight in eliminating [the afflictions], is itself eliminated, and mental fitness and mental pliancy arise due to this antidote."[1] "Mental dysfunction" refers to the unwieldiness, rigidness, tightness, and heaviness of the mind. That dysfunction is banished, "and mental fitness and mental pliancy arise due to this antidote." With the elimination of mental dysfunction, there is a release of energy that emerges from a deeper source than your coarse human mind and body.

Asaṅga continues, "Due to its occurrence, vital energies of the great elements that are conducive to the arising of physical pliancy course through the body." This refers to the release of energy that was already there but trapped because of the five obscurations, as well as the obscurations of the subtle energies, or prāṇas. These vital energies of the great elements—earth, water, fire, air, and space—"that are conducive to the arising of physical pliancy course through the body." Further, "Because of their movement, one is freed of physical dysfunction affiliated with mental afflictions that obstruct delight in meditation, and it seems as if the entire body were filled with physical pliancy as the antidote for that."[2] In this way, there is an emergence and outflowing of these karmic energies, which are manifesting in a release of physical and mental pliancy that was previously hidden by the obscurations and their corresponding blockages of the prāṇa.

It requires a bit of sustained effort to continue resting in awareness of awareness, to take the mind as the path, and to practice mindfulness of breathing. But by persevering in meditation in a gradual, sustained fashion, when you come to the culmination of your śamatha practice, it releases far more energy than you put into it.

Asaṅga continues, "When that first arises, having taken delight in the extraordinary mental joy in superb mental engagement, there is supreme mental pleasure in the accompanying meditative object. At that time, that is called *the mind.*" That is, now you have a mind—not the other way around. What you had before was a mind that was enslaved by the bondage of illusory appearances and conceptualization—the mind had you.

Moreover, "That which arises first immediately thereafter is the force of pliancy, which incrementally becomes subtler." There is a "force of pliancy," like an explosion of energy coursing through the body that gradually settles and "incrementally becomes subtler." He continues, "Pliancy occurs in the body, following it like a shadow. The extraordinary mental joy is relinquished, and the mind, having a serene aspect, becomes stabilized in śamatha with respect to the meditative object."[3] In other words, your body and mind are utterly calm and the "serene aspect," which is the very meaning of śamatha, "becomes stabilized in śamatha with respect to the meditative object." Now you have achieved śamatha.

Asaṅga then states that "the entire continuum and flow of your attention, focused in single-pointedness and internally focused in the śamatha of the mind, should sequentially be signless, devoid of ideation, and calm. Direct your attention in that way [and] due to the absence of mindfulness and of mental engagement, when that object is dissolved and removed, the mind is placed in the absence of appearances."[4] When he writes, "mindfulness and mental engagement," this refers to the two factors of the coarse mind. And "when that object is dissolved and removed, the mind is placed in the absence of appearances," which points to the dissolution, or the fusion, of your coarse mind as it dissolves into the underlying continuum of the substrate consciousness. There is a fusion, and in that fusion or dissolution, this enormous eruption of bliss, luminosity, nonconceptuality, energy, and pliancy occurs. In other words, you get more out of it than you put into it, as with nuclear fusion.

Asaṅga says that this is signless. Jé Tsongkhapa (1357–1419) in his *Concise Presentation of the Stages of the Path to Enlightenment* writes, "Here, *signs* refer to the ten signs of the five objects, including visual form, of the three poisons, of male and of female. This is the way they vanish: at first a variety of signs of the objects such as visual forms appear, and as soon as they appear, they naturally subside and are purified. Finally, when you settle in meditative equipoise, only the aspects of sheer cognizance, luminosity, and bliss of the mind appear, without the appearance of the signs of visual form, sound, and so on."[5] This is a complete implosion of all the mental and sensory appearances of the desire realm, fusing into this subtle continuum. Then, out of that emerges an enormous energy, bliss, and so on.

We saw earlier that the Fourth Paṇchen Lama, Lozang Chökyi Gyaltsen, writes in his autocommentary to his root text on Mahāmudrā, "By sustaining the practice in that way, the essential nature of meditative equipoise, not being obscured by anything, is lucid and very clear." That is, the nature of meditative equipoise is not contained, obstructed, or limited by anything. He continues, "Not being determined in any way as a physical entity, it is a clear vacuity like space. Moreover, a meditative experience arises in which whatever good or bad objects of the five senses may emerge, they appear clearly and vividly, as if they were reflections in a lucid mirror." In other words, when you come out of meditation, all objects of the five senses appear as dreamlike, empty appearances. He continues, "a meditative experience arises in which . . . one is free from the identification of anything as 'this is this' or 'this is not that.'" When you are dwelling in that nonconceptual consciousness, the demarcations of "this is" or " this is not" are gone. He then states, "Such samādhi, however stable—if not imbued with the bliss of mental and physical pliancy—is said to be single-pointedness of the mind of the desire realm. On the other hand, samādhi that is so imbued [with mental and physical pliancy] is said to be śamatha. This is the source of many positive attributes, such as extrasensory perception, paranormal abilities, and so forth."

Regarding your meditation practice, if you find that you are too tired to practice longer each day, then that means you are putting more energy into the practice than you are getting out of it. This is not a sustainable approach. Instead, when resting in awareness, give just enough effort to release all the grasping, appropriation, and reification that arises. Recognize thoughts pertaining to the past, present, and future as being simply thoughts pertaining to the past, present, and future, without letting the mind be drawn to these three times. By giving just enough effort—without pushing too hard with hopes and fears, or else becoming so lax that practice is dull—then practice becomes both sustainable and continuous. It is an ongoing process of gently tuning your practice such that you do not fall into the extremes of laxity and excitation but instead gently and steadily remain resting in awareness.

Until you have realized and are able to dwell in pristine awareness, you cannot practice effectively without exerting any effort at all. You must find the subtle balance in your practice so that you give just enough not to be moved, trapped, or carried away by thoughts, emotions, hopes, fears, and all manner of mental afflictions. Then peace of mind arises. Note that even when the mind is not peaceful, awareness is peaceful by nature. Even when your environment or other people's behaviors are not peaceful, you will continue to rest in awareness, which is protected from the stormy winds of samsara. This peace of mind leads to a sense of well-being and joy that is energizing. Then you will have energy to practice more and more each day, instead of becoming tired from pushing through practice with an active sense of doing.

This is a nuclear fusion within your own mind, in which you give just enough effort to release your mind of all grasping so that the natural stillness, clarity, and luminosity of awareness can shine forth and empower you, and then you can hardly bear to be off the cushion. Then your challenge becomes one of not grasping for more and more time to meditate but rather to see things like cooking, cleaning, and other mundane activities as an opportunity to maintain an unbroken flow of mindfulness without slipping into the habitual patterns of being a sentient being—without slipping into and being carried away by conceptualization and thus becoming exhausted. Conceptualization is exhausting—not meditation.

SECURING THE FIVE INNER CONDITIONS FOR ŚAMATHA

Düdjom Rinpoché described how to choose a conducive outer environment and how to cultivate a conducive inner space for achieving śamatha, but it is worthwhile to look more deeply into the importance of a conducive inner environment, for this is far more difficult to obtain than a suitable physical retreat place.

The outer environment is undoubtedly important, but all the perfect outer circumstances will *not* give rise to the achievement of śamatha unless you have integrated them with the proper internal conditions for achieving śamatha. This is the key to success, which is given in all of the lamrim literature.

There are five inner conditions for the achievement of śamatha. The first is to have few desires for anything in samsara, keeping in mind that the virtuous desire, aspiration, and intention associated with bodhicitta is a foundational support for your practice within the context of the Mahāyāna and Dzogchen. The second is to be content with resting continuously in the sheer luminosity and cognizance of awareness. The third is to have few concerns and activities for anything outside your formal practice. The fourth is to have pure ethical discipline, which means practicing nonviolence and benevolence in all actions of body, speech, and mind. And fifth is to dispense completely with conceptualization involving desire and so on.

First of all, when you are in retreat—in formal meditation and in between sessions during the post-meditative state—have few desires for anything that you do not have. This does include having too much desire for the fruits and success of progress in practice—if you are grasping to that with your conditioned mind. When you are practicing, you are to release desires even for a particular outcome and instead simply practice in the present moment. Desires also include, more obviously, desires for external things such as having more companionship, wanting to check the internet, wanting to buy this or that thing, and so on. As long as you are desiring to do or obtain something else, that is going to be an obstacle to progress.

On the other hand, the flipside of having few desires for what you do not have is the importance of experiencing contentment with what you have already. In the context of śamatha practice, can you be content resting in the immediacy of the present moment from moment to moment, session to session, day to day, month to month? Can you be content resting in your closest approximation to nirvana, or do you start missing samsara? If you miss samsara, it will inevitably catch up with you and lure you back in.

Next, having few concerns and activities outside of your formal practice, both on and off the cushion, is crucial. If you have concerns and activities, this is bound to erode, undermine, and unravel the coherence and composure of your practice. So, keep it as simple as possible. Śamatha is, in fact, a solitary practice. It is achieved in solitude with simplicity.

Then there is the importance of having pure ethical discipline. This refers to practicing nonviolence and benevolence on the subtlest levels in all activities of body, speech, and mind, with respect to all the sentient beings you encounter or are aware of in your space of retreat.

The final inner condition is to dispense completely with conceptualization involving desire and so on, both on the cushion and off the cushion. This is probably the most difficult of the requisite internal conditions for achieving śamatha.

To elucidate this point, let's turn to Dromtönpa and Atiśa in their dialogue titled *Cutting the Root of Suffering and Equalizing Excitation and Laxity*. In the midst of this conversation, Dromtönpa, a former incarnation of His Holiness the Dalai Lama, asked his guru, Atiśa, a former incarnation of the Paṇchen Lama, "What is the root of the mental afflictions that is to be relinquished?" Atiśa responds, "Drom, it is this great conceptualization."[6] In other words, the root of mental afflictions is the flow of both coarse and subtle conceptualization (Skt. *vikalpa*), which entails the obsessive and compulsive arising of thoughts. Delusionally, you are trapped in them, thinking that the thoughts are the whole truth and nothing but the truth. Undoubtedly, thinking can be very useful, such as the thinking required to cultivate the four immeasurables, thinking in terms of planning your grocery needs, and so on. But be sure that when you pick up conceptualization, always promptly put it back down again when you have finished what is required, even in the context of analytical meditation. Here, Atiśa is asserting that the great flow of conceptualization is the root of mental afflictions—be it craving, ignorance, delusion, reification, grasping to true existence, and so forth. The obsessive, compulsive, delusional fixation on thinking is the "root of the mental afflictions that is to be relinquished."

Dromtönpa then asked, "Master, what is the method of destroying this?" and Atiśa responds, "Drom, none other than vanquishing it as soon as it arises." Here, he is not saying that one shouldn't think at all. Rather, thoughts may be very useful. They may arise as aids on the path and can certainly be transformed into the path, especially when used constructively to discover the absence of inherent existence of phenomena during meditation on vipaśyanā. From the perspective of pristine awareness, moreover, thoughts are seen as expressions of dharmakāya, so there is nothing inherently wrong with them. Instead, Atiśa is referring to the reifying conceptualization that leads you back into the rut of thinking like a sentient being. Vanquish *that* as soon as it arises. That is, release the identification with and appropriation of it. Release your very identity as the thinker because every time you are the thinker, you are reaffirming your existence as a sentient being, which ultimately veils and obscures your deeper identity as a buddha.

Then, Dromtönpa asks his final question in this particular exchange, saying, "Master, how is it relinquished by means of its antidote?" In other words, how do you vanquish conceptualization? Atiśa responds, "Drom, by means of striking it down with no hesitation whatsoever. All paths, moreover, are traversed by means of this single path, and all aspirations are concentrated into this single one as well." In essence, then, this practice is very simple, but it is couched within authentic refuge, bodhicitta, the four revolutions in outlook, the four immeasurables, lojong, and within whatever understanding you have of the view—the dreamlike nature of phenomena and the illusion-like nature of your own identity.

SEEKING GUIDANCE FROM YOUR INNER GURU

When embarking on your personal śamatha retreat, questions may arise. Maybe you have the opportunity to ask your personal, outer guru or maybe that opportunity is not available to you while in retreat. Regardless, here is some practical guidance on how you can begin to cultivate trust in your inner guru for guidance, as has been done by yogis for many centuries.

When a question arises, perhaps in regard to a lack of clarity, an indecision, uncertainty, or challenge arising, first try to clarify and articulate the question as clearly and succinctly as you can. What exactly is it you want to know? Holding that in mind, simply rest in awareness and let the question dissolve. Do not hold on to it, but from the space of awareness, release it and simply rest in that awareness, observing what may come up in response. If something arises that seems like it may be a response to the question posed, test that with your prajñā, or your discerning intelligence, to see if it is in accordance with the teachings. Is this appropriate, sound, authentic, and good advice? If it passes the test of investigating its value and authenticity with intelligence, then follow the inner guidance. From there, continue to probe with prajñā to see whether or not following that advice turns out to be beneficial, harmful, or simply neutral.

In other words, when you pose the question clearly and see what arises, respond to it in exactly the way you would to any of the teachings you receive from your gurus. That is, test the teachings by first hearing them and then thinking about them. Are they sound and authentic teachings? If so, put them into practice and experience firsthand whether or not they are beneficial. Do not accept the guru's words with blind faith. Whether it is your inner guru speaking from the depths of your own pristine awareness or any of your gurus speaking to you in an "I-thou" relationship, recognize that there is essentially the same method of discernment taking place. When in the depths of silent retreat, this especially is the time to take to heart the Dzogchen aphorism, "Do not look outside yourself for the buddha."

Appendix 3: Distinguishing Dimensions of Consciousness

Distinguishing between Coarse Mental Consciousness and the Substrate Consciousness

In order to better understand the crucial distinction between coarse mental consciousness and the substrate consciousness (Skt. *ālayavijñāna*), begin by gaining a conceptual understanding of each one. Once you have gained a conceptual understanding from hearing, or reading, and reflecting upon this distinction so that your understanding is clear, it is time to plunge directly into meditation. From here, you are better able to distinguish between the flow of the coarse mental consciousness you have as a human being and that of the substrate consciousness.

A major distinction is that unlike coarse mental consciousness, which occurs during the waking and dream states, the substrate consciousness never merges with the sensory and mental appearances that it illuminates, such as when you ordinarily look at something, reify it, and therefore view it as objectively real. When viewed from the perspective of coarse mental consciousness, the same occurs for thoughts, emotions, hopes, fears, memories, and so on—they arise, you merge with them, and hence, by way of dualistic grasping, samsara is perpetuated. The substrate consciousness, however, illuminates all these sensory and mental appearances, but it never merges with them. It is the conditioned stillness in the midst of motion.

Then, consider how the coarse human mind is subject to coarse impermanence in the sense that it has a beginning in the womb and an end at death. Your mind, the mind you identify with—which is so tied up with your personality, your memories, and your hopes and fears about the future, this mind, this little short story—began in the womb, and it will end at death.

Yet, with the first emergence of a human mind in a human embryo, its appropriative cause—that from which it arose and which turns into a human mind—is not a human mind but a prehuman mentation, which in turn emerges derivatively from something else—namely, the substrate consciousness. The latter is like a "stem consciousness" that could be configured into any type of mind, depending on the projecting karma and the correlated physical basis by which it is configured. It first transforms into subtle mentation and then coarse mentation, which are the faculties in immediate dependence upon which the conditioned human mind emerges.

Likewise, in the dying process, the human mind disappears and turns into something that is not a human mind—namely, post-human mentation, which then devolves back into the substrate consciousness from which it arose. A similar process occurs in the transition from deep sleep to the waking state and back to deep sleep.

Further, from moment to moment, a kind of "kinetic energy," or movement, of human mental processes emerges from the "potential energy," or relative stillness, of habitual propensities (Skt. *vāsana*) and dissolves back into such propensities, which are stored in the substrate (Skt. *ālaya*). On occasion the mind becomes relatively still, as in deep sleep or during the intervals between thoughts, but that is always a superficial, fleeting, unstable stillness, which vanishes as soon as the mind is set in motion again by the awakening of habitual propensities and mental formations (Skt. *saṃskāra*), along with their subtle physiological correlates, the karmic energies (Skt. *karmavāyu*). This is the core internal process of causation within the mind.

According to the Pāli canon, when the Buddha declared that the mind is always luminous but is adventitiously obscured by defilements, he was referring to the *bhavaṅga*, or the ground of becoming, which most likely corresponds to the substrate described in Mahāyāna literature. In Dzogchen, a distinction is first made between the substrate, the relative inner space of the mind, and the substrate consciousness. In light of that distinction, the bhavaṅga, or "ground of becoming," from the Theravāda tradition corresponds more closely to the substrate than to the substrate consciousness, while the corresponding Pāli term *javana* (which I have referred to as the "kinetic energy" of the mind) refers to "the karmically active state in which defilements 'arrive' like visitors arriving at a house."[1]

The substrate consciousness, characterized by its sheer luminosity and sheer cognizance, transcends coarse impermanence, for unlike the coarse human mind, it has neither a beginning nor an end, and it never emerges from or dissolves into anything other than prior and subsequent moments of its own continuum. That is, its appropriative causes and appropriative effects are always successive moments in the continuum of the substrate consciousness, so that substrate consciousness never disappears. Rather, like matter and energy—two other fundamental constituents of the natural world—throughout all its permutations, this conditioned consciousness is always conserved.

In that sense, on a coarse level, it is unchanging because it is always the substrate consciousness, never diverging from its relative, essential nature of luminosity and cognizance. Nevertheless, the substrate consciousness is subject to subtle impermanence, for it is ever arising and passing from instant to instant, with prior moments of the substrate consciousness transforming into subsequent moments of the substrate consciousness, along with the habitual propensities whose energy it perpetuates. On a coarse level, it never merges with the ever-changing movements of objective sensory and mental appearances and of the coarse, subjective mental processes it illuminates, even though it is repeatedly obscured by them—just as from Earth, the sun is obscured by clouds even while its own luminosity is unwavering. But on a subtle level, the substrate consciousness is ever-changing, moment by moment, like all other conditioned, nonphysical and physical phenomena throughout the worlds of samsara.

In order to dissolve the coarse mind into the substrate, one can take the classic Dzogchen śamatha practice of "taking the impure mind as the path," which is done by resting in the stillness of awareness while simultaneously noting the movements of the mind without being distracted by them or identifying with them. This practice is taught in *The Vajra Essence* by the Lake-Born Vajra, a speech emanation of Padmasambhava. The culmination of the practice, when śamatha is fully achieved, is described as follows:

> O, Vajra of Mind, the bonds of mindfulness and firmly main-
> tained attention are gradually dissolved by the power of medita-
> tive experiences until finally—because the ordinary mind of an
> ordinary sentient being, as it were, disappears—thoughts go dor-
> mant, and roving concepts subside into the space of awareness.
> You then slip into the blank vacuity of the substrate, in which
> self, others, and objects disappear. The state that becomes man-
> ifest, in which the appearances of self, others, and objects have
> vanished, and in which there is an inwardly focused grasping to

the experiences of vacuity and luminosity, is the *substrate consciousness*. Some teachers say that the substrate to which you descend is the "one taste" or "freedom from conceptual elaboration," but others say it is ethically unspecified. Whatever they call it, in truth you have come to the essential nature of the mind.[2]

By "essential nature of the mind," he is referring to its relative, not ultimate, essential nature. Simply resting in the sheer luminosity and cognizance of awareness results not in the realization of pristine awareness but rather in this subtle continuum of conditioned mental consciousness known as the substrate consciousness, which carries on from one lifetime to the next.

A further distinction is made in Dzogchen between the actual substrate, which corresponds to the absence of mindfulness, and the temporarily luminous substrate, which corresponds to self-illuminating mindfulness. The former is an ethically unspecified state, like immaterial space, in which the radiance and creative expressions of awareness are impeded, while the latter is transient and luminous, in which luminosity emerges from the vacuity of the substrate. In this context, the actual substrate and the temporarily luminous substrate alternatingly serve as each other's appropriative cause and appropriated effect, with each one manifesting successively in a beginningless cycle until both dissolve irreversibly into the ground of pristine awareness with the fourth vision of tögal, which is the final extinction of all impure appearances into the actual nature of reality.

In the course of samsara, when a being in the intermediate period enters into the union of the egg and sperm of its prospective human parents, the stream of its substrate consciousness dissolves back into the actual substrate, or ālaya, which is immaterial like space—a blank, unthinking void, in which one is free of clinging to the experiences of cognition and mentation. At conception, there arises from the substrate radiant, clear consciousness itself, which serves as the basis for the emergence of appearances, and this is the substrate consciousness.

In *The Vajra Essence*, the Lake-Born Vajra further explains,

> Moreover, no objects are determined that are not expressions of its own luminosity, and while it can give rise to all kinds of appearances, it does not enter into any objects. This is like the way that planets and stars are able to emerge in lucid, clear water; like the way that reflections are able to appear in a lucid, clear

mirror; and like the way that physical worlds and their sentient inhabitants are able to emerge in lucid, clear space. In the same way, appearances are able to emerge in the empty, clear substrate consciousness.[3]

During the process of gestation, mentation (Skt. *manas*) emerges from the substrate consciousness, as do the five modes of sensory consciousness, during which the embryo gradually evolves into a human fetus and mentation evolves into a human mind. Confusing this dimension of consciousness for primordial consciousness is like mistaking a quartz crystal for a diamond.

DISTINGUISHING BETWEEN CONDITIONED CONSCIOUSNESS AND PRIMORDIAL CONSCIOUSNESS

Regarding the distinction between conditioned consciousness and primordial consciousness, the substrate consciousness—which is simply the subtlest form of conditioned consciousness—does not merge with appearances to it, but it retains the propensities to cling to, merge with, and reify its own conditioned qualities of bliss, luminosity, and nonconceptuality. Whereas, if you release all identification with, attachment to, and reification of these mental processes, which are the fundamental allures of samsara and are deeper than the allures of the desire realm, then you may cut through this subtle, conditioned mind to the very subtle, unconditioned mind of primordial consciousness—and this is done without analysis. The ability to realize emptiness without reliance upon analysis is a distinctive quality of both Dzogchen and Mahāmudrā, the paths that provide a direct, nonconceptual route to this realization.

The primordial consciousness that is pristine awareness transcends even the subtle impermanence of the substrate consciousness, for its luminosity is timeless and forever unchanging, so it is transcendentally still. According to Dzogchen, it has no appropriative causes or effects, nor any contributing conditions, nor does it arise and pass from moment to moment. Much as the movements of the coarse human mind obscure the relative stillness, nonconceptuality, and luminosity of the substrate consciousness, so do the subtle movements of the substrate consciousness, with its qualities of a conditioned phenomenon, obscure the primordial stillness of pristine awareness. Only by releasing all coarse mental grasping and reification of ordinary mental processes and sensory appearances can the ever-present luminosity of the substrate consciousness be revealed. And only by releasing all subtle mental grasping—which reifies even such subtle subjective states as the substrate consciousness itself—can the primordial, timeless luminosity of pristine awareness be revealed. Such release of all grasping to signs of dual appearance is natural liberation. As Śāntideva writes, "Surrendering everything is nirvana, and my mind seeks nirvana. Surrendering everything at once—this is the greatest gift to sentient beings."[4]

Moreover, the luminosity and cognizance of consciousness is the one invariant of all states of consciousness: during waking, sleeping, the bardo, and in future lifetimes. You need not be lucid for luminosity and cognizance to be present, as they are there unceasingly. Moreover, it is the one aspect common to the dualistic mind of a sentient being and the primordially non-dual mind of a buddha. The mind of a buddha is luminous and cognizant, and the mind of a sentient being is luminous and cognizant. If you dwell in that luminosity and cognizance, then you are dwelling right where there is a common ground between your own existence as a sentient being and your own existence as a buddha.

Whether you are primarily focusing on mindfulness of breathing, taking the mind as the path, or unelaborated śamatha without a sign, be aware of this sheer luminosity and cognizance of consciousness. It is your closest approximation to the actual nature of the mind, or cittatā, which is nirvana, while all transitory appearances to your awareness represent samsara. So, all mental and sensory appearances, which you look to with the dualistic grasping of hope and fear, desire and aversion, and so forth, are tokens of samsara. If you penetrate into the actual nature of appearances and rest in the sheer, unelaborated awareness of them, imbued with the luminosity and cognizance of consciousness, then that is nirvana. By focusing solely and continuously, free of distraction, on this simple flow of luminosity and cognizance, which is a ray of pristine awareness, the coarse mind dissolves into the substrate consciousness and śamatha is achieved. These are quintessential pith instructions.

Breaking the Habit of Thinking You Are a Sentient Being

If you want to stop being a sentient being, then stop acting like a sentient being. And if you want to be a buddha, then start acting like a buddha.

Sentient beings think a lot; buddhas do not. Buddhas are aware of the thoughts of sentient beings, but do not think them. From a Dzogchen perspective, sentient beings do not "have the potential" to become buddhas through a process of evolution any more than someone who does not exist has the potential to exist. In other words, you simply have to be freed from the delusion that you have ever been a sentient being, and then your actual nature as a buddha can fully manifest. While still caught in the illusion of being a sentient being, you cannot and do not transform into a buddha.

When you rest in awareness of awareness, you are gazing directly at nirvana, though you may not recognize it as such. When you gaze at the appearances to awareness—including your own thoughts—you are gazing at the illusions of samsara, conjured up by your own karma and mental afflictions. Inevitably you are bound to reify these mere appearances, perpetuating the cycle of samsara.

As we saw earlier, Yangthang Rinpoché wrote in his pith instructions, *A Summary of the View, Meditation, and Conduct,* "If you wish to look into the mirror of the actual nature of your mind, do not look outward. Rather, look inward. Looking outward involves the delusion of reification. By looking inward, you observe your own mind."[5] In other words, if you are constantly looking outward to try to find understanding within the realm of mental and sensory appearances, then you are bound to reify whatever you are looking at, thinking about, listening to, and so on. These are merely the objects that you designate on the basis of appearances, and yet you will surely reify these appearances to awareness. Not only will you reify them, but, in the process, you will reify the one who is reifying them—that is, you reify the object, and in so doing, you also reify the subject, thereby binding yourself with the fetters of delusion. Conversely, by drawing your awareness inward to come to know the actual nature of your mind, free from the shackles of appearances, you set yourself free from the restrictions of dualistic cognition that keep you stuck in samsara, thinking you are a sentient being. Thus, you may actualize your own identity as a perfect buddha.

Appendix 4: Twenty-Seven Samayas of the Root Guru's Body, Speech, and Mind Particular to the Great Perfection Tradition of the Old Translation School[1]

Düdjom Rinpoché

Translated by Eva Natanya

The following explanation provides the essential content to understand this sentence in Düdjom Rinpoché's *Extracting the Vital Essence of Accomplishment*: "Although there are many kinds of Secret Mantra samayas, in brief, they are synthesized as the samayas of your root guru's enlightened body, speech, and mind."

The root samaya is known as such because one binds (or vows) one's own body, speech, and mind inseparably with the three vajras—namely, the holy body, speech, and mind of the guru, who is the synthesis of all buddhas. Moreover, it is known as such because the word *guru* means "heavy"—that is, if one degenerates, or falls away, in the relationship with the guru, it is difficult to purify.

Enlightened Body

Outer: One vows to abandon (1) stealing, (2) sexual activity, and (3) killing.

Inner: One vows to abandon (4) disparaging one's parents, brothers, sisters, or one's own body; (5) disparaging phenomena or the person; (6) beating one's own body, or tormenting and mistreating oneself with mortifications.

Secret: One vows to abandon (7) striking, or even threatening to strike, the body of a member of one's vajra family, or else disparaging their clothing or adornments; (8) harming the spouse or spiritual partner of one's guru; (9) stepping on or over the shadow of one's guru or behaving unconscientiously with one's body or speech in the presence of the guru.

ENLIGHTENED SPEECH

Outer: One vows to abandon (10) lying, (11) divisive speech, and (12) harsh speech.

Inner: One vows to abandon abusing or repudiating (13) anyone who speaks the Dharma, (14) contemplates its meaning, or (15) meditates upon the nature of existence.

Secret: One vows to abandon condemning or violating (16) the words of one's vajra siblings, (17) the words of the spiritual partner or attendants of one's guru, and (18) the holy speech of one's guru.

ENLIGHTENED MIND

Outer: One vows to abandon (19) ill will, (20) covetousness, and (21) wrong views.

Inner: One vows to abandon (22) improper conduct, in the sense of unconscientious or crude behavior; (23) incorrect meditation, beset by laxity, excitation, and the obscurations of mistaken pitfalls; (24) wrong views—namely, eternalism, nihilism, or grasping to extremes.

Secret: One vows to abandon failing to bring to mind, within each period of the day and night (i.e., six sessions) (25) the view, meditation, and conduct; (26) one's chosen deity; and (27) guru yoga, together with affectionate love for one's vajra brothers and sisters.

NOTES

PREFACE

1. For more details on the past and future lifetimes of Düdjom Rinpoché, see Lama Tharchin Rinpoché's foreword to Ron Garry, trans., *Wisdom Nectar: Dudjom Rinpoché's Heart Advice* (Boulder: Snow Lion, 2005), 1–9; Khenpo Tsewang Dongyal Rinpoche, *Light of Fearless Indestructible Wisdom: The Life and Legacy of His Holiness Dudjom Rinpoche* (Boulder: Shambhala, 2008), 32, 47–55; and Thinley Norbu, *The Ruby Rosary: Joyfully Accepted by Vidyādharas and Ḍākinīs as the Ornament of a Necklace* (Boulder: Shambhala, 2022), 141–259. The Tibetan source for this account is Dungsé Thinley Norbu Rinpoché, *'Khrungs rabs gsol 'debs muktika'i do shal gyi 'grel pa rig 'dzin mkha' 'gro dgyes pa'i mgul rgyan padma rāga'i phreng ba*, in *The Collected Works of Dungse Thinley Norbu Rinpoche*, vol. 1 (Hong Kong: Hong kong gyi ling dpe skrun tshad yod kung si, 2009), esp. 215–21 and 409–15.

2. Khenpo Tsewang Dongyal Rinpoche, *Light of Fearless Indestructible Wisdom*, 89–90. See also https://treasuryoflives.org/biographies/view/Dudjom-Rinpoche.

3. This Sanskrit mantra, which is classically uttered in empowerments, means "May this [realization] remain firmly within you."

4. See especially Khenpo Tsewang Dongyal Rinpoche's *Light of Fearless Indestructible Wisdom*.

5. *Śamatha* (pronounced "shamata") can be explained briefly as follows: By focusing the attention continuously, without being diverted to other objects, the mind eventually rests naturally upon its chosen object. When the exceptional joy and bliss of pliancy in body and mind arises, then this concentration (or *samādhi*) becomes śamatha. This arises simply from maintaining concentration of the mind inwardly, without being distracted, but it does not rely upon fathoming the actual nature of any phenomenon.

6. *Vipaśyanā* (pronounced "vipashyana") can be defined as the wisdom imbued with the exceptional bliss of pliancy that arises in dependence upon śamatha and comes about by the power of discerningly investigating the phenomenon upon which it focuses.

7. Karma pa dbang phyug rdo rje, *Phyag chen rgyas pa nges don rgya mtsho* (Sarnath, India: Vajra Vidyā Institute Library, 2006), 102.

3. THE PREPARATION

1. *Aṅguttara Nikāya* 1.49–50, *Pabhassara Sutta*. Citations to the *Aṅguttara Nikāya* are in the form of the volume number (e.g. the Book of Ones), followed by the verse numbers within the particular sutta and then the Pāli name of the sutta. This accords with the numbering system used at https://www.accesstoinsight .org/tipitaka/an/index.html.
2. See B. Alan Wallace, trans., *The Vajra Essence*, vol. 3 of *Dūdjom Lingpa's Visions of the Great Perfection* (New York: Wisdom, 2015). A revised edition translated together with Eva Natanya is forthcoming from Wisdom Publications.
3. Alfred North Whitehead, *Science and the Modern World* (Cambridge: Cambridge University Press, 1929), 233.
4. *Aṅguttara Nikāya* 1.48, *Lahu-parivaṭṭa Sutta*.
5. See chap. 7, vv. 47–48, of Śāntideva, *A Guide to the Bodhisattva Way of Life*, trans. Vesna A. Wallace and B. Alan Wallace (Ithaca, NY: Snow Lion, 1997), 83 (translation slightly modified).
6. B. Alan Wallace, *The Art of Transforming the Mind: A Meditator's Guide to the Tibetan Practice of Lojong* (Boston: Shambhala, 2022), 243 (translation modified).
7. For English translations of both texts mentioned in this paragraph, see B. Alan Wallace and Eva Natanya, *Śamatha and Vipaśyanā: An Anthology of Pith Instructions* (New York: Wisdom, 2025).
8. See B. Alan Wallace, *Dzokchen: A Commentary on Dūdjom Rinpoché's Illumination of Primordial Wisdom* (New York: Wisdom, 2024), 14–15.
9. Asaṅga, *Śrāvakabhūmi, Rnal 'byor spyod pa'i sa las nyan thos kyi sa*, in *Bstan 'gyur* (*Gser bris ma*), vol. 138, 238. An earlier version of my translation of this entire section was published in B. Alan Wallace, *Minding Closely: The Four Applications of Mindfulness* (Boulder: Shambhala, 2021), 321–33.
10. "Train in calming the movements of your respiration just until you do not notice them, thereby settling your speech in its natural state." See B. Alan Wallace, *Open Mind: View and Meditation in the Lineage of Lerab Lingpa* (Somerville, MA: Wisdom, 2017), 25 (translation slightly modified).
11. As the Buddha said in the *Ānāpānasati Sutta* (*Majjhima Nikāya* 118), "Breathing in long, one understands: 'the in-breath is long'; breathing out long, one understands: 'the out-breath is long.' Breathing in short, one understands: 'the in-breath is short'; breathing out short, one understands: 'the out-breath is short.'" This citation refers to the 118th discourse of the *Majjhima Nikāya* in accord with the numbering system found at https://www.accesstoinsight.org/tipitaka/mn /index.html.
12. "One trains: 'experiencing the whole body I shall breathe in'; one trains: 'experiencing the whole body I shall breathe out.'" See *Majjhima Nikāya* 118.

13. Arthur C. Clarke, *Profiles of the Future: An Inquiry into the Limits of the Possible* (London: Pan Books, 1973), 39n.

14. *Mahāyānottaratantraśāstra, Theg pa chen po rgyud bla ma'i bstan bcos*, v. 27.

5. THE MAIN PRACTICE: MEDITATION

1. See B. Alan Wallace, trans., *The Vajra Essence*, vol. 3 of *Düdjom Lingpa's Visions of the Great Perfection* (Somerville, MA: Wisdom, 2015), 21.

2. See B. Alan Wallace and Eva Natanya, trans., "The Great Commentary to Mingyur Dorjé's *Buddhahood in the Palm of Your Hand*," in *Śamatha and Vipaśyanā: An Anthology of Pith Instructions* (New York: Wisdom, 2025).

3. The five obscurations are (1) fixation on the allures of the desire realm, (2) malevolence, (3) laxity and dullness, (4) excitation and anxiety, and (5) afflictive uncertainty. They are known as "obscurations" because they obscure the natural purity and luminosity of the substrate consciousness. Achieving śamatha is sufficient to subdue them and replace them with the five dhyāna factors, which act as their natural antidotes, respectively. The five dhyāna factors come into their full power with the achievement of śamatha and especially in the form-realm concentration of the first dhyāna. They are single-pointed attention, well-being, the faculty of coarse investigation, joy, and the faculty of subtle analysis.

4. This great vidyādhara, whose Sanskrit name is reconstructed as Pramodavajra or Prahevajra, stands at the root of the Dzogchen lineage as it was passed to human beings on this planet. He is said not to have had a human father but to have been born to a virgin daughter of the king of Oḍḍiyāna through the divine intervention of Vajrapāṇi, likely sometime in the seventh century C.E. The foundational Dzogchen work attributed to him is *The Three Phrases That Strike the Crucial Points*, which he gave to Mañjuśrīmitra as a miraculous text enclosed within a tiny golden casket, just after his body had dissolved into rainbow light.

6. THE MAIN PRACTICE: CONDUCT

1. John 14:6.

2. See "Conservation of Energy," The Feynman Lectures, Caltech, updated 2013, https://www.feynmanlectures.caltech.edu/I_04.html. These lectures were originally published as R. P. Feynman, R. B. Leighton, and M. L. Sands, *The Feynman Lectures on Physics* (Reading, MA: Addison-Wesley, 1963).

3. See B. Alan Wallace and Eva Natanya, trans., "How to Establish the Ground of Being by Way of the View," in *Śamatha and Vipaśyanā: An Anthology of Pith Instructions* (New York: Wisdom, 2025).

4. B. Alan Wallace, *Open Mind: View and Meditation in the Lineage of Lerab Lingpa* (Somerville, MA: Wisdom, 2017), 25 (translation slightly modified).

5. For a thorough presentation of this method, see B. Alan Wallace and Eva

Natanya, trans., "Taking the Aspect of the Mind as the Path," in *Śamatha and Vipaśyanā: An Anthology of Pith Instructions* (New York: Wisdom, 2025).

6. See B. Alan Wallace and Eva Natanya, trans., "A Summary of the View, Meditation, and Conduct," in *Śamatha and Vipaśyanā* (New York: Wisdom, 2025).

7. See B. Alan Wallace, *Dzokchen: A Commentary on Düdjom Rinpoché's Illumination of Primordial Wisdom* (New York: Wisdom, 2024), 11.

8. *Saṃyutta Nikāya* 54.9, *Vesālī Sutta*. Citations to the *Saṃyutta Nikāya* are in the form of the number of the *saṃyutta* grouping, followed by the verse number within that *saṃyutta*, and then the Pāli name of the sutta. This accords with the numbering system used at https://www.accesstoinsight.org/tipitaka/sn/index.html.

9. See B. Alan Wallace, *The Art of Transforming the Mind: A Meditator's Guide to the Tibetan Practice of Lojong* (Boston: Shambhala, 2022), 73.

10. Niels Bohr, *Atomic Theory and the Description of Nature* (Cambridge: Cambridge University Press, 1961), 56–57.

11. Bohr, *Atomic Theory*, 57.

12. Werner Heisenberg, *Physics and Beyond: Encounters and Conversations* (New York: Harper and Row, 1971), 206.

13. *Bodhicittavivāraṇa*, v. 34.

14. Translated and paraphrased from the *Monlam Grand Tibetan Dictionary's* Tibetan-language entry for *gzhon nu bum sku*, "youthful vase kāya," https://monlamdictionary.com.

15. See B. Alan Wallace, trans., *The Enlightened View of Samantabhadra*, vol. 1 of *Düdjom Lingpa's Visions of the Great Perfection* (Somerville, MA: Wisdom, 2015), 211–12 (translation slightly modified).

16. See B. Alan Wallace and Eva Natanya, trans., "Taking the Aspect of the Mind as the Path," in *Śamatha and Vipaśyanā: An Anthology of Pith Instructions* (New York: Wisdom, 2025).

17. B. Alan Wallace, trans., *The Vajra Essence*, vol. 3 of *Düdjom Lingpa's Visions of the Great Perfection* (Somerville, MA: Wisdom, 2015), 21.

18. Wallace, trans., *The Vajra Essence*, 21 (translation slightly modified).

7. POST-MEDITATIVE PRACTICE

1. See Ngari Panchen Pema Wangyi Gyalpo, *Perfect Conduct: Ascertaining the Three Vows*, with commentary by His Holiness Dudjom Rinpoche, Jigdral Yeshe Dorje, translated by Khenpo Gyurme Samdrub and Sangye Khandro (Boston: Wisdom, 1996).

2. *Sutta Nipāta* 1.8, *Karaṇīya Mettā Sutta*. The *Sutta Nipāta* constitutes the fifth book of the *Khuddaka Nikāya*, and the citation here refers to the chapter and verse within that book, according to the numbering system found at https://www.accesstoinsight.org/tipitaka/kn/snp/index.html.

3. Tsenshab Tsewang Samdrup (Mtshan zhabs tshe dbang bsam grub), *Sdom gsum bslab bya nor bu'i 'od 'phreng*, in *Sdom gsum dka' gnas nyes ltung phyir bcos dang bslab byas brgyan pa snying nor 'dul 'dzin lag bcangs* (Karnataka, India: Drepung Loseling Educational Society, 1998). Note that the explanations of these secondary misdeeds differ somewhat across Gelukpa and Nyingma lineages, but the more deeply one understands the trainings as applied to one's own practice, the more easily one can see the complementarity between different lineages of explanation rather than any fundamental contradictions between them.

4. Tsenshab Tsewang Samdrup, *Sdom gsum bslab bya nor bu'i 'od 'phreng*, 100.

5. Tsenshab Tsewang Samdrup, *Sdom gsum bslab bya nor bu'i 'od 'phreng*, 104.

6. An earlier version of this translation appeared in Venerable Gyatrul Rinpoche, *Meditation, Transformation, and Dream Yoga*, trans. Sangye Khandro and B. Alan Wallace, 2nd ed. (Ithaca, NY: Snow Lion, 2002), 20 (translation modified).

7. For this sequence of quotations, see B. Alan Wallace, trans., *The Vajra Essence*, vol. 3 of *Düdjom Lingpa's Visions of the Great Perfection* (Somerville, MA: Wisdom, 2015), 185 (translation slightly modified).

8. See Wallace, trans., *The Vajra Essence*, 262 (translation slightly modified): "Depending on their faculties, some remain unconscious in that state for six hours, twelve hours, one full day, or two or three days. However long you stay there, that is the phase at which you dissolve into the actual substrate to which you descend. Following that is the *dissolution of the [dark] near-attainment into the clear light*."

9. See Wallace, trans., *The Vajra Essence*, 263 (translation slightly modified): "The number of days one remains in meditation in the clear light of the dying process corresponds to the stability and duration of one's present practice. Those who have achieved stability of practice lasting throughout a day and night may achieve stability lasting seven human days at death. But for those who have not entered the path, the clear light will not appear for longer than the time it takes to eat a bowl of food."

10. The other three māras are the māra of mental afflictions, the māra of the appropriated aggregates, and the māra of the Lord of Death.

11. On June 9, 2000, His Holiness Penor Rinpoché Kyabjé Drubwang Pema Norbu granted a Medicine Buddha empowerment from the *terma* lineage of Mingyur Dorjé, who had received the initiation and transmission in a direct vision of the Medicine Buddha. I was the English-language interpreter for this empowerment and so heard this statement firsthand.

8. COMMENTATOR'S CONCLUSION

1. Traktung Dudjom Lingpa, *A Clear Mirror: The Visionary Autobiography of a Tibetan Master*, trans. Chönyi Drolma (Kathmandu: Rangjung Yeshe, 2011), 181.

APPENDIX 1: THE SCIENCE OF DHARMA: METEOROLOGY, ASTRONOMY, AND COSMOLOGY

1. See this verse as quoted in Tsong kha pa, *The Great Treatise on the Stages of the Path of Enlightenment* (Ithaca, NY: Snow Lion, 2000), 1:75: "It is said that one who is nonpartisan, intelligent, and diligent / Is a vessel for listening to the teachings. / The good qualities of the instructor do not appear otherwise / Nor do those of fellow listeners."

2. See chap. 5, vv. 48–53 of Śāntideva, *A Guide to the Bodhisattva Way of Life*, trans. Vesna A. Wallace and B. Alan Wallace (Ithaca, NY: Snow Lion, 1997), 53: "When one sees one's own mind to be attached or repulsed, then one should neither act nor speak, but remain still like a piece of wood. / When my mind is haughty, sarcastic, full of conceit and arrogance, ridiculing, evasive, and deceitful, / When it is inclined to boast, or when it is contemptuous of others, abusive, and irritable, then I should remain still like a piece of wood. / When my mind seeks material gain, honor, and fame, or when it seeks attendants and service, then I will remain still like a piece of wood. / When my mind is averse to the interests of others and seeks my own self-interest, or when it wishes to speak out of a desire for an audience, then I will remain still like a piece of wood. / When it is impatient, indolent, timid, impudent, garrulous, or biased in my own favor, then I will remain still like a piece of wood."

3. This was stated in the first of five Messenger lectures at Cornell University on "The Future of Fundamental Physics," on October 4, 2010. http://www.cornell.edu/video/nima-arkani-hamed-quantum-mechanics-and-spacetime.

APPENDIX 2: THE NUCLEAR FUSION OF ŚAMATHA

1. See B. Alan Wallace, *Balancing the Mind: A Tibetan Buddhist Approach to Refining Attention* (Ithaca, NY: Snow Lion, 2005), 202.

2. Wallace, *Balancing the Mind*, 202.

3. Wallace, 203 (translation slightly modified).

4. Wallace, 206.

5. Wallace, 207 (translation slightly modified).

6. See B. Alan Wallace and Eva Natanya, trans., "Cutting the Root of Suffering and Equalizing Excitation and Laxity," in *Śamatha and Vipaśyanā: An Anthology of Pith Instructions* (New York: Wisdom, 2025).

APPENDIX 3: DISTINGUISHING DIMENSIONS OF CONSCIOUSNESS

1. Peter Harvey, *The Selfless Mind: Personality, Consciousness and Nirvana in Early Buddhism* (Surrey, UK: Curzon Press, 1995), 170.

2. See Wallace, trans., *The Vajra Essence*, vol. 3 of *Düdjom Lingpa's Visions of the Great Perfection* (Somerville, MA: Wisdom, 2015), 28 (translation modified).

3. See Wallace, trans., *The Vajra Essence*, 67–68 (translation modified).

4. This is chap. 3, v. 11. See Śāntideva, *A Guide to the Bodhisattva Way of Life*, trans. Vesna A. Wallace and B. Alan Wallace (Ithaca, NY: Snow Lion, 1997), 34. Here, the first line is translated from the Sanskrit and the second line from the Tibetan.

5. See B. Alan Wallace and Eva Natanya, trans., "A Summary of the View, Meditation, and Conduct," in *Śamatha and Vipaśyanā: An Anthology of Pith Instructions* (New York: Wisdom, 2025).

APPENDIX 4: TWENTY-SEVEN SAMAYAS OF THE ROOT GURU'S BODY, SPEECH, AND MIND

1. Based closely on Düdjom Rinpoché, *A Vessel of the Ambrosia of Good Explanation That Dispels the Mental Anguish of Beginners: A Word-for-Word Commentary on the Treatise "Ascertaining the Three Sets of Vows," Sdom gsum rnam par nges pa'i bstan bcos kyi 'bru 'grel blo gros gsar bu'i yid kyi gdung sel legs bshad bdud rtsi'i za ma tog*, in *The Collected Writings and Revelations of H. H. Bdud 'joms rin po che 'jigs bral ye shes rdo rje*, vol. 4 (*nga*), 346–48 (Kalimpong: Dupjung Lama, 1979–85).

BIBLIOGRAPHY

SOURCE TEXTS

Extracting the Vital Essence of Accomplishment: Concise and Clear Advice for Practice in a Mountain Retreat. Ri chos bslab bya nyams len dmar khrid go bder brjod pa grub pa'i bcud len. In *The Collected Writings and Revelations of H. H. Bdud 'joms rin po che 'jigs bral ye shes rdo rje,* vol. 13 (*pa*), 443–68. Kalimpong: Dupjung Lama, 1979–85.

A Vessel of the Ambrosia of Good Explanation That Dispels the Mental Anguish of Beginners: A Word for Word Commentary on the Treatise "Ascertaining the Three Sets of Vows." Sdom gsum rnam par nges pa'i bstan bcos kyi 'bru 'grel blo gros gsar bu'i yid kyi gdung sel legs bshad bdud rtsi'i za ma tog. In *The Collected Writings and Revelations of H. H. Bdud 'joms rin po che 'jigs bral ye shes rdo rje,* vol. 4 (*nga*), 1–407. Kalimpong: Dupjung Lama, 1979–85.

FOR FURTHER READING

Aśvaghoṣa. *The Buddha-Carita, or Life of Buddha.* Edited and translated by Edward B. Cowell and E. H. Johnston. Arranged by Ānandajoti Bhikku. Online edition, 2005. https://ancient-buddhist-texts.net/Texts-and-Translations/Buddhacarita/Buddhacarita.pdf.

Düdjom Lingpa. *Düdjom Lingpa's Visions of the Great Perfection.* Translated by B. Alan Wallace and Eva Natanya. 3 vols. Rev. ed. New York: Wisdom, forthcoming.

Dudjom Lingpa, Traktung. *A Clear Mirror: The Visionary Autobiography of a Tibetan Master.* Translated by Chönyi Drolma. Kathmandu: Rangjung Yeshe, 2011.

Dudjom Jigdral Yeshé Dorjé. *Wisdom Nectar: Dudjom Rinpoché's Heart Advice.* Translated by Ron Garry. Boulder: Shambhala, 2005.

Dudjom Rinpoche, Jigdrel Yeshe Dorje. *A Torch Lighting the Way to Freedom: Complete Instructions on the Preliminary Practice of the Profound and Secret* Heart Essence of the Dakini. Translated by the Padmakara Translation Group. Boulder: Shambhala, 2016.

Harvey, Peter. *The Selfless Mind: Personality, Consciousness and Nirvana in Early Buddhism.* Surrey, UK: Curzon Press, 1995.

Khenpo Tsewang Dongyal Rinpoche. *Light of Fearless Indestructible Wisdom: The Life and Legacy of His Holiness Dudjom Rinpoche.* Boulder: Shambhala, 2008.

Ñāṇamoli, Bhikkhu. *The Life of the Buddha According to the Pāli Canon.* Onalaska, WA: Buddhist Publication Society Pariyatti Editions, 1992.

Ngari Panchen, Pema Wangyi Gyalpo. *Perfect Conduct: Ascertaining the Three Vows.* Commentary by His Holiness Dudjom Rinpoche, Jigdral Yeshe Dorje. Translated by Khenpo Gyurme Samdrub and Sangye Khandro. Boston: Wisdom, 1996.

Śāntideva. *A Guide to the Bodhisattva Way of Life.* Translated by Vesna A. Wallace and B. Alan Wallace. Ithaca, NY: Snow Lion, 1997.

Stevenson, Ian. *Where Reincarnation and Biology Intersect.* New York: Praeger, 1997.

Thinley Norbu. *The Ruby Rosary: Joyfully Accepted by Vidyādharas and Ḍākinīs as the Ornament of a Necklace.* Boulder: Shambhala, 2022.

Tsong-kha-pa. *The Great Treatise on the Stages of the Path of Enlightenment.* Translated by the Lamrim Chenmo Translation Committee. 3 vols. Ithaca, NY: Snow Lion, 2000–2004.

Vajirajñāna Mahāthera, Paravahera. *Buddhist Meditation in Theory and Practice: A General Exposition According to the Pāli Canon of the Theravādin School.* Charleston, SC: Charleston Buddhist Fellowship, 2010.

Wallace, B. Alan. *The Art of Transforming the Mind: A Meditator's Guide to the Tibetan Practice of Lojong.* Boston: Shambhala, 2022.

——. *Balancing the Mind: A Tibetan Buddhist Approach to Refining Attention.* Ithaca, NY: Snow Lion, 2005.

——. *Dzokchen: A Commentary on Düdjom Rinpoché's Illumination of Primordial Wisdom.* New York: Wisdom, 2024.

——. *Hidden Dimensions: The Unification of Physics and Consciousness.* New York: Columbia University Press, 2007.

——. *Minding Closely: The Four Applications of Mindfulness.* Boulder: Shambhala, 2021.

——. *Open Mind: View and Meditation in the Lineage of Lerab Lingpa.* Edited by Eva Natanya. Somerville, MA: Wisdom, 2017.

——. *The Taboo of Subjectivity: Toward a New Science of Consciousness.* New York: Oxford University Press, 2000.

Wallace, B. Alan and Eva Natanya. *Śamatha and Vipaśyanā: An Anthology of Pith Instructions.* New York: Wisdom, 2025.

FOR FURTHER STUDY

If you would like to hear, study, and practice further teachings on Dzogchen with Lama Alan Wallace, you can listen to the audio recordings from his eight-week retreats offered through the Santa Barbara Institute from 2016–2023: https://sbinstitute.com/product-category/retreats/

Index

About the Author

B. Alan Wallace is president of the Santa Barbara Institute for Consciousness Studies, as well as the Center for Contemplative Research. He trained for many years as a monk in Buddhist monasteries in India and Switzerland. He has taught Buddhist theory and practice in Europe and America since 1976 and has served as interpreter for numerous Tibetan scholars and contemplatives, including His Holiness the Dalai Lama.

After graduating summa cum laude from Amherst College, where he studied physics and the philosophy of science, he earned his MA and PhD in religious studies at Stanford University. He has edited, translated, authored, and contributed to more than forty books on Tibetan Buddhism, medicine, language, and culture, and the interface between science and religion.

After teaching for four years in the Department of Religious Studies at the University of California, Santa Barbara, he founded the Santa Barbara Institute for Consciousness Studies and later the Center for Contemplative Research. Both organizations focus on the interface between contemplative and scientific ways of exploring the mind and its potentials, and the latter has created a conducive environment for dedicated practitioners to remain in long-term meditation retreat with the aspiration to reach the Mahāyāna path in this lifetime.